SATHER CLASSICAL LECTURES

Volume Thirty-eight

THE SOUND OF GREEK

Studies in the Greek Theory and Practice
of Euphony

THE SOUND OF GREEK

Studies in the Greek Theory and Practice of Euphony

by W. B. STANFORD

UNIVERSITY OF CALIFORNIA PRESS
BERKELEY AND LOS ANGELES 1967

UNIVERSITY OF CALIFORNIA PRESS
BERKELEY AND LOS ANGELES, CALIFORNIA

CAMBRIDGE UNIVERSITY PRESS
LONDON, ENGLAND

Preface

THE FIRST six chapters of this book incorporate the Sather Lectures which I had the honour of giving in Berkeley in the spring semester of 1966, with some amplification and revision. The seventh chapter, the Appendix, and the sound recording have been added by permission of the Sather Committee.

Perhaps I should offer an apology for the absence of scientific linguistic analysis in a book with this title, though I hope my subtitle will prevent any misunderstanding. Originally I did, optimistically, plan to apply principles of modern phonetics to the theory and practice of the ancient Greeks in matters of euphony. But it soon became clear that a choice had to be made between an aesthetic and a scientific approach. Since my primary purpose was to explore the minds of the Greek rhetoricians and poets, I decided to follow Calliope and not Hermes. So, apart from a few references to modern phonetics and acoustics, the book is mainly confined to literary and musical topics.

I should like to record my indebtedness to many scholars on both sides of the Atlantic for information and advice, especially to Professors Joseph Fontenrose, J. T. Hooker, W. K. Pritchett, and Charles Witke in Berkeley; to Professors W. S. Allen, E. G. Turner, R. P. Winnington-Ingram, and Mr. F. R. Dale, in England; and to my colleagues Brian Boydell, D. W. Greene, J. V. Luce, J. D. Pheifer, E. G. Quin, and L. J. D. Richardson in Trinity College, Dublin. All these helped me in several ways. Mr. J. F. Walters of the University of California Press greatly improved my text by his suggestions. Mr. R. McKirahan of Berkeley typed my manuscript with admirable promptitude and accuracy. I owe special thanks to my wife, who checked the manuscript, typescript, and printed text with indefatigable care. Professor L. J. D. Richardson also removed many errors at the proof stage, and Mr. Michael O'Regan advised me on some French questions. Others to whom I am indebted for help on specific points are mentioned in the notes.

Cold print cannot adequately express the deep gratitude of my wife and myself to the many friends in Berkeley and elsewhere in the United States whose cordial and generous hospitality made our visit so unforgettably enjoyable. To them I offer the dedication of this book as a token of our friendship—especially to the Fontenroses, the Pritchetts, Maud Senior, Camille Durney, George and Ruth Sharp, ad Lionnel Pearson.

Dublin   W. B. STANFORD
October, 1966

Contents

I. The Primacy of the Spoken Word   1

II. Speech and Music   27

III. Theoretical Aspects of Euphony   48

IV. Euphony in Practice   74

V. Mimesis in Words   99

VI. Matters of Pronunciation   122

VII. The Speaking Voice   140

Appendix: Remarks on the Pronunciation of the Greek Pitch Accent   157

Selective Bibliography   161

Indexes

A. General Index   165

B. Selective Index of Passages from Greek and Latin Authors   169

C. Selective Index of Greek and Latin Words   172

Synopsis of Record   175

I

The Primacy of the
Spoken Word

IN OUR WORLD of printed books we mostly study and enjoy
literature in silence. We do sometimes hear the sound of poetry and of good
prose in the classroom and in the theatre, and when we listen to the radio.
But most of our literary experience, as adults at any rate, is silent. We sit
in a library or at home; our eyes move quickly over black marks on a white
page; and our mind takes in an author's thoughts and images. When we
were children at school, our teachers taught us to aim at rapid reading:
the sooner we got through the elementary stage of sounding the words as
we went along, the better, they said. In any educational book on the
psychology of reading you will probably find a section called something like
"Training to Decrease Vocalization." [1]

We take all this for granted, and undoubtedly we gain great benefits
from this silent, rapid reading. So when we are studying the classical lit-
eratures of Greece and Rome we generally aim at reading them in just the
same way. We use our eyes, but not our ears and our voices.[2] We are what
has been aptly called "eye-philologists," not "ear-philologists." [3]

But that is not how Plato or Cicero or Aristophanes or Plautus used to
read books to themselves. In ancient Greece and Rome reading without
speaking the words seems to have been a rare accomplishment,[4] and it
remained so until well into the Middle Ages. Normally, it seems, an ancient
Greek or Roman had to pronounce each syllable before he could understand
a written word. The written letters informed his voice;[5] then his voice informed his ear; and finally his ear, together with the muscular movements
of his vocal organs, conveyed the message to his brain—"just like young
children at school," you may be thinking. Yes, but in several other ways,

too, the Greeks were—as the Egyptian priest says to Solon in Plato's *Timaios*[6]—"always children . . . all young in spirit"; and some of the charm and wisdom of their literature and art comes from that childlike—but not childish—nature.

Reading aloud, then, was the general rule even for private study. Probably among well-practised readers their eyes, voices, ears, and minds received the message almost simultaneously. We know, in fact, that their eyes moved on ahead of the speaking voice, and we know from our best authority on education in the classical world, Quintilian, that this separation of faculties could be rather a strain on the ancient reader.[7] Quintilian did not foresee that the quicker-moving eye would someday completely abandon the slower voice.

But apparently silent reading was not entirely impossible in ancient times, if one made a special effort. The earliest named silent reader in Europe is, as one might have expected, a man of supreme genius, Julius Caesar—who once was seen to read a letter to himself in that way.[8] Later some unnamed Roman senators under Augustus were expected to be able to do the same. There are also one or two other possible, but dubious, references to the silent reading of brief personal messages. But in every case the circumstances were exceptional, and in no case was the reader reading a work of literature. Oddly enough, the Romans seem to have been better than the Greeks at this, if we can trust the scanty evidence. There is no clear reference at all to silent reading by any Greek, named or unnamed, until after the fourth century A.D.[9]

The earliest description of anyone reading a literary work—as distinct from a short message—silently is as late as A.D. 384. Augustine in his *Confessions*, describing how St. Ambrose used to spend his leisure time, remarks, "When he was reading, his eyes were led over the pages and his heart searched into the meaning, but his voice and tongue were silent." [10] Augustine obviously found this very unusual: in fact, he seems never to have seen or heard of anything like it before. He wonders why Ambrose adopted it—was he trying to save his voice, or did he want to avoid interruption by anyone who might want to question him if he read interesting things aloud?

Two years afterward Augustine himself had apparently learned this rare accomplishment. In the famous incident of his conversion, when he heard the voice saying, "Take up and read, take up and read," he tells us: "I snatched up the Apostle's book; I opened it, and in silence I read . . ." [11] So the first specific literary text that we know to have been read silently in Europe was Paul's Epistle to the Romans, chapter xiii, verse 13. But for long after that year A.D. 386 silent reading seems to have remained rare and difficult for most people.[12]

So it seems that our accepted ideal for reading—swiftly, soundlessly, visually—was alien to classical antiquity, among the Greeks at any rate. It is certainly never recommended by any classical writer on literary theory and practice. So far as we can judge, the necessity of reading aloud prevailed at all levels of writing. Even a Greek schoolboy in Egypt when he was writing one of those poignant personal letters which have been recovered among the papyri[13] knew that his parents normally would have to pronounce every word of what he had written before they could understand it. So if he was a wily schoolboy he would take the trouble to make the sound of his words pleasant, as well as their meaning. And, needless to say, at the other extreme of literature any great writer, knowing that every syllable he wrote must be spoken and heard even by the private reader, was bound to choose his language with scrupulous attention to euphony in the widest sense of that word (which we must examine closely later on). A scribe, too, when he was copying a manuscript by himself and not from dictation, would have to pronounce the text if he wished to understand it as well as copy it. Perhaps authors also normally spoke their words aloud as they composed.[14]

In other words, our classical texts were never intended by their authors to be read only by the eye and brain like algebraical formulae or Chinese ideograms. Written words were more like memory-aids to remind readers of certain sounds.[15] As Quintilian puts it: "The use of letters is to preserve vocal sounds and to return them to readers as something left on trust." [16] In modern terms, they resembled a tape-recording waiting to be played on someone's vocal organs.

All this means that the actual substance, the physical material, which historians like Herodotos and philosophers like Plato—as well as every ancient poet and orator—used for conveying their thoughts and feelings and their sense of formal beauty was primarily and essentially vocal sound, as literally as the materials of the ancient Greek sculptors were marble, bronze, gold, and ivory. When Pindar spoke of the "far-flashing façade" [17] of a poem, he made that phrase out of specific sounds as surely as the architects and masons of Athens made the far-flashing façade of the Parthenon from Pentelic marble. The poet intended much more too, of course. He also wished to convey a conceptual meaning that would fill the hearer's mind with glorious images and ideas, just as the workers on the Parthenon were building a habitation for a great goddess and a great ideal. But a Parthenon built from wood or a Pindaric ode made from silent letter-symbols would have been radically different from what Pheidias and Pindar created. Every good artist exploits the potentialities of his material and is influenced by it, whether he be a Chinese sculptor exploring the special qualities of a particular piece of jade or a Theocritean shepherd composing a tune on his new Panpipes. One of the most spellbinding of modern poets, Dylan Thomas, has well expressed this relationship between the artist and his material and his final composition:

What I like to do is to treat words as a craftsman does his wood or stone or what-have-you, to hew, carve, mould, coil, polish, and plane them into patterns, sequences, sculptures, fugues of sound expressing some lyrical impulse, some spiritual doubt or conviction, some dimly-reached truth I must try to reach and realise.[18]

There I believe he speaks, though in modern terms, for the authors of ancient Greece.

But though all classical Greek authors composed for the ear, not all by any means aimed at producing the equal of the Parthenon or the Delphic Charioteer in terms of beautiful sounds. There were some who minimized the euphonic element, like architects who build only for usefulness. One does not look for subtle sound-effects in the *Posterior Analytics* of Aristotle or in Euclid's *Elements*, though for all I know they may be there for the seeking, and certainly if those writers had violated fundamental principles of euphony they would have been stigmatized as uncouth by their contemporaries. But such writings are not in the central arena of Greek literature, where every author who wished to win and hold a wide audience had to exploit the aesthetic and emotive powers of sound finely and fully. Even so austere a writer as Thucydides used these aural sophistries—as some regard them—no less subtly than the mellifluous Phrynichos and the sensuous Sappho. All classical Greek authors were in this way euphuists.

What concerns us, then, is not a superficial matter of assonance or alliteration or onomatopoeia and the like. It is the very substance itself of Greek literature. If we read Greek literature silently we are doing something almost as inadequate as studying the Venetian painters in black and white reproductions. If we do read it aloud but read it—as so many at present do—with attention only to the metre, ignoring the other elements of euphony, we might as well be thumping out a Bach toccata and fugue on a xylophone. There is this great difference, of course, that in music the sound is everything, while in literature it is generally subordinate to the conceptual meaning. But what I shall be mainly arguing is that the poetic meaning in the fullest sense often depends much more on the sound of the words than is generally recognized. To put it in mythological terms: the marriage of Cadmus, bringer of the alphabet to Greece, and Harmonia, personification of musical form, was a marriage of true and equal consorts.

Here I must meet an objection which is bound to come to mind. Even if one grants that sound was the basic material of Greek literature, can we study that material with any certainty? We can still go and see and handle the stones of the Acropolis—changed a good deal, to be sure, by weather and rough usage—but how can we recapture the sounds that Aeschylus used when he produced and acted in his tragedies in the Theatre of Dionysos, or of Demosthenes when he spoke on the Pnyx? The objection is justified only up to a point. Though in the absence of accurate sound-recordings we can never exactly recapture personal intonations from the distant past, yet, as I hope to establish later, we have enough evidence about how the ancient Greeks used their voices to allow us to recapture more than a little of their vocal world. Our knowledge is very far from being perfect. But should that deter us from trying to hear and speak ancient Greek as closely as possible to the original?

Yet some of the most authoritative of contemporary scholars consider all efforts to recapture the sound of ancient Greek useless and futile. The mere sound of Greek literature, they say, has little or nothing to do with its literary value: silent reading can give us all that matters; and if we do sometimes have to read aloud or recite passages from the ancient authors, it is not worth while trying to pronounce them as the ancients did. Here is a characteristic quotation, all the more challenging because it comes from one of the most erudite and respected of classical scholars of our century, Paul Maas:

For those people in whose cultural life ancient Greek still plays a part, even an approximately correct pronunciation of it is impossible, particularly in respect of the musical accent. It follows that in pronouncing it we should not aim at correctness [I repeat that amazing advice from one scholar to others—"we should not aim at correctness"!], but at making it intelligible to our living fellow countrymen. The easiest way of doing this is to pronounce Greek words just as we should pronounce a similar combination of letters in our own language. Until quite lately this has been the general practice, but there is now quite a strong movement against it, started by philologists. This movement is doomed to failure, both by its own inconsistency and by the waste of time and effort which it sacrifices to a phantom, thereby impeding the chief purpose of study, which is to understand the texts. The same applies to rhythm, only in this case it costs us more to give up all hope of achieving correctness.[19]

If those assertions were true, then most of what follows in these lectures would be a waste of time, a sacrifice to a phantom. To fortify my own resolution I hasten to cite two even more authoritative writers. Plato says, "What makes each of us a grammarian is knowledge of the number and variety of vocal sounds indicated by the letters of the alphabet";[20] and Aristotle introduces his discussion of style in his *Poetics* like this:

These [the letters, which for him are the basic elements of style] differ in the conformations and position of the mouth, in roughness and smoothness, in length and shortness, and, further, in the high, low and middle accentuation. Detailed discussion of these matters is appropriate to metrical studies.[21]

Clearly, Aristotle assumes here that all his disciples would be familiar with matters of euphony as expounded by the metricians. Perhaps there is a touch of philosophic scorn in his phrase "appropriate to metrical studies." [22] But he certainly did not mean "These things don't matter at all." And is there not some irony for us now in his delegation of questions of euphony to the metricians? It is our metricians who have reduced the study of Greek sound-effects almost entirely to a single one of Aristotle's three phonetic categories, namely, "length and shortness." And it is the metricians who have taken the traditional term "prosody," *prosodia*, which in classical Greek meant the sound of speech in general, or else its melodic qualities in particular, and have narrowed it down to metrical quantity or else to stress.[23] They have jettisoned those other fundamental factors in euphonic language, the sound-quality and pitch-variation which Aristotle also mentions. Indeed, what has happened in most areas of literary education, and especially in classical education, is that "quantity" like a tyrant has driven out his former co-regents, melody and timbre, drumming them into exile with the remorseless tumptity-tum of his long and short syllables. The injustice is all the more flagrant because often what masquerades as the sound of the classical metres is a deplorable travesty of what the Greek poets and prose-rhythmicists intended, as I hope to show in a later chapter.

    To return to the assertion that it doesn't matter how we hear or speak ancient Greek. Three main arguments are offered to support this contention. One is that even an approximately correct restoration of the ancient pronunciations is impossible in practice; or at any rate that the effort required for mastering the ancient sounds would be too arduous for learners. This I hope to refute in my last chapter. A second argument goes like this: the evidence for the sounds of ancient Greek is insufficient to establish fully and precisely what the classical pronunciations were; we can never be quite certain that we are reproducing the kind of Greek spoken by a citizen of Periclean Athens; so we'll just pronounce Greek like our own language, more or less. But is this a fair argument? Have we full and precise information about, say, life in early Troy, or about all that happened in the battle of Marathon, or about the contents of Euripides' *Hypsipyle*? We certainly have not. Yet few scholars will for that reason recommend that we should cease to study and theorize on such topics, or suggest that we should discuss Marathon as if it had been fought with tanks and machine guns or treat the *Hypsipyle* as if Euripides composed it on a typewriter. Yet that is very like what serious scholars have recommended for the reading of Greek aloud: "we should not aim at correctness"—amazing words from a scholar of high reputation, and one superbly skilled in making the best of tattered fragments of papyrus.

A third argument is the most radical of all, namely, that the movement to revive interest in the theory and practice of ancient Greek pronunciation is "a waste of time and effort"; it impedes "the chief purpose of study, which is to understand the texts." A strange contrast here with the insistence of the ancient Greek grammarians on the fundamental and primary importance of "orthoëpy" (ὀρθοέπεια), that is, correct reading according to intonation, timbre-quality, and quantity, as the prerequisite of literary appreciation; and a strange reaction to the frequent ancient Greek mockery of barbarians who garbled the correct pronunciation of Greek![24] Were the ancient teachers wrong? Were they as backward and primitive in their insistence on the value of the spoken word, as they were—perhaps—in using chariots rather than automobiles, arrows rather than explosive missiles? Are the powers of vocal sound merely trivial—a touch of onomatopoeia here, a dash of alliteration there—or do those sounds reach deep into the creative processes of the author and into the unconscious mind of the hearer? In the rest of this book I shall try to show that the second view is nearer the truth, and that our modern obsession with eye-philology to the detriment of ear-philology needs to be reconsidered, if our aim is to fully understand Greek literary theory and practice.

Here I turn from apologetics to historical fact, to offer a brief survey of Greek theories on the sound of words. For the present my concern will be with the philosophers, scientists, rhetoricians, literary critics, and grammarians. I shall postpone to later chapters consideration of what the creative writers did with the superb phonetic resources of ancient Greek.

The actual beginning of Greek speculation on euphony and phonetics is unknown.[25] Clearly, Homer and Hesiod thoroughly understood the practical use of the chief euphonic resources of Greek; and so, too, did the succeeding poets of the seventh and sixth centuries. The first person recorded as having shown a doctrinaire interest in a matter of euphony was Lasos of Hermione,[26] who came to Athens under the Peisistratids about 520 B.C. There he became the teacher of *mousiké* in its widest sense, that is, the study of literature as well as music. Together with some pupils of a Pythagorean from South Italy—the earlier Pythagoreans may have studied speech-phonetics as well as musical acoustics—he examined the speed of the vibrations of strings when emitting a note, and he also introduced some revolutionary new developments in rhythm and harmony, showing a special interest in the tempo of dithyrambic song. His interest in euphony is indicated by his celebrated "asigmatic odes" in which the sibilant *s* was entirely avoided.[27] Pindar, perhaps a pupil of his, probably refers to this in his remark that "formerly the *san* [the Doric name for the Greek sibilant, presumably here a poetic synonym for *sigma*] issued undetected [literally, 'as a base coin'] from the lips of men." [28] This doctrinaire objection to what was later called sigmatism often recurs in ancient Greek literary criticism. More than four hundred years after Lasos and Pindar, Dionysios of Halicarnassos remarks: "Sigma is an unpleasant disagreeable letter, and positively painful when used to excess." [29] Perhaps this aesthetic objection to the sibilant even goes back to the earliest stages in the evolution of the Greek language, for early Greek eliminated or modified initial and medial *s* in some cases where it was retained in other Indo-European languages as will be illustrated in chapter iii. Though, needless to say, no modern philologist would be inclined to believe that some proto-Greek dictator proclaimed: "*S* is an ugly sound: we must purge our language of it," yet it may not be entirely fanciful to see in those very early reductions of sibilance the unconscious beginnings of the aesthetic antipathy first formulated by Lasos. There is, in fact, an objective acoustic basis for the prejudice: the rougher sibilants emit in pronunciation a larger proportion of the higher partials (or "overtones," or "harmonics") than the other Indo-European speech-sounds, and phonemes in which these partials predominate are regarded by modern acousticians as being harsh and penetrating. No Greek writer, so far as I know, gave this explanation, and the actual existence of these higher overtones can only be proved by modern instruments. But the Greeks with their superbly sensitive and well-trained ears could certainly detect some of them.

Fifty years or so after Lasos, in the second half of the fifth century, there is evidence for a wide interest in phonology and euphony. Two kinds of investigators were prominent. On the one hand, philosophers and scientists studied language as an embodiment of nature and truth; on the other, the sophists and rhetoricians viewed it as an instrument for rhetorical persuasion and pleasure-giving. Among the philosophers, Herakleitos without formulating any specific theories of sound seems to have believed, like certain early

Pythagoreans, that there was a direct natural connexion between words and their referents (as will be illustrated in a few moments when we consider Plato's *Cratylos*). The word etymology, ἐτυμολογία, truth-in-words, enshrines this attitude. Believing in it, anyone in search of metaphysical truth would not scorn to find with Herakleitos significance in the fact that a word meaning "in concord," ξυνῷ, resembled ξὺν νῷ, "with intelligence," or to note that the word for a bow (whose purpose is to cause death), βιός, is paradoxically distinguished from the word for life, βίος, only by a variation in the pitch-accent.[30] We may smile and consider the resemblances fortuitous. But this belief in etymology at least had the useful effect of leading serious-minded thinkers to study phonetic questions.

The doctrine of a natural kinship between words and their referents was opposed by Demokritos, who asserted that words are only conventional signs for things, decided on by convention (θέσει) and not produced by nature (φύσει). But this scepticism toward "truth-in-words" did not deter him from linguistic studies. On the contrary he composed studies on vocal sounds, on rhythm, on harmony (which included speech-intonations), and— most important for the present enquiry—on the beauty of words and on euphonious and cacophonous letters.[31] Unfortunately no significant details survive from these studies, but much of the phonetic theory expounded in later authors may derive from them. Demokritos himself apparently had a highly individualistic manner as a teacher: he pronounced *gamma* in a markedly Ionian way as *gemma*, and *mu* as *mō*, and coined terms like "extremely *delta*-ish" or "*theta*-ish" (δέλτατος and θήτατος).[32]

In Athens during the last quarter of the fifth century the Sophists were exploring many aspects of the sound of words. Hippias discussed questions of accentuation and spelling, and explained problematical passages in Homer by suggesting variant pronunciations (not variant "readings" then).[33] Protagoras wrote a treatise on "rightness in speech" (Περὶ ὀρθοεπείας) which may have included matters of pronunciation and euphony.[34] Prodikos gave lectures on a similar topic, and Gorgias with proverbial virtuosity showed how elaborately and effectively a prose-speaker could use effects of rhythm and assonance to influence his audiences.[35] His pupil Licymnios wrote specifically on "effective wording" (εὐέπεια).

In the second half of the fifth century in Athens interest in phonetics and spelling was widespread enough to encourage dramatists to use it in the theatre. One writer of comedies, Callias,[36] produced a play called a *Letter Tragedy* or a *Letter Show* in which a chorus of women characters sang combinations of consonants and vowels like βα, βε, βη, βι, βο, βυ, βω; γα, γε, γη, γι, γο, γυ, γω. Apparently his chorus spelled these syllables out with music and dancing in strophes and antistrophes, while some of the speeches were concerned with the pronunciation and the shapes of the letters. Sophocles and Euripides also made some dramatic use of letter-shapes and spelling.[37]

Toward the end of the fifth century the politician and orator Archinos, who in 403/2 successfully proposed the decree that the Ionic alphabet should become the official script in Athens, became the first—so far as surviving records go—to examine an aspect of ancient phonetics which is of great importance for us now.[38] He studied what parts of the mouth were used in producing various syllables, thereby introducing a kind of analysis that gives us some of our best clues for the pronouncing of ancient Greek. This sort of thing could have its comic aspects, as the comedians soon saw. Aristophanes gives us a glimpse of a blasé young man pronouncing a word, κρέμαιο, with lips wide apart in a drawling affected way.[39] Similarly Socrates in Plato's *Cratylos* incurs some gentle mockery for his facial expression while pronouncing βουλαπτεροῦν.[40] He looked, we are told, as if he were "going to whistle the pipe-prelude of the *nomos* to Athena." One can see the pursed lips for the βου- and -ροῦν and the raised tongue for the -λ- almost as clearly as in one of those rather repulsive illustrations in modern studies on phonetics. Pericles, if we can trust a late source, prudently avoided such grimaces: he used to practice in front of a mirror to minimize facial contortions in pronouncing *sigma*.[41]

The comic writers found useful material in other aspects of phonetics and pronunciation. They gibed at the efforts of barbarians to pronounce Greek, and they caricatured various speech defects like the inability of Alcibiades to pronounce *rho* correctly, saying *kolax* for *korax*. A famous comic incident in the fifth century resulted from a single slip by an actor in mispronouncing the pitch accent in a play by Euripides. We shall examine this more closely later. Meanwhile we may note that Athenian audiences were obviously quick to notice and appraise nuances in speech-sounds.

The earliest fully extant discussion of the sound of words in Greek comes in the *Cratylos* of Plato. Socrates is asked to join in a discussion on whether words have a natural affinity[42] with what they denote or are merely conventional and arbitrary signs as Demokritos believed. In other words, did the original inventors of words—Plato assumes a much more rational approach to language in primitive times than modern linguists would accept—choose their sounds to express natural qualities of the things they wished to describe, as in "bow-wow," "buzz," or "murmur," or did they not? One of the questioners in the dialogue believes that there is "a natural rightness in descriptive words, alike for everyone, both Greeks and barbarians." His opponent maintains that words are merely "a bit of people's voices sounded at a thing," and that this sound is accepted by common agreement as the name for the thing concerned.

Socrates in accepting the invitation to give his views begins with some ironical self-depreciation about not being really qualified to discuss verbal correctness since he has only attended Prodikos' one-drachma course of lectures on the subject, not the superior fifty-drachma course. Then he settles down to analyzing the problem. First he argues—and wins agreement—that a descriptive word is a kind of instrument (ὄργανον): as a weaver uses a shuttle or weaving rod (κερκίς) to separate the confused threads of warp and woof on his loom, so a teacher uses a descriptive word to separate the elements of reality (or the world of being, or whatever Plato means by the term οὐσία here), or as we would say, to identify things.[43] Now, Socrates continues, any craftsman, when he is making instruments, shapes and adapts them to suit the material they are to be used on, though he also constantly keeps in mind the ideal form for such instruments in general. So, too, the original name-giver should understand how to express in sounds and syllables the name that fits each object's nature, while at the same time remembering the essential purpose of naming, which is to separate out the elements of reality. It seems, then, that words should have a natural affinity with their referents. But what is this affinity?

In trying to answer this question Socrates first discusses the meanings of words from the etymological point of view very fancifully, and perhaps even playfully at times, as when he derives ᾿Αθηνᾶ from ἁ θεονόα "she who is the intellect of god," and Ἄρτεμις from ἄροτον μισεῖ, "she hates sexual intercourse." [44]

This part of the dialogue has little to say in detail about the sound of words, except for some useful remarks on the pitch accent and on the interchanges of certain vowels and consonants in the Attic dialect.[45] But there is a general assumption underlying all this etymological speculation that similarities in sound indicate affinities in meaning, as for example in the famous body-tomb equation (σῶμα-σῆμα) where the implicit reasoning seems to be that the words σῶμα and σῆμα sound like each other because the body is in fact a kind of tomb for the soul. The similarity in sound is assumed to imply a similarity in the nature of the referents. Every reader of Greek literature knows how deeply this belief—or superstition, if you like—in etymological truth—or etymological fallacy, if you prefer—was rooted in the thoughts and emotions of the Hellenes. We recall how names like Aias and Pentheus and Achilles and Helen and Odysseus were solemnly believed to have expressed the destinies of their bearers. Indeed, what seems to us little more than a mere jingle or a pun could reverberate like the voice of destiny to a Greek tragedian and his audience. This was essentially a matter of sound, not of spelling, of hearing a name instead of seeing it, and in fact some of Socrates' farfetched etymologies seem much less absurd when spoken and not simply read by the eye alone.[46]

Socrates now comes to a difficulty in the etymological method of analyzing words by breaking them up—or "bashing them asunder," as Hermogenes vigorously puts it—into their meaningful constituents. To take a modern example, one can deduce the meaning of a compound word like "hippocamp" if one knows that it comes from two roots meaning "horse" and "curve"— a horse with a curve, i.e., a sea horse whether as a mythological mount for sea gods or as an actual marine animal. But you cannot use the same method with uncompounded words like Shakespeare's "strake" or "frush," or, to take Socrates' example, the Greek words ἰόν and ῥέον. How then can we determine whether simple words have a natural affinity with their referents or not? Some of them are clearly mimetic like "buzz" and "murmur" as already mentioned. But what about words like "cat," "dog," "man," "girl"?

To meet this difficulty Socrates expounds a theory which some modern linguists still regard as one of the best explanations of how words were originally formed. He first offers a new definition of descriptive words. Instead of his earlier definition of a word as "an instrument for distinguishing the elements of reality," he suggests that a word is a vocal imitation or re-presentation (μίμημα φωνῇ) of its object.[47] In other words, he turns from semantics to phonetics. Here our special theme comes into the centre of the picture.

Socrates begins by pointing out that we can mime things by gestures of the hand or body. Similarly a descriptive word may be regarded as a vocal gesture. Some are mere mimicries of sounds, like baa-baa, cock-a-doodle-doo, and such. But another kind of word goes much deeper and represents more general qualities, such as flow, motion, restraint—qualities which, he claims, are nearer to the essential reality (οὐσία) of things.[48]

The first type he dismisses as a musical rather than a verbal kind of *mimesis*.[49] He concentrates on the second type, that is, the phonetic expression of the inner nature of things. He illustrates what he means—having first modestly, or perhaps mock-modestly, remarked that he considers his views outrageous and ludicrous—by showing that certain letters naturally express physical qualities: *r* expresses motion because in pronouncing this letter the tongue is least at rest and most strongly vibrated; *i* is apt for thin and narrow things (presumably from the position of the lips); *o* expresses round things, and indicates the notion of internality, as in ἔνδον and ἐντός; *t* and *d* express binding and stopping, on account of the thrust and pressure of the tongue.[50] Letters, he thinks, can even suggest ethical or dimensional qualities: *omega* (in which the mouth is widest) may express grandeur; *eta*, length.[51] Earlier he had surmised that *epsilon*, *eta*, and *zeta* had more magnificent sounds than *iota* and *delta*.[52]

He shows how these natural sound-gestures are found in various words. For example in the initial *gl* of the words γλισχρόν ("glutinous"), γλοιῶδες ("gluey"), and γλυκύ ("sweet") the *gamma*, which holds back the movement of the tongue, indicates the nature of the gluey quality of γλισχρόν and γλοιῶδες and the viscous sweetness of γλυκύ, while the *lambda* with its gliding movement gives an impression of liquidity.[53] Similarly Socrates suggests that the strong breath required in the letters φ, ψ, σ and ζ has mimetic force in words like ψυχρόν (cold that makes one sh-sh-shiver), ζέον (s-s-s-seething: Homer improves on this when he uses σίζ' [*sisd*] to express how the eye of poor Polyphemos sizzled under the red-hot stake), and σείεσθαι (sh-sh-shake) and so on.[54]

This kind of thing—and I have only cited some of the more plausible examples—is likely to evoke contempt rather than admiration among linguists today. We cannot always be sure that Socrates himself is quite serious about it. Yet no matter how small its scientific value may be, poets have always used these phonetic affinities between words and their objects skillfully and effectively, as later chapters will, I hope, show. Indeed, when Socrates goes on to describe how his hypothetical name-giver might have gone about his work of giving apt names to things, what he says is essentially true of a poet selecting the right word for his concepts. Part of what he says is particularly relevant, so I must quote it in full. After stating that name-givers must be able to separate the letters into vowels, mutes, and semi-vowels, and to distinguish various differences in the vowels themselves, he says:

When we have properly investigated all these things we must understand how to apply each letter according to its likeness, whether one applies a single letter to a single object or mixes many letters together, like painters who when they want to produce a likeness sometimes use only purple (ὄστρεον), sometimes some other colour, and sometimes mix many colours together whenever they are preparing flesh-coloured pigment or something else of the kind—as each picture demands each colour, I suppose. In the same way we also shall apply letters to things, one letter to one thing if it seems necessary or else several letters together forming what, as you know, are called syllables, and then putting syllables together, from which both nouns and verbs are composed. Then again from the nouns and verbs we shall eventually construct something great and fine and complete (μέγα . . . καλὸν . . . ὅλον).

It looks very much as if here Plato is drawing on his own experience as a literary artist. Compare a modern poet, Paul Valéry, describing how he used to choose a word:

> I seek a word, says the poet, which should be: feminine, of two syllables, containing *p* or *f*, ending in a mute, and synonym of breaking, separation; and not learned or uncommon. Six conditions ate least.[55]

After Socrates' analysis of letter-sounds, the dialogue begins to move in another direction. So far Socrates has been illustrating, and to some extent upholding, Cratylos' belief in the natural fitness of names. Now he begins to demolish it. He argues that just as the mimesis which painters produce with colours can be inexact, so the mimesis that word-makers produce with words can be false, if the maker of words is incompetent. Besides, words often lose their primary forms by subsequent phonetic changes. And further, against the theory that letters are vocal gestures corresponding to their referents, one can point to Greek words which contain the letter *rho* (which has been accepted as expressive of movement) and *lambda* (accepted as expressing smoothness) that have the meaning "hard to move" or "harsh" like σκληρός. Further, the sounds of words vary from dialect to dialect: the Eretrians call σκληρότης, σκληρότηρ.[56] How does that fit in with the previous statement that ρ and σ have different mimetic qualities? It seems, then, that there are times when the sound of words may have no natural affinity with their referents. So to some extent Demokritos was right in arguing that words were conventional signs. Socrates goes on to conclude that descriptive names are not a safe guide toward reality at all, being only likenesses at best. Linguistics yields to metaphysics.

I have dealt at some length with this dialogue for two reasons. First, it shows how questions about the sound of words in relation to their meaning were familiar to fifth-century Greeks, for Socrates alludes to predecessors in this study and also assumes familiarity with it among his hearers. Secondly, in this dialogue Plato, as so often elsewhere, sows the seeds of many far-reaching theories which later writers, ancient and modern, accepted and expanded. Specially valuable for our enquiry is his recognition that the phonetic qualities of Greek words should be considered in the light of three main properties: ease of pronunciation,[57] beauty of sound, and mimetic power. These three become major criteria in later classical discussions, and remain so to this day. But in the end Socrates makes it clear that in his opinion phonetics and linguistics in general are not of supreme importance for the philosophic seeker after reality. In this regard two incidental remarks of his may serve as preliminary warnings against overvaluing the importance of my further enquiries in these lectures. He reminds us that there are "people who value ease of pronunciation more than truth," and he condemns others "who care nothing for the truth but only for the way they shape their mouths." But with all due deference I would add a third type which hardly existed in Plato's time: those who care nothing for the physical substance of words and thereby miss a good deal of what authors are trying to convey to them.

Three centuries and more after Plato wrote his *Cratylos* a Greek author from Asia Minor, Dionysios of Halicarnassos, who had become a teacher of rhetoric in Augustan Rome, produced his celebrated treatise *On Putting Words Together* (i.e., fitting words into their most euphonically effective sequences).[58] It is a supremely valuable work for our present study, and we shall continually return to it. Dionysios' chief aim is to show in what ways skillfully composed sequences of words can create an effect of beauty and pleasure. In other words his main interest is neither in the metaphysical truth that Plato sought, nor in the practical persuasiveness that most teachers of rhetoric taught, but in something lying between the two—the aesthetic aspect of words, or, as he calls it, "the poetical element, pleasant to the tongue and honey-sweet to the hearing." He is conscious that Platonists might blame him for neglecting higher reality, so in his first chapter he affirms:

The love of beauty (τὸ φιλόκαλον) attached to literary diction blossoms in the days of our youth no less than in later life. For every young person's spirit (ψυχή) is naturally inclined to be excited about loveliness of verbal expression and receives instinctive impulses, like divine inspirations (ἐνθουσιώδεις), toward that loveliness.[59]

Here his language hints at mysticism, at the strange overpowering force of cults like those of Dionysos and Cybele; and later he speaks of the power of melody and rhythm to cast a spell (κηλεῖν)[60] on the listener, a term that other writers use of Orpheus and the Sirens. Modern readers may recall how the young Heinrich Schliemann was captivated by the mere sound of Homer as recited by a stranger and received an "impulse" that led him to discover Homer's Troy. Dionysios is deeply convinced of this almost magical power in words. "Who," he asks in speaking of verbal melody, "is not swayed and held as if by a magical incantation (ἄγεται καὶ γοητεύεται)[61] by one melody of speech and quite unaffected in such a way by another, or placated by one sort of rhythm and exasperated by others?"

In most of his treatise Dionysios is occupied with exploring the sources and techniques of this compelling power in the sound of words. He finds three chief factors—melody (especially as prescribed by the Greek pitch-accent), rhythm, and variety.[62] These we must examine closely in the next chapter. As components of the pleasure that words can give he mentions[63] "fresh loveliness" (ὥραν), "charm" (χάριν), "ease of pronunciation" (εὐστομίαν), and "sweetness" (γλυκύτητα). From these are derived the higher qualities of "beauty" (τὸ καλόν), "magnificence" (μεγαλοπρέπειαν), "weightiness" (βάρος), "impressiveness" (σεμνολογίαν), "worthiness" (ἀξίωμα), and "mellowness" (πίνον). All these, he claims, can be created in the mind and spirit of the hearer by the sound of words as well as by their conceptual meaning.

If Dionysios had confined himself to abstractions and generalizations such as I have selected, many scholars might be apt to brush him aside as a mere essayist. But he substantiates his views in detail and in doing so gives us some of the most valuable information we have about Greek pronunciation and euphony. In discussing the tone-quality of various letters—for example, the roughness of *xi*, the sweetness of *lambda*, and the ugliness of *sigma*—he describes how the vocal organs should be shaped and used in pronouncing them: invaluable evidence, though not always quite satisfactory, for ancient Greek phonetics. Also, he analyzes the rhythms of poetry and prose—speaking of the stately anapaest, the virile and grave baccheios, the mean and unimpressive trochee, the effeminate and unattractive amphibrach, and so on. Here again many scholars may deny the basis of his argument—namely, that metrical feet have special ethical or emotional qualities—but his detailed remarks contain much valuable factual information, and he undoubtedly voices the general doctrine of antiquity.

Sometimes Dionysios goes to almost ridiculous lengths in his analysis of the significance of special sound-effects. When, for example, he spends more than a hundred and fifty words in extracting the euphonic qualities of the very ordinary and unemphatic word πέμπετε in a passage from Pindar,[64] even a sympathetic reader may begin to lose patience. This oversubtlety is a temptation—to be avoided, I hope, in what follows here—for all writers on the euphonic power of words. As a warning I shall also quote a modern critic's strictures:

Provided . . . that a sentence is fine in sense, and fine in rhythm, and easy to articulate—not congested with consonants nor disfigured by jingles, I doubt if it will gain quite so much further beauty or effectiveness from the actual sounds of its syllables—from vowel-play and dentals and labials and the rest of it—as precious persons who revel in this sort of subtlety sometimes suppose. The whole business is liable to degenerate into mere foppery and frippery. [65]

Those are sobering words: but if Dionysios heard them he might ask whether this attack on euphonic elaboration would have been so effective without the contemptuous *p-r* alliteration in "precious persons" and without the hissing sibilance of "this sort of subtlety sometimes suppose" and the close phonetic parallelism of "foppery and frippery." (Indeed, Dionysios might claim that the last two words are merely translations of two words of his own.) [66] Also, as he easily shows, some of the most eminent authors— prose authors [67] as well as poets—were known to have taken great pains to achieve beauty and effectiveness in the sound of their words.

Later there will be good reason to return often to Dionysios' treatise for illumination and instruction. Here we must leave him for the moment to glance briefly at other writers on the sound of Greek after Plato's time. Aristotle was obviously not greatly interested in the subject. Essentially an intellectualist, he did not concern himself much with the mere form of words, except for their rhythmical properties. But, as we have seen, he assumes in his hearers and pupils a sound knowledge of the euphonic qual- ities of words, as implied in the quotation from his *Poetics* cited earlier. Similarly in his *Rhetoric* [68] he refers to the importance of both the right choice of words for an orator and the effective management of the voice, [69] especially with regard to volume of sound, modulation of pitch, rhythm, and assonance. But in general he prefers to study the logic and semantics of language, not its aesthetic or sensuous aspects. He believes that he has chosen the loftier road—and so we should all agree. If we had to make a rigid choice between exploring the mind of the ancients and exploring the sounds they used for expressing their mind, then we should choose the content and not the form, what they say and not how they say it. But Aristotle never suggested that we should ignore the lowlier road: he simply pointed his pupils to others who could guide them in it—who could play Martha to his Mary.

Some of his pupils did not despise the Martha role. His nephew Theo- phrastos (whose name is said to have been given to him by Aristotle him- self for reasons of euphony instead of his cacophonous original name Tyrtamos) wrote on the pitch-accent and on euphony; [70] and the treatise on harmonics by Aristotle's pupil Aristoxenos includes valuable remarks on the intonations of speech. The Alexandrian scholars often discuss ques- tions of pronunciation in the classical poems. The earliest Greek gram- marian whose work has substantially survived, Dionysios the Thracian, emphasizes that the first essential of a literary education is correct reading aloud with careful observance of the accents, the quantities, the use of the breath, and the appropriate emotional tones.[71] His successors continued to insist that this was the foundation of all the other literary arts and graces. Yet this is the foundation which many of our present teachers either never lay at all or else lay crookedly, when they say that silent reading is sufficient or that incorrect pronunciation doesn't matter.

Interest in the sound of Greek, whether as a grammatical or rhetorical or aesthetic or philosophic question, continued until the latest periods of pagan Greece and Rome. Among other more notable exponents were Crates of Mallos (whose visit to Rome in the mid-second century B.C. stimulated interest in Greek euphonic studies),[72] Philodemos of Gadara,[73] Demetrios, Cicero, Quintilian, "Longinus," and Aulus Gellius.[74] (But some had occasional misgivings about paying close attention to mere sounds. Cicero remarks to a friend who was studying a treatise on accentuation: "I can't help asking what bearing that acute and grave study of yours has on the *summum bonum*.") [75] The Stoics in general were particularly interested in matters of phonetics and euphony because of their belief in the doctrine of etymology.[76] Their opponents, the Epicureans, tended to depreciate any cult of euphony. In the second century A.D. a humorous writer could still find material for comedy in mere phonetics. Lucian in one of his dialogues[77] presents a lawsuit between *Sigma* and *Tau* before the presiding Court of the Seven Vowels, where Sigma accuses Tau of stealing his property, especially in Attica where πράττω has been substituted for πράσσω and θάλαττα for θάλασσα and so on.

Many of these writers—and others not mentioned here—will help in our later enquiries. What I have already said will, I hope, suffice to answer any charge that questions of pronunciation and euphony are negligible for the study of Greek literature so far as theory is concerned. To conclude I quote from perhaps the most judicious and sensible of all writers of this topic, Quintilian. After a discussion of the sound of words he remarks with characteristic Roman sobriety:

Again the thought comes back to me that there will be people who regard what I have said as excessively trivial and even hindering those who are working on something greater. I myself do not believe that one should descend to excessive worrying or futile quibblings about these matters. Minds can be made into mincemeat by them . . . [Then he mentions men like Gaius Caesar and Cicero who thought it worth while to pay attention to such things.] Studies of this kind harm only those who stick in them, not those who pass through them. [78]

As we proceed I shall not try to persuade any student of the classics to "stick" in questions of mere sound, or to worry or to quibble about them. But I will try to re-establish the claim made by the founders of our grammatical science that if we wish to understand and enjoy classical literature fully we must learn to speak it and hear it as perfectly as we can. Our habits of silent reading and of inadequate pronunciation have, I believe, weakened the power and attractiveness of Greek literature, especially for our younger students. So my chief aim is to help in restoring what Wordsworth called "the living voice" [79] to a language and a literature too often treated as if it were written for the eye and not for the ear.

ABBREVIATIONS USED IN THE NOTES AND BIBLIOGRAPHY

AJP	*American Journal of Philology*
CJ	*Classical Journal*
CP	*Classical Philology*
CQ	*Classical Quarterly*
CR	*Classical Review*
CW	*Classical Weekly*
GR	*Greece and Rome*
HSCP	*Harvard Studies in Classical Philology*
IF	*Indogermanische Forschungen*
JHS	*Journal of Hellenic Studies*
LSJ	H. G. Liddell and Robert Scott, *Greek-English Lexicon* 9th ed., rev. H. Stuart Jones and Roderick McKenzie, 1940
Ph	*Philologus*
P–W	Pauly–Wissowa–Kroll, *Realencyclopädie der klassischen Altertumswissenschaft*
REG	*Revue des Etudes Grecques*
RhM	*Rheinisches Museum*
RPh	*Revue de Philologie*
SO	*Symbolae Osloenses*
TAPA	*Transactions and Proceedings of the American Philological Association*
WS	*Wiener Studien*

NOTES TO CHAPTER I

[1] See, e.g., John Anthony O'Brien, *Silent Reading* (New York, 1921).
[2] Cf. A. W. Verrall, *The Bacchants of Euripides and Other Essays* (Cambridge, 1910)

246: "The habit of silent reading has made us slow to catch the sound of what is written. And moreover, used to language and poetry constructed on principles not merely different from the Greek, but diametrically opposed, our attention, even if given to the sound, brings us no natural and instinctive report. To logic, rhetoric, pathos we are alive; and upon these heads the tragic poets are criticised; but as to noise we will not notice it, not even if we are bidden and bidden again."

[3] I take the terms "eye-philologists" and "ear-philologists" from Jespersen 23 f. How little the ear counts among modern rhetoricians is exemplified in the neglect of all matters of verbal sound except rhythm in so full a manual as Cleanth Brooks and Robert Penn Warren, *Modern Rhetoric* (New York, 1949).

[4] On the extreme rarity of silent reading in antiquity see, especially, Balogh; also Norden 6; Eugene S. McCartney, "On Reading and Praying Audibly," *C P* XLIII (1948) 184–187; G. L. Hendrikson, "Ancient Reading," *C J* XXV (1929/30) 182–190. On references to reading aloud in the Aristophanic scholia see W. G. Rutherford, *A Chapter in the History of Annotation* (London, 1905) 97–179. See further in nn. 8–12 *infra*. To this day in rural parts of Greece (as in other countries) peasants often have to pronounce written words, or at least shape them with their mouths, before they can understand them; see, e.g., Xan Fielding, *The Stronghold* (London, 1955) 151. Silent reading without movement of the lips is canonically forbidden for religious exercises by some Christians and Moslems (Balogh 104). As Hendrikson notes, there are many intermediate gradations between silent reading and full speech. Some doctors forbid patients suffering from throat ailments to read at all, because they believe that some movement of the throat is likely to occur.

[5] Letters of the alphabet are generally defined as "voices": see the scholia on Dionysios Thrax (Hilgard) 31,6; 182,13; 316,25; Donatus, *Inst.* 48,33 (Keil); Priscian II 3 (p. 6 Hertz); Marius Victorinus (Keil) 6,5,5 and 30; Aeschylus, *Seven* 434, 468; Euripides fr. 370 (Nauck); also Hendrikson (as cited in n. 4 *supra*) on the use of ἀκούω with reference to understanding written speech; Balogh 202–208; and LSJ at λέγω III 8. "Aristotle," *Problems* 10,39 defines letters as πάθη τῆς φωνῆς.

[6] *Timaios* 22B. The reference is primarily to the comparative newness of the history and traditions of Greece compared with Egypt, but the aphorism is broadly true of the Greek approach to life and art.

[7] Quintilian 1,1,34: in reading, he says, it is necessary for the eye to look on ahead of the speaking voice, and so the attention has to be divided (*dividenda intentio animi*). Cf. Horace, *Satires* 2,5,55. In the second century A.D. Lucian (*Adv. Indoct.* 2) speaks of one who reads "very quickly (πάνυ ἐπιτρέχων), your eye going in advance of your mouth," but adds that this is no advantage if one fails to appreciate the merits and defects of each passage. Cf. Horace, *Satires* 2,5,55, *veloci percurre oculo*.

[8] For Julius Caesar's silent reading (σιωπῇ) see Plutarch, *Brutus* 5. For that of the senators (*taciti*) see Suetonius, *Augustus* 39. Similar references to silent reading of non-literary documents are in Horace, *Satires* 2,5,68 and Ovid, *Heroides* 21,1 f. (=Aristainetos 1,10: p. 140 Hercher). But *tacitus* in some—perhaps even all— of these may not preclude a low murmur without distinct words to any hearer: cf. n. 4 *supra*. In Horace, *Sat.* 1,6,122 f. presumably a literary text is being read:

but *tacitum* there is frequently (and, I believe, rightly) taken as "in quiet moments," for in *Sat.* 1,3,64 f., where a literary text is also presumably in mind, *legentem* is contrasted with *tacitum*: one is not *tacitus* when *legens*. See further in Balogh 90 f., 98.

⁹ Two passages (not cited by Balogh) from fifth- and fourth-century Greek have been cited as evidence of ability to read written messages silently. The first is in Euripides, *I.T.* 763:

αὐτὴ [ἡ γραφή] φράσει σιγῶσα τἀγγεγραμμένα

but the silence referred to is that of the written letters which cannot actually speak by themselves, and not that of a reader. The second is in Antiphanes fr. 196 (Edmonds) which refers to letters in a written message as

ἄφωνα δ'ὄντα . . . τοῖς πόρρω λαλεῖ
οἷς βούλεθ'' ἕτερος δ'ἂν τύχῃ τις πλησίον
ἑστὼς ἀναγιγνώσκοντος οὐκ ἀκούσεται.

But Edmonds (correctly, I believe) renders the last two lines "Though dumb, they speak far off to whom they choose, And, near their reader, you'll not hear his news," i.e., you will not be able to gather the actual message when listening to someone reading the letters (aloud, but not loudly, to himself: see the end of n. 4 *supra*), not that you will not hear any sound from the reader. Both quotations are variations on the paradox that though letters are silent yet in a sense they have a voice. The earliest certain Greek reference to silent reading is in Aristainetos (as cited in n. 8 *supra*), and that is not earlier than the fifth century A.D.

¹⁰ *Confessions* 6,3. See Additional Note, *infra*.

¹¹ *Confessions*, 8,12. Balogh takes Augustine's silent reading here as an indication of his rejection of the old rhetorical method of reading aloud with enjoyment of the euphony. But probably Ambrose's example influenced him, too. For the later belief that the Devil tried to hinder monks from the pious practice of silent reading see the amusing passages cited by Chaytor (see n. 12 *infra*).

¹² On the continuation of reading aloud as normal practice until well into the Middle Ages see Balogh and also H. J. Chaytor, *From Script to Print* (Cambridge, 1945) and "The Medieval Reader and Textual Criticism," *Bulletin of the John Rylands Library* 26 (1941/42) 49–56, and Ludwig Bieler, "A Grammarian's Craft," *Classical Folia* (New York, 1965) 30 f.

¹³ See S. Witkowski, *Epistulae Privatae Graecae* (Leipzig, 1911).

¹⁴ For evidence in support of the likelihood that authors in antiquity generally spoke their words aloud while writing them Balogh 213 quotes Ovid, *Heroides* 18, 19–20; Petronius, *Satyricon* 115 (where the poet Eumolpius while writing poetry makes "an extraordinary noise like the bellowing of a wild animal trying to get out"); and Theodoretos *Graecarum affectionum curatio* 1,29 (p. 13 Raeder) on Socrates' stammering (βατταρίζοντα) as he wrote. Cf. Dylan Thomas' way of "muttering, whispering, intoning, bellowing" when composing a poem (Fitz-Gibbon 220) and Swift, *Journal to Stella* for 7 March 1710–11.

¹⁵ On writing as primarily a mnemonic see, e.g., Quintilian 1,7,31 and "Plutarch," *On Music* 2, where γραμματική is defined as a τέχνης ἐπιτηδείου γραμμαῖς τὰς

φωνὰς δημιουργεῖν καὶ ταμιεύειν τῇ ἀναμνήσει. Cf. Lasserre 152. On ancient objections to writing as a vehicle for recording the spoken word see J. A. Notopoulos, "Mnemosyne in Oral Literature," *TAPA* LXIX (1938) 465–493. The key passage, as he notes, is Plato, *Phaidros* 274c with its distinction between the static memory (ὑπόμνησις) preservable by writing, and the creative memory (μνήμη) which works through the spoken word. See also Havelock 42 ff., 93, 100–103, 146, 167 ff. On the λέξις γραφική see Sonkowsky. S. H. Butcher in his lively essay on "The Written and the Spoken Word," in *Some Aspects of the Greek Genius* (3d ed.; London, 1904), contrasts the Egyptian reverence for hieroglyphs (in which the signs represent sight, not sound) with the utilitarian Greek attitude to the alphabet, and discusses Plato's views on the defects of writing as a means of conveying truth. There is a clear contrast between the artistic care with which the ancient Egyptians (like modern Chinese poets with their ideograms) drew and arranged their hieroglyphs and the careless scattering of letters in early Greek inscriptions. The first reference to writing in Greek literature is unfavorable— σήματα λυγρά in *Iliad* 6,168, with reference to a written (literally, "scratched") message.

[16] Quintilian 1,7,31.

[17] *Olympians* 6,4: πρόσωπον τηλαυγές.

[18] FitzGibbon 325.

[19] Maas, 55 f.; cf. 57 f. See chap. ii, n. 76.

[20] Plato, *Philebos* 17c: cf. 18b. In 51c he ranks the pleasures of the ear second to those of the eye, but above those of the other senses.

[21] Aristotle, *Poetics* 20, 1456b 30–34, I translate his δασύτητι and ψιλότητι as "roughness" and "smoothness" (not as "rough and smooth breathings"), as in Aristotle, *De audibilibus* 804b 8–11 and Dionysios Thrax 12,5 (Uhlig) and scholia.

[22] For disdain toward "lovers of hearing" see Aristotle, *Rhetoric* 3,1,1403b 20 ff. and Plato, *Republic* 5, 476b. Aristotle suffered from a speech defect himself (see chap. vii, n. 12), which may partly explain his attitude to matters of euphony.

[23] Cf. Maas 72: "Prosody is the study of language from the metrical point of view." Against this see the far wider definitions of *prosodia* in Dionysios Thrax 12 (and scholia *ad loc*.), Herodian 1,5, Aulus Gellius 13,6, and others cited by Hanschke 78–89. For stress in Greek see Index.

[24] On the importance of correct reading, orthoëpy (ὀρθοέπεια), with due regard to pitch, quality, and quantity, as the primary requisite of a literary education see Dionysios Thrax 1 f. and the scholia; Dionysios, *Antiquit.* 1,90; Quintilian 1,5,33 and 1,6,20 (with F. H. Colson's notes *ad loc*.) and 1,8,1 ff.; also Philodemos, *Rhet.* 1,186 (Sudhaus). The distinction made by LSJ at ὀρθοέπεια and ὀρθοεπεῖν is not as sharp as suggested there: ὀρθοέπεια in its earliest use (i.e., in the title of Demokritos' book, Diels-Kranz 2,91,27) could refer to either pronunciation or diction. See further in chap. vii.

[25] I have omitted reference to mythical and early historical "inventors" of the alphabet or special letters, e.g., Prometheus, Cadmus, Cecrops, Linus, Palamedes, Danaos, Simonides, for which see: Schmid-Stählin 1,1,522 n. 1; A. Kleingunther, ΠΡΩΤΟΣ ΕΤΡΕΤΗΣ, *Ph.* Supplementband XXVI 1; Schwyzer 137 f.; and Dornseiff, *Alph.* 2 ff. On the origins of the alphabet in general see L. H. Jeffery, *The Local Scripts of Archaic Greece* (Oxford, 1961) 2, and J. A. Bundgård, "Why Did

25

the Art of Writing Spread to the West?" *Analecta Romana Instituti Danici*, Vol. III (1965).

[26] On Lasos see Lasserre 34 ff.; Schmid-Stählin 1,1,545,2; Diels-Kranz, index at *Lasos*. For his studies in the vibrations of strings and his connexions with Pythagorean doctrines see Diels-Kranz 1,110,5 ff.; B. L. van der Waerden, "Die Harmonienlehre der Pythagoreer," *Hermes* LXXVIII (1945) 165–199; Lasserre 35 f., Hanschke 93; and Dornseiff, *Alph.* 20 ff., 32 ff.

[27] On Lasos' asigmatic odes see G. A. Privitera, "L'asigmatismo di Laso e di Pindaro in Clearco fr 88 Wehrli," *Rivista di Cultura Classica e Medioevale* VI (1949) 164–170 and Schmid-Stählin 1,1,544.

[28] Pindar fr. 61,1 f. (Bowra): see Privitera (as cited in n. 27 *supra*), Schmid-Stählin 1,1,544, n. 11, and Wilamowitz, *Pindaros* 342; and cf. Herodotos 1,139. I take it that by his phrase τὸ σὰν κίβδαλον Pindar means that the *s*-sound passed as good currency for poetry (i.e., as euphonically acceptable) until detected as being base metal.

[29] Dionysios 14,146,12.

[30] For Herakleitos on ξυνῷ and βίος see Diels-Kranz 1,176,5 f. and 1,161,6 f.

[31] For the titles of Demokritos' books on *Mousiké* see Diels-Kranz 2,91,25 ff. They include: Περὶ καλλοσύνης ἐπέων, Περὶ εὐφώνων καὶ δυσφώνων γραμμάτων, Περὶ Ὁμήρου ἢ ὀρθοεπείης καὶ γλωσσέων.

[32] Demokritos' pronunciation, etc.: Diels-Kranz 2,146,17 and 19–21; 2,167,15; 2,146,22–24.

[33] Hippias on accentuation and spelling: see Aristotle, *Poetics* 25,1461A 22 ff. (οὐ and οὔ, δίδομεν and διδόμεν); Plato, *Hippias Major* 285c. It is clear from Aristotle, *Soph. El.* 166B 1 and 177B 35 ff. (τὸ μὲν ὀξύτερον, τὸ δὲ βαρύτερον ῥηθέν) that, the criterion in the οὔ/οὐ ambiguity was one of accent, not of breathing.

[34] For Protagoras see Plato, *Phaidros* 166B.

[35] For Gorgias see John C. Robertson, *The Gorgianic Figures in Early Greek Prose* (Baltimore, 1893), Norden 16 ff., Schmid-Stählin 1,3,57 ff.

[36] Callias' *Letter Tragedy* is described in Athenaios 10,454C–F, 448B, 276A (= Edmonds, *Fragments of Attic Comedy* I, 176–181). See Dornseiff, *Alph.* 67 for similar "syllabaries" in the papyri: he doubts that Callias' work was really for the theatre.

[37] Soph. fr. 117 (Nauck); Eurip. fr. 382 (Nauck).

[38] For Archinos on the positions of the vocal organs in speech see Diels-Kranz 1,458n. on 1.4 (citing Syrianus on Aristotle, *Metaphysics* N 6 1092B 26 ff.) and H. Usener, *RhM* XXV (1870) 90–92: cf. Blass 114, n. 7.

[39] On the wide lips of Pheidippides see *Clouds* 870 ff. and cf. Blass 54. Cf. Diogenes Laertius, *Lives* 7,28: τὸ μέντοι στόμα μὴ διέλκειν (it being a sign of garrulity and exaggeration). Cf. p. 142.

[40] On Socrates' facial expression see *Cratylos* 417E.

[41] Eustathios on *Iliad* 10,409 cites Aelius Dionysios for Pericles' avoidance of facial contortions. He also quotes Aelius as suggesting that Homer used the form θεά and not θεή in the first line of the *Iliad* "so that he might not narrow the orotundity by drawing his lips closer together" (ἵνα μὴ συστείλας τὰ χείλη στενὸν τὸν ὄγκον ποιοίη).

[42] "A natural affinity": ὀρθότητά τινα τῶν ὀνομάτων . . . φύσει πεφυκυῖαν: *Cratylos*

383A–B. I translate ὀνομάτων as "descriptive words," not simply as "names," here, because Socrates later includes verbs and adjectives in the discussion. On the dispute whether words originated φύσει or θέσει see W. S. Allen, "Ancient Ideas on the Origin and Development of Language," *Transactions of the Philological Society*, 1948, 35–60, and Detlev Fehling, *RhM* CVIII (1965) 212–229. For the Pythagorean origin of the φύσει view and its refutation by Demokritos see Proclus on *Cratylos* 16 p. 5,25, cited by Diels-Kranz II 148,8.

[43] Socrates on names as instruments: *Cratylos* 388B–C.

[44] Ἀθηνᾶ: 407B. Ἄρτεμις: 406B. σῶμα-σῆμα: 400B–C.

[45] Remarks on accentuation: 399B, 416B. On vowel-quality: in 398D it is implied that in "old Attic" ἥρως was only slightly different in pronunciation from ἔρως; similarly in 418B–C ἡμέρα is said to have been pronounced ἱμέρα or ἐμέρα by οἱ ἀρχαιότατοι, and δέον like διόν (419A): cf. 411E, 426C, 398B, 406C, and 437A. For other interchanges of ε, ει, η, and ι cf. Sturtevant 26,34. In 410C it is stated that in old Attic ὧραι was pronounced ὅραι; cf. 420B. In 418C–E and 419B we are told that the older Attic δ was sometimes changed later to ζ. In 421B–C Socrates says some people pronounce οὐκ ὄν as οὐκ ἰόν. Blass 109 n. 1 notes evidence in 427A for similarity between δ and τ. On p. 95 he suggests emendations in 412A and 437A, substituting τὸ ῄ (i.e., the rough breathing) for τὸ εἶ. See chap. iii, n. 5.

[46] "Less absurd": e.g., the coincidence of the pitch accent helps to make ἀτειρές similar to Ἀτρεύς (395C) and δαήμονες to δαίμονες (398B). Even the derivation of ἄνθρωπος from ἀναθρῶν ἃ ὄπωπε is not utterly outrageous if one allows for apocope, synizesis, and elimination of the repeated syllable (as in ἀμ[φι]φορεύς), making the second phrase ἀνθρωνωπε. The pronunciation of Ἑρμῆς as Εἰρέμης (408B) by "anaptyxis" to justify an etymology from εἴρειν ἐμήσατο is paralleled by the inscriptional form hερεμῆς: see Lejeune 177 n. 1, and cf. pp. 61 f. *infra*.

[47] "A vocal imitation": 423B. For words containing gesture-letters see 422E ff.; for an elaborate modern development of this theory of the origin of speech see Paget 132 ff.; cf. Tylor 160 ff.

[48] Early views on the onomatopoeic and gestural theory of the origin of language are discussed by Allen (as cited in n. 42 *supra*) 46 ff. Aulus Gellius, *Attic Nights* 10,4 gives examples in Latin, as, *vos* with an outward movement of the lips and breath, *nos* with both lips and breath held back *quasi intra nosmet* (so, too, *tu/ego*, *tibi/mihi*). Cf. Tylor 220 ff.

[49] Socrates, who is thinking almost entirely in terms of the sound of words, not of the appearance of letters (see n. 51 *infra*), does not consider the fact that the shapes of letters can imitate the shapes of their referents. For Greek interest in symbolical aspects of the shapes of letters cf. my *Greek Metaphor* 62–69; also *CR* L (1936) 109–112 and Dornseiff, *Buchst. and Alph.* As evidence for emphasis on the sound of words, note that the derivation of Ἥρα in 404C only works if the word is sounded.

[50] For Socrates' examples of mimetic letters see 426C–427C.

[51] For the "grandeur" assigned to *alpha* and the "lengthiness" assigned to *eta* (τὸ δ' αὖ ἄλφα τῷ μεγάλῳ ἀπέδωκε καὶ τῷ μήκει τὸ ἦτα) see 427C; possibly 407B assumes the same notion. Plutarch in discussing the question why *alpha* comes first in the alphabet (*Quaestiones conviviales* 9,2) notes that it is the first of articulate sounds to be clearly pronounced by infants (cf. Berry 20), which he takes to

be one of the reasons for its coming first in the alphabetic table. Theodosios of Alexandria Περὶ γραμματικῆς (p. 1 Goettling) says that God opened man's mouth for speech with *alpha* because it is spoken with the mouth opened widest. Socrates gives as his reason for ascribing greatness to *alpha* and lengthiness to *eta*, ὅτι μεγάλα τὰ γράμματα (427c). Méridier (*Platon: œuvres complètes*, V, *Cratyle* [Paris, 1950] 25) rightly takes this as referring to the sound of the letters (so, too, Allen [as cited in n. 42 *supra*], citing the scholium to Dionysios Thrax, Hilgard 198), not to their size as visual signs (as H. N. Fowler takes it, in *Plato* [London and New York, 1926] VI 147: cf. his note on pp. 56 f., where he accuses Plato, without clear evidence, of "confusing pronunciation with spelling" in "several passages of the dialogue"). In fact, *alpha* and *eta* are not notably larger than the other letters, but still the mouth would have been wider open in pronouncing them than in pronouncing most of the others. Perhaps the "Doric" associations of *alpha* also had some influence in enhancing its prestige: cf. chap. iii, nn. 97–99.

52 For the greater magnificence (μεγαλοπρεπέστερα) of *epsilon*, *eta*, and *zeta* see 418c.

53 On γλ-, etc., see 427B.

54 See 424c ff.

55 *Autres Rhumbs* (Paris, 1934) 143.

56 σκληρότης-σκληρότηρ: 434c.

57 See chap. iii, n. 5.

58 On Dionysios' Περὶ συνθέσεως in general see especially the excellent introduction, translation, notes, and glossary in Rhys Roberts' edition. I have used his translation extensively with some alterations. See also Bonner and Grube.

59 "The love of beauty," etc.: 1,66,16 ff. The general idea goes back to Plato.

60 κηλεῖν: 11,124,13.

61 ἄγεται καὶ γοητεύεται: 11,122,16. Cf. 12,134,9 ff., where Dionysios says that an author either should "join together words that are melodious (εὐμελῆ), rhythmical (εὔρυθμα) and euphonious (εὔφωνα), by which the hearing is touched with a feeling of sweetness and softness . . . or he should intertwine and interweave those which have no such natural effect with those that can so bewitch (γοητεύεται) the ear that the unattractiveness of the one set is overshadowed by the grace of the other." For the same use of ἄγεται cf. 11,124,25: "the hearing is swayed by the rhythms." For these metaphors from magic see p. 78 f.

62 Three chief factors: 11,120,19 f. and 11,122,11 f. and 23; see further at the beginning of chap. iii *infra*. The fourth factor, "appropriateness" (τὸ πρέπον), is of a different kind, and I do not discuss it here (see Wilkinson 50 ff.). On the "ethos" of rhythm see further 115.

63 ὥραν, etc.: see 11,120,20 ff.

64 For the analysis of πέμπετε see 22,220,16 ff.

65 F. L. Lucas, *Style* (London, 1955) 250, with special reference to prose. But he goes on to consider some clear cases of expressive alliteration. Alexander Pope's famous indictment of those who "by numbers judge a poet's song" (*An Essay on Criticism*, II 137 ff.) does not mean that "numbers" should be neglected by poet or critic, for see the same *Essay* II 164 ff. and his special praise for Dionysios: "See Dionysius Homer's thoughts refine, And call new beauties forth from every line" (III 106 f.).

66 The words are σκευωρίαν and φλυαρίαν (25,264,7), which Roberts translates as

"niggling and peddling": perhaps "finicality and triviality" would be better.

[67] Plato and Isocrates: see Roberts' note on p. 266.

[68] Aristotle, *Rhetoric* 3,1,1403B 2–1404A 39. See also 1407B 12 (ὅλως δὲ δεῖ εὐανάγνωστον εἶναι τὸ γεγραμμένον καὶ εὔφραστον), 1408B 5, 1410A 24 ff., 1412A ff.

[69] On ὑπόκρισις see chap. vii.

[70] Theophrastos on euphony: see J. Stroux, *De Theophrasti virtutibus dicendi* (Leipzig, 1912) and Roberts' note on Dionysios 16,164,22. For the change of name from Tyrtamos to Theophrastos see Strabo 13,618 and Kourmoules 201. But Diogenes Laertius, *Lives* 5,38 says he was called Theophrastos διὰ τὸ τῆς φράσεως θεσπέσιον. Dionysios says that Theophrastos considered some words were beautiful by nature and others paltry and ignoble by nature, with reference, it seems, to euphony. Aristoxenos: see p. 28.

[71] πρῶτον ἀνάγνωσις ἐντριβὴς κατὰ προσῳδιάν: Dionysios Thrax 1 and see scholia *ad loc.*: cf. nn. 24 and 68 *supra*.

[72] Crates' treatise Περὶ φωνῆς is mentioned by Diogenes Laertius, *Lives* 7,44. See Schmid-Stählin 2,1,269 ff. and Grube 132, 136, 150.

[73] On Philodemos' notable references to matters of euphony (owing to the mutilation of the papyri it is often hard to determine which of the views expressed are his own) see Gomperz; Jensen; Schmid-Stählin 2,1,371–374; Grube 193–206, 222 n. 7; Hausrath; Sudhaus (especially pp. 33, 150, 162, 198), and H. M. Hubbell, "The Rhetoric of Philodemos," *Transactions of the Connecticut Academy* 23 (1920) 243–382.

[74] See Index at *Demetrios* and the other names cited.

[75] Cicero, *Ad Atticum* 12,6,2. But Atticus might have replied, "Any *bonum* may contribute to the *summum bonum*."

[76] On the Stoics' interest in euphony see Grube 135 ff. and Phillip De Lacy, "Stoic Views . . ." 252 ff.; on that of the Epicureans see Dionysios 24, p. 250, 4 ff. with Roberts' note, and De Lacy, "The Epicurean Analysis of Language" *AJP* LX (1939) 85–92. For later quotations from other authors cited in this paragraph see Index. For Latin views in general see Wilkinson.

[77] *Judgement of the Vowels.*

[78] Quintilian 1,7,33–35.

[79] *The Prelude* VI 99: see chap. vi, n. 40 and cf. Balogh 203 ff. for similar phrases referring to the embodiment of the voices of the ancient in written texts.

ADDITIONAL NOTE TO CHAPTER I

On silent and audible reading see also E. G. Turner, *Ancient Books in the Fifth and Fourth Centuries B.C.* (London, 1951), and W. J. Verdenius, *Studium Generale* 19 (1966), 103–114, especially p. 114.

II
Speech and Music

"The science of public oratory is, after all, a kind of musical science":[1] so remarks one of our best helpers, Dionysios of Halicarnassos. On the same principle Quintilian strongly emphasized the necessity for orators to be familiar with both the theory and the practice of music.[2] Like a singer, the speaker should be a master of melody as well as of rhythm if he wants to win his cases. To illustrate the importance of a skillfully modulated voice Quintilian recalls that a celebrated Roman orator when making a speech used to keep a man with a pitch pipe beside him to warn him by sounding it if his voice went off the best pitch-levels.[3]

While rhetoricians had to remind their matter-of-fact pupils that oratory and music were sisters, writers on poetry hardly needed to emphasize the kinship. Poetry's earliest name in Greek, ἀοιδή, primarily meant "song"; and the poet was called a singer (ἀοιδός) long before he was called a maker (ποιητής). For the Greeks, poetry, song, and dance, like the three Graces, often went together.[4] (Perhaps that is why the two Muses whose names sound like early Greek formations are Terpsichore, "she who delights in the choral dance," and Calliope, "she of the beautiful voice.") The most famous opening lines in Greek and Roman literature—the *Iliad*'s "Sing, Muse, the wrath . . ." and the *Aeneid*'s "I sing of arms and the man . . ." —always reminded ancient readers of this primordial marriage of music and words.

In Greek and Roman education music and poetry were kept together in the discipline called *mousiké*.[5] Though gradually they drew apart, as each became more elaborately studied and systematized, and as the written word ousted the spoken word, yet it was not until the end of the Middle Ages that the theory of music ceased to be an essential part of education. Unhappily now in our own time the average student is often far worse educated in the understanding and appreciation of music than any schoolboy of ancient Greece. When our school children learn what we call "music," often all they learn is to play an instrument, an aim which the classical educators certainly did not consider supreme. In ancient times what mattered most was the understanding of the principles of music in general. As a result of our present neglect of training in musical appreciation we may often, when we read poetry, fail to notice sound-effects which the classical writers and critics assumed would be obvious to every educated reader.

Artistic language, as they saw it, was a kind of music. But speech and song are not exactly the same. What is the basic difference between them?[6] Aristoxenos, Aristotle's pupil, was the first, so far as we know, to give a satisfactory answer. He distinguished between speaking and singing by the way in which the pitch of the voice changes in each. When the voice is speaking, he says, it "seems to the senses to traverse a certain space in such a manner that it does not become stationary at any point, not even at the extremities of its progress . . . but passes on into silence in unbroken continuity." This he calls "the continuous movement" (ἡ συνεχὴς κίνησις). In contrast, when the voice is singing "the process seems to be of exactly the opposite nature: the voice in its progress stations itself at a certain pitch, and then again at another, and it pursues this process all the time . . ." This he calls movement by intervals (ἡ διαστηματικὴ κίνησις). In other words, as he puts it later, "in normal conversation we avoid bringing the [pitch of the] voice to a steady point unless occasionally forced by strong feeling to resort to such a movement, whereas in singing we act in precisely the opposite way, avoiding continuous movement [between the notes] and making the voice become, as far as possible, absolutely stationary [on each note]."

This is a fundamental distinction, but it is too rigid. As Aristoxenos saw, there is a kind of song-melody in speech (λογῶδές τι μέλος), especially in ancient Greek with its melodic word-accent. A later musicologist, Aristides Quintilianus, developing this notion, spoke of a tone of the voice lying between singing and speaking.[7] He described it as "the intermediate voice-movement, the one in which we make our readings of poetry"—an important indication for us of how we should recite passages from the ancient poets. Presumably what he chiefly meant was a way of speaking which pronounced the Greek pitch-accents more like musical notes than ordinary speech-tones.

In English we do not have a built-in tonic accent in separate words. But our sentence intonation can provide a kind of melody in speech, too. A hundred years, or so, ago many admired Gladstone's mighty organ-voice and were impressed when they heard Tennyson "mouthing out his hollow *oes* and *aes*" in reading his own poems.[8] Similarly W. B. Yeats almost intoned when he recited his own work, and James Joyce, who had a fine tenor voice, almost sang. Nowadays such intonations from a contemporary poet or orator would probably be disliked.

On the other hand, as the ancient critics saw, the musicality of speech can be exaggerated. Quintilian recalls that Gaius Caesar once remarked to a teacher of rhetoric who was overdoing it: "If you are singing, you are singing badly; if you are reading, you are singing." [9] And Plutarch complains that many sophists of his time by exaggerating the tunefulness of their enunciation put their hearers into a kind of ecstasy, thereby "giving their hearers an empty pleasure and gaining for themselves an even more empty renown." [10] Even a saint could be led astray by this vocal music: Augustine says that he was tempted to neglect the substance of Ambrose's discourses by the sweetness (*suavitas*) of his speech.[11] These, however, were unusual cases. In general the best orators and reciters of the ancient world probably spoke like the orotund, melodious speakers of our nineteenth century—"echoing loud and clear like the trumpet at the Olympic games," to quote one Greek description—and not with the studiously casual tones of the present time. Once again contemporary fashions make it hard for us to appreciate the full richness of the sounds of ancient Greek.

From what the Greek musicologists said, it is clear that one cannot always draw a clear line of separation between speech and song; there is a central area where the two kinds of utterance meet. This is the area where ancient poetry and oratory chiefly moved, and in it they probably kept closer to the sound of music than to the sound of plain conversation. Most of the ancient critics would probably have endorsed the following words by one of the most musical of modern poets, Paul Valéry:

˙ . . in studying a piece of poetry, one should never take as a beginning or point of departure ordinary discourse or current speech and then rise from the level of prose to the desired poetic tone; on the contrary, I believe one should start from song, put oneself in the attitude of the singer, tune one's voice to the fullness of musical sound, and from that point descend to the slightly less vibrant state suitable to verse.[12]

The kinship between music and spoken literature can be viewed in another way. Both speech and music depend for their acoustic effect mainly on five elements: speed of delivery (fast or slow), intensity (loud or soft), pitch-variation (high or low), rhythmic variation (long or short, stressed or unstressed), and what I call timbre-quality or simply quality (rough or smooth, bright or dull).[13] For example, in speaking the well-known line of Yeats,

I will arise and go now and go to Innisfree,

one can gabble it double-quick, or drag it out intolerably; one can bellow it or whisper it; one can monotone it or run it up or down a scale; one can stress all the syllables (like a child learning to read) or reduce its wavering rhythm to crude iambics; and one can pronounce the vowels and consonants gruffly or mellifluously. If any one of the five musical elements that I have mentioned is seriously distorted in reading this line, or any other carefully constructed line of poetry, its poetic intention may be spoiled, except insofar as it makes a factual statement. "But surely that factual statement is what matters most?" some may ask. The answer is no. Nobody, except perhaps Yeat's more affectionate relations and friends, would have been interested in the rather commonplace homesickness he describes in his Innisfree poem if it had not been expressed in a delicate wavering word-music, which caught the ear of the literary world as something new and beautiful.

Of these five musical elements in speech the most musical in the commonest sense of that word is variation in the pitch of the voice, a "dimmer kind of song" (*cantus obscurior*),[14] as Cicero called it. In this respect the ancient Greek language had a special feature of its own, unknown in most of the languages of modern Europe—a fixed pitch-accent on all important words. So a Greek poet, unlike an English-speaking poet who must trust in his reader's good education to say a word like Innisfree with the highest tone on the last syllable, had a built-in basic melody in almost every word he used, a melody which no reader would neglect or distort except through ignorance or incompetence. According to this fixed accentuation the voice had to glide upward or downward (I am making some pre-suppositions here)[15] within a gamut of a fifth—i.e., three and a half musical tones, from *doh* to *soh* in the tonic sol-fa notation or, say, from C to G—in pronouncing all except some unimportant parts of speech. This melodic pattern was learned by the Greeks from infancy as an integral part of the word. It would be as bad a linguistic lapse for an ancient Athenian to say Εὐριπιδής (with the rising glide on the last vowel) instead of Εὐριπίδης (with the rise on the second-last) as for an Englishman to say Montgoméry for Montgómery or for a modern Greek to say Evreépïdes instead of Evrïpeédes. In fact, linguistic barbarism is sometimes defined specifically as a distortion of the pitch-accent.[16]

The pitch-accent in ancient Greek had two functions, one practical, one aesthetic. Aesthetically, it prescribed a basic melodic pattern in all Greek words. Practically, it served to distinguish between words like βίος, "a life," and βιός, "a bow," in which the other phonetic elements were identical. There were many thousands[17] of such words in ancient Greek if we count the verbal inflexions which had different accentuations as well as the nouns, pronouns, verbs, and adverbs. In the declension of the verb βασιλεύειν, for example, βασίλευσαι, βασιλεῦσαι, and βασιλεύσαι have different meanings (imperative, infinitive, and optative). According to some ancient grammarians a few adjectives also showed this kind of variation, as, μοχθηρός, "unfortunate," and μόχθηρος, "worthless, bad," with the proparoxytone forms showing greater emotional force.[18]

One would hardly have expected any humour in so strictly phonetic a matter as this. But I think we can perhaps find some. Why are the genitives plural of the Greek words for a creditor and an anchovy irregularly accented—χρήστων and ἀφύων, instead of χρηστῶν and ἀφυῶν according to the rule for almost all other first-declension nouns? Perhaps because if you accented them regularly (χρηστῶν and ἀφυῶν) they would be identical with the genitives of the words for "good men" (χρηστοί, χρηστῶν) and "untalented men" (ἀφυεῖς, ἀφυῶν). Now who in ancient Athens would be charitable enough to use the same word for a creditor and for a decent chap? Or who would be brutal enough to add to the miseries of untalented citizens in that highly talented city by identifying them, even if only in the genitive plural, with a very small fish?

In cases like these, ancient Greek was obviously nearer to the tone-languages of the Far East or of Africa than to Irish, English, German, or the Romance languages. In China if a missionary preaching a sermon in the four-tone Peking Mandarin speech should use the wrong tone in pronouncing the word for "lord," chŭ (with a falling-rising pitch-variation), and, instead, say chū (with a level tone), he would delight any atheists in his congregation, for chū means "pig." [19] Ribald laughter of this kind actually occurred in Athens in 408 B.C. During the first performance of Euripides' *Orestes* an actor, instead of saying γαλήν' with a rising inflection on the second syllable, said γαλῆν with a rising-falling inflection on it, and thereby changed the meaning of the whole line from "After the storm I see calm weather" to something like "I see a pussycat." [20] The audience burst into a roar of mocking laughter—an incident which probably helped to drive Euripides into exile soon afterward. So much could turn on a lapse in the pitch-accent. In the sixth book of the *Odyssey*, similarly, Odysseus owed his escape to a mishearing of his pseudonym Οὖτις, "no man," as οὔτις, "nobody." [21]

Occasionally a daring speaker would purposely alter the intonation of a word for a calculated effect. Demosthenes in his speech *On the Crown* is said to have asked the question "Is Aeschines a guest-friend of Philip or a traitor?" with a deliberate mispronunciation of the word for a traitor, μισθωτός, as μίσθωτος (as if in English instead of "mércenary" one were to say mercénary"). The listeners, quick to correct him, are said to have shouted back μισθωτός,[22] giving him the answer he wanted. Similarly he is said to have pronounced the name of Ἀσκληπιός as Ἀσκλήπιος in order to emphasize that he was a benign (ἤπιος) god. Several famous puns, too, depended on a similar distortion of the pitch-accent, as I shall illustrate later. Such devices are the equivalent of introducing a dissonance in music for a calculated effect.

There were other conditions under which the regular pitch-accent was purposely varied. Strong emotion could change an oxytone word like ἀληθές to proparoxytone ἄληθες in an indignant question, as in Aeschylus' outburst at Euripides in the *Frogs* of Aristophanes:

$$\text{ἄληθες ὦ παῖ τῆς ἀρουραίας θεοῦ,}^{24}$$

for which an English equivalent would be "really" with a rapidly rising inflection, or "indeed" with a rapidly falling one. Perhaps this kind of excitability was partly the reason why the volatile fifth-century Athenians moved the accent backward on words like ἑτοῖμος, ἐρῆμος, making them proparoxytones,[24] as also in χάριεν, "that's fine," for normal χαρίεν.[25] A similar tendency is found in vocatives like Σώκρατες.[26]

It is fortunate for us, if we value the euphony of ancient Greek, that these basic pitch-variations are preserved in the signs whose invention is attributed to Aristophanes of Byzantium at Alexandria about 200 B.C. His three simple marks for the acute, grave, and circumflex tones could not, of course, indicate all the infinitely subtle pitch-variations of living speech.[27] These vary from person to person, from mood to mood, from time to time, and from place to place. But thanks to his ingenious and easily workable system, from our manuscripts of ancient Greek we can still speak and hear the fundamental tone-variations of Greek. Should we not be grateful to him? And should readers of the many modern languages that have borrowed his accent-signs not be grateful, too? One might naturally have thought so. But at least one eminent scholar in a recent publication takes a different view, and my impression is that it is shared by others. This is what he says about Aristophanes of Byzantium:

One of his more dubious titles to fame is that he invented the Greek accents. They were intended to preserve the already fading pitch-accentuation of classical Greek and his system has survived to this day to plague every student of Greek.[28]

Small thanks there for one of the most brilliant innovations in the history of writing! It is hardly the fault of Aristophanes that later teachers of

Greek came to regard his dynamic musical notation as a sprinkling of meaningless marks either not pronounced at all or else mispronounced. Aristophanes knew, like Dionysios and every other reputable literary critic in classical and Hellenistic times, that the pitch-accent was an essential element in Greek for expressing meaning in the widest sense—conceptual, aesthetic, and emotional. That is why he invented his accents, not to plague us. More must be said about their aesthetic and emotional effects in a later chapter. For the moment let me only emphasize that Dionysios, when he comes to discuss the sources of beauty and charm in his treatise on composition which is so valuable to us in our present quest, twice puts word-melody,[29] not rhythm, first of all, and it is through the simple and ingenious notation of Aristophanes of Byzantium that we can still hear something of this word-melody in ancient Greek.

A second element shared by both music and speech is what I call timbre-quality. Others prefer to speak of it as timbre or sound-texture or tone-colour (the German *Klangfarbe*). The classical Greeks had no regular term for it,[30] using instead specific descriptions like "rough," "smooth," "pleasing" or "unpleasing," "beautiful" or "ugly." Dionysios comments on it like this:

Different sounds affect the hearing with many different sensations of sweetness (γλυκαίνουσιν), bitterness (πικραίνουσι), roughness (τραχύνουσι), smoothness (λεαίνουσι), and so on. The reason for this lies partly in the nature of the letters which make up speech and partly in the extremely various forms in which syllables are combined together.[31]

Later he speaks of sounds that are soft or rigid or astringent or mouth-watering (μαλακαί, σκληραί, στύφουσαι, διαχέουσαι). As will be more fully discussed in the next chapter, he gives a detailed analysis of the euphonic and cacophonic qualities of the separate letters, finding some beautiful and noble, others ugly and mean. To justify his judgements Dionysios describes the physical processes which produce the various sounds. The sound of *omega*, for example, he says, is superior to that of *upsilon* because "in pronouncing it the mouth is rounded, the lips are contracted, and the impact of the breath is on the edge of the mouth," [32] while in pronouncing *upsilon* there is a more marked contraction of the lips and "the sound is strangled and comes out thin." Worst of all is *iota* because, he says, the breath strikes the teeth, not the lips. Modern students of phonetics and acoustics are unlikely to accept such arguments for inherent beauty or ugliness, pleasantness or unpleasantness, in vocal sounds. They prefer to discuss the physical causes of these differences of quality in terms of overtones (or "partials" or "harmonics") and formants.[33] But some modern investigators do cautiously use descriptions like "rough" and "smooth," correlating them with variations in the shape of sound waves as recorded on a sound spectrograph.

Without mechanical aids for analyzing and recording the nature of sounds, the Greeks had to rely on sensitive ears,[34] musical training, and a knowledge of surface anatomy for their researches in the causes and effects of quality. They also had a remarkable talent for describing sounds in terms of other sense-experiences by means of what are now called syn-aesthetic[35] or intersensal metaphors. Thus by analogy with the sense of touch they described tone-qualities as "rough," "smooth," "sleek," "sharp," "piercing," and "blunt." [36] More elaborately Homer spoke of screams as being "woolly," [37] just as much later in time Dante spoke of "hairy" or "shaggy" words.[38] Besides this, they found analogies for tone-qualities in visual sensations, describing voices as "bright" or "shining" (λαμπρός),[39] as in later days Crashaw wrote of "a sparkling noyse." [40] (This quality of brightness in tone was observed by physicians of the Hippocratic school in making medical diagnoses.)[41] Colour-terms were also used to describe kinds of voice-tones—"white," "gray," "dusky." [42]

We find similar equations between sound and taste. A favourite analogue for pleasant-sounding voices was honey, μέλι.[43] So in the Homeric poems the Siren's song is "honey-speaking" (μελίγηρυν) and orators speak with tones like honey. More ingeniously Sextus Empiricus compared a tune con-taining discordant notes to a mixture of honey and vinegar (ὀξύμελι: like the Chinese "sweet-and-sour" foods), and tunes consisting entirely of con-cordant notes he compared to mixtures of honey and wine or water (οἰνόμελι, ὑδρόμελι, old English "hydromel").[44] Aeschylus may have compared the sound of bitter lamentation to the taste of resin—a comparison which may displease modern retsina-lovers.[45] But perhaps, following a clue in Dionysios when he speaks of sounds that distort the face,[46] we should seek the basis of comparison not in a shared bitterness or astringency, but in a similarity between the distorted faces of the mourners and of those who taste over-resinated wine.

Analogies between sound and smell are rarer. The most striking I know is that used by Agias, the writer on music, who, according to Athenaios,[47] said that burnt storax had an odour in the Phrygian mode.

Other synaesthetic descriptions of sounds are taken from a sense of weight (βαρύs and βαρυ- compounds) and in one case apparently from com-pression of close-packed moving particles—a kind of auditory swarm-feeling (*Schwärmerei*). This is in the word ἀδινός used to describe the voices of the Sirens and intense lamentations, as well as a swarm of bees and a flock of sheep.[48] John Clare gives something of this effect in reverse when he describes warmth in terms of noise—

The ruthless heat seems twittering by.[49]

One metaphorical description of tone-quality has baffled the commentators. Homer describes the voice of the cicada as a "lily voice," ὄπα λειριόεσσαν.[50] Is it a metaphor based on some similarity between sound and touch and so to be translated "fine-textured as the petals of a lily"? Or between sound and shape—"shapely as a lily"? Or between sound and colour—"white as a lily"? (Modern phoneticians speak of "white" noise, but in a different sense.) It would take us too far afield to try to decide this now. Whatever the phrase precisely means, it shows brilliant originality, and implies a high degree of sensitivity and imaginativeness in perceiving nuances of tone-quality.

The more elaborate of these metaphors apparently refer to the qualities of a speaking voice, not to the timbre-qualities of particular words or syllables. But for practical purposes in a world of universal reading aloud, voice-quality and word-quality were closely interconnected so far as literary composition and performance were concerned. If an author wanted to describe a rough object or a harsh voice or a person with a rough character he would normally—as I hope to show later—choose words whose qualities as well as their meaning suggested those qualities. So, too, a professional performer would naturally choose a role whose language suited his own voice and temperament. The same principle would hold for preachers and sophists: even the most golden-mouthed Chrysostom would not get far with leaden language.

From an author's point of view, then—and that is our chief concern here—in terms of quality alone, as distinct from pitch-variation and rhythm, the Greek language provided something like the variety in sounds which a musician has at his disposal in the different instruments of a modern orchestra. Thus a Pindar or a Demosthenes could use the noble *alpha*'s and *omega*'s like trumpets or horns, the slender *upsilon*'s and *iota*'s like flutes or piccolos, the sombre *eta*'s like cellos, the *mu*'s and *nu*'s like violas, the *lambda*'s and *rho*'s like violins, the dental consonants like light percussion instruments, the aspirates like oboes. Perhaps many may think these comparisons inexact and the whole analogy rather farfetched. But the basic idea comes from suggestions by classical rhetoricians, and is, I am convinced, broadly valid, provided that we remember the fundamental distinction between the musician's orchestra and the author's speech-sounds: the freedom of the author to choose the best sounds for musical or mimetic effect is severely limited by the fact that he usually—but not always—wants primarily to convey a conceptual meaning; for the musician, in contrast, the meaning is entirely in the sound (except in so-called "programme music"). Also an author in choosing suitable qualities is mainly confined to the prefabricated patterns in existing words. But sometimes, like a musician taking liberties with the conventional uses of an orchestra, he changes existing words or invents new ones to get the kind of quality or pitch-variation or rhythm that he wants. That is why, for example, Aristophanes coined a word like βομβαλοβομβάξ[51] to express contempt for pretentious language, and why Homer introduced the harsh form τετραχθά[52] when he wanted to describe the shattering of a sword in battle. What they were aiming at was a special effect in tone-quality—or so at least I hope to show later.

The third of the basic elements shared by speech and music is what musicians call tempo, and literary critics call speed or rate of delivery. We need not delay long over it, because most authors assume—perhaps rashly at times—that the reader's ear or voice will take their words at the right speed. Musicians are more careful; they tell the executant when they want him to play *presto* or *adagio* and when to have an *accelerando* or *rallentando*; and since the invention of the metronome in the early nineteenth century they have been able to indicate the tempo with mathematical precision.

Almost no precise information survives about speech speeds in ancient Greek.[53] Presumably, as in modern times, poetry and oratory went more slowly than everyday speech, except in moments of passionate eloquence or of comic garrulity (as in the πνῖγος of the Old Comedy, and in modern patter songs). But how many hexameters did Homer or the rhapsodes speak to the minute?[54] One can only guess: there is no firm evidence. Or how long did an actor take to deliver an iambic line of average length? Here some scholars think we have better information. Galen, quoting an earlier medical writer, says that there is a similarity between the systolic and diastolic beats of the pulse and the arsis and thesis of a metrical foot. This could be taken to mean that about 72 iambic feet were recited per minute—assuming that the normal ancient Greek pulse rate was like our own.[55] But this rate, below 150 syllables per minute, would be extremely slow; and, anyway, Galen's words do not clearly imply anything more than a general comparison of the short-long beat of an iambic foot with the weak-strong beat of the diastolic and systolic movements of the pulse, or possibly with the unequal lengths of the intervals between the two pulse beats, which are roughly in the proportion of three to five. Probably the comparison is based on stress-rhythm or quantitative-rhythm, not on tempo. Yet whatever Galen's exact meaning may be, his statement emphasizes the fact that even in our blood stream there is both stress and time. Our pulse beat is a built-in measure of rhythm. There is nothing similar for the other elements of sound.

An ingenious attempt has been made to calculate the speed of Greek oratory by reference to the amounts of time, measured by water clock, which are known to have been allotted to certain speeches.[56] If we accept this method—but the capacity of water clocks may not always have been the same as that of the specimen found in the Athenian agora—then it appears that Demosthenes delivered his speech *On the Crown* at about 150 words, or something like 350 syllables, per minute, which is faster than the average English conversational speed of 300 syllables a minute. Aeschines and Isocrates were rather slower in some of their speeches, at just under 300.

Sometimes we are given indications of speed by statements in the text of poems or speeches. In the *Iliad* we have a memorable comparison between the oratorical styles of Menelaos and Odysseus.[57] Menelaos, we are told, spoke at a running speed (ἐπιτροχάδην), saying little, but saying it clearly (λιγέως) and without stumbling at any word. Odysseus, on the contrary, seemed tongue-tied and even stupid at first, but when eventually he let his great voice (ὄπα . . . μεγάλην) go out from his chest then the words came thick and fast[58] as the winter's snow—a superb simile for overwhelming, relentless eloquence. Most famous, perhaps, of all references to rate of speaking is the remark in Aristotle's description of the high-minded man (μεγαλόψυχος): "his voice is deep and his speech steady . . . for a high and quick voice is a sign of haste and eagerness." [59] We find similar remarks in the writers on physiognomy.[60]

Speed is one of the less important factors in the euphonic exploitation of language. But every time we read a passage of Greek aloud we must consciously or unconsciously make a decision about how fast or slow it should go, and where one should reintroduce an *accelerando* or a *rallentando*. Our decision will depend partly on non-linguistic conditions—especially on matters of characterization and of emotional atmosphere. But the nature of the words themselves, their sound-texture and ease of articulation as well as their quantities, will prescribe a faster or a slower speed. For example, phrases like

> Come, and trip it as ye go

and

> αὖτις ἔπειτα πέδονδε κυλίνδετο,

with their light, thin syllables, clearly demand a faster rate of recitation—
or of listening by the inner ear—than, say,

> Yet once more, O ye laurels, and once more

and

> λᾶαν βαστάζοντα.

The speed must be rightly judged as well as the metre and timbre-quality, if
such lines are to have their full poetic effect.[61]

The fourth element shared by speech and music is intensity, the degree
of loudness or softness resulting from variations in the force with which
the air is emitted from the lungs. It can be measured in terms of decibels
or units of electrical energy.[62] The ancient Greeks had no scientific means
of measuring or recording it, not even one so crude as a water clock for
measuring time. They could only use terms like "with a loud voice" [63] or
various kinds of metaphor and simile. In this respect I know of no description more charming than one in Theocritos' idyll about the Argonauts.[64]
It occurs after the lad Hylas has been drawn down under what another
poet has euphoniously called

> the glassy, cool, translucent wave

by those water-nymphs with the lovely-sounding names,

> Eunika and Malis and Nycheia with springtime in her eyes

> Εὐνίκα καὶ Μαλὶς ἔαρ θ'ὁρῶσα Νύχεια.

Hercules comes looking for him in the adjacent woods. He calls again and
again for Hylas. Then from under the pool

> Three times the boy replied, but his voice came faint out of the water, and
> though nearby he seemed very far away.

Scientifically absurd, but poetically how superb!

In general this element of intensity with its potentialities of *crescendo* and
diminuendo, *fortissimo* and *pianissimo*, is the least important of the main
five factors in Greek linguistic euphony so far as composition is concerned.
It is more a matter of performance (ὑπόκρισις, *pronuntiatio*),[65] than of diction (λέξις, *elocutio*), like speed of speech. A person playing the part of
Stentor the herald, or of Heracles, or of the poet Aeschylus in the *Frogs*
of Aristophanes, or of a rustic boor, such as Theophrastos describes,[66]
would naturally speak with a loud voice. Here, as elsewhere, the two com-
plementary aspects of euphonious speech—skillfully chosen language,
which is the author's part, and appropriate delivery, which is the performer's
part—are not to be entirely separated. An author may at times choose

certain words or letters in a phrase for the sake of some inherent capacity for loudness or softness, just as when a Theocritean shepherd calls σίττα to his flock,[67] or when any Greek says *pst* to attract notice, he is exploiting the notorious carrying-power of the sibilant *s*. Similarly when Xenophon gives a list of names suitable for hounds,[68] they are all disyllabic and phonetically apt for calling at a distance.

To illustrate how important in oratory can be the four elements I have been discussing—pitch-variation, quality, speed, and intensity, together with rhythm, which will be considered next—here is a description of the style adopted by the most diabolically influential demagogue of our time:

The opening moves of every speech he made were hesitant. The attitude of his body was stiff, he was feeling his way like a blind man; his voice was muted and monotonous. After a few minutes, this apparent unwillingness to communicate gave way to a steadier, louder flow of sentences; the speaker's muscles visibly relaxed, and he was soon to begin using his right arm in gestures that resembled blows aimed at an invisible nail. Then the flow increased into a torrent; the punch-line was delivered in a loud, sometimes hoarse, high-pitched voice; the end was abrupt. A new paragraph, another train of thought, was then introduced in a softer voice, though not in the same halting manner as the opening of the speech; the clockwork was again seen by the spellbound audience to unwind itself, the *crescendo* was once more achieved, and wiped out by a wide sweep of the right arm. The onslaught on the eardrums of the audience was tremendous: it was estimated that the frequency of Hitler's voice in a typical sentence was 228 vibrations per second, whereas 200 vibrations is the usual frequency of a voice raised in anger.[69]

Classical students will recognize some of the features of this: the hesitant opening followed by torrential eloquence resembles the technique of Odysseus already mentioned; the hoarse high-pitched voice could be Cleon's. But when supported by all the swarm-emotion of bands playing, troops marching, torches blazing, thousands of voices intoning *Sieg Heil, Sieg Heil, Sieg Heil*, like an incantation, its effect was more powerfully and disastrously emotive than anything classical Greece or Rome ever experienced. Basically it was the sheer sound of Hitler's voice together with the carefully created atmosphere of rhythmical movements and shouts which inflamed a civilized people to a Dionysiac orgy of destruction, as surely as in the *Bacchai* of Euripides it was the singing and shouting and dancing, and the sound of the deep-voiced hand drums of the maenads, that roused the women of Thebes to tear a young prince asunder.

Last of the five elements that speech shares with music—but by far the most carefully studied by classical students at present—is rhythm. And what is rhythm? If I were to try to answer that question thoroughly and with full consideration for the conflicting views from ancient times to the present day, I should have space for nothing else in the chapters that follow. I must define it brusquely as a recognizable pattern of strongly emphasized and less strongly emphasized sounds. In classical Greek the stronger emphasis was chiefly—perhaps almost entirely—a matter of duration: in other words, the rhythmical patterns were made from long (or "heavy") syllables and short (or "light") syllables. This contrasts with English, where the emphasis is achieved by stress and is primarily a matter of loudness.

Here another far-reaching question emerges. Was any stress-element operative in classical Greek speech, and, if so, was it linked to lengthened quantity or to the pitch-accent (as it is in modern Greek)?[70] There does not seem to be enough evidence for any firm decision, though the belief that Greek quantitative lengthening involved some stress seems to be gaining ground. What we do know for certain is, of course, that in later Greek a stress accent mostly supplanted the pitch-accent, though not entirely.[71] "Metre," corresponding to musical "time" (duple, triple, quadruple, and so on), is, of course, the name we give the measurement of rhythm in speech; in fact, the word means simply "measurement." For several reasons the study of metre has tended to monopolize the phonetic analysis of ancient literature in our schools. First, it can be easily demonstrated and taught visually without the help of scientific instruments. Beating time with hand or foot comes naturally to everyone—just "Observe the beat of my thumb," as Horace says.[72] In making such movements we are probably going back to one of the original sources of rhythmical speech—the adaptation of words to a regular movement in marching or dancing or working.[73] Indeed, the best way to teach and learn the simpler Greek metres is to step them out, waltzing to pure iambics or trochees, fox-trotting to dactyls, spondees, and anapaests. When we do that, the feet become really feet, and other Greek metrical terms like βάσις and θέσις and ἄρσις regain their original force.

A second reason why quantitative metre is comparatively easy to teach is that it can be explained in quasi-mathematical terms. If a teacher accepts the conventional belief that a long syllable always took exactly twice the time for a short syllable—which no conscientious metrician accepts without reservations in view of statements to the contrary among the testimonia[74]— then it is simplicity itself to analyze lines in neat patterns of "longs" and "shorts" on a blackboard or a page.

But there are times when a teacher or lecturer cannot avoid quoting some metrical phrases, when long and short marks or numbers will not suffice.

What happens then? More often than not, so far as I can discover, what
is offered to the listening ear is a travesty of classical quantitative metre.
Whether the teacher is an Anglicizer in his pronunciation, or a Neo-Hel-
lenist, or even sometimes when he thinks he is a faithful Erasmian (I shall
discuss these terms in chapter vi),[75] he probably marks his Greek metres
not by lengthening long syllables, but by stressing them—indeed, he has
been advised to do so by an eminent metrician.[76]

Let us hear how this stress-accentuation distorts the authentic rhythms.
The ancient evidence classifies the dactylic hexameter as a metre of quadruple time approximately. If, then, we count, as every learner should, four
beats to each foot, as if the feet were bars in music, we get this steady
marching rhythm:

Ἄνδρα μοι ἔννεπε Μοῦσα πολύτροπον ὅς μάλα πολλά.
1-2 3   4 1-2 3 4   1-2 3   4 1-2 3 4   1-2 3   4 1-2 3+

But those who substitute a stressed syllable for the first long syllable in
each foot tend to speak the dactyls as if they were tribrachs (or trochees
with resolution) and the spondees as if there were trochees, changing the
rhythm to three beats to the bar, thus:

Ἄνδρα μοι ἔννεπε Μοῦσα πολύτροπον ὃς μάλα πολλά.
1   2   3 1 2 3   1   2   3 1 2 3   1   2 3   1   2+

We find the same rhythm undisguised in a typical English hexameter like

Thís is the fórest primévical. The múrmuring pínes and the hémlocks . . .

which—to adapt Bentley's comment on Pope's *Iliad*—is a pretty metre,
but you must not call it Homer's. Tennyson's ear was not deceived, and
he wrote in parody:

These lame hexameters the strong-wing'd music of Homer!
No—but a most burlesque barbarous experiment.
When was a harsher sound ever heard, ye Muses, in England,
When did a frog coarser croak upon our Helicon? [77]

We hear a similar kind of distortion when iambic trimeters are pronounced
with this unclassical "stressed-longs" rhythm. Let us hear the effect of this.
Sophocles no doubt gave careful consideration to the sound of the first line
of his *Antigone*. It is a stately rhythm consisting of two four-beat spondees
and four three-beat iambs—or, if you prefer, of two heavy *metra* and one
light—

ὦ κοινὸν αὐτάδελφον Ἰσμήνης κάρα
1-2 3-4 1   2-3 1 2-3   1   2-3 1-2 3-4   1 2-3

The voice naturally lingers on the prolonged *o* and *e* sounds of the two spondees. But how does it sound with stress instead of quantity? It becomes a senile senarius of six monotonous iambs (or even pyrrhics), as if it were:

ὦ κοινὸν αὐτάδελφο’Ι νσμήνης κάρα—
1 2-3 1   2-3 1   2-3 1 2-3 1 2-3   1 2-3

ti-tum, ti-tum, ti-tum, ti-tum, ti-tum, ti-tum. Even worse is what the Neo-Hellenizers make of it: they disrupt the metre into something like the following chaos:

óh keenón aftádelphon Isméenes kára,
1-2   3 1-2 3 1-2 3   1   1   1-2 3 1-2 3

which is almost entirely trochaic. (I assume that the stress accents cause some increase in duration.)

The fact is: when stress takes over from quantity, much of the variety and subtlety of poetic music may be lost. Humpty Dumpty becomes patron of the epic and tragic line instead of Calliope and Melpomene. Unless we respect the classical observance of quantity, pitch-variation, and tone-quality as a whole, we are in danger of reducing Greek poetry to the kind of clattering music that Bottom liked in *A Midsummer Night's Dream:* "I have a reasonable good ear in music. Let's have the tongs and the bones." [78]

I certainly do not intend to depreciate the force and value of rhythm in the sound of Greek poetry or oratory. But I do condemn and oppose the postclassical tendency to let metrical studies completely overshadow other aspects of euphony. The best of the Greek rhetoricians never practised or preached any exclusive policy of that kind. Though they gave most attention to matters of rhythm—partly, I think, because it was the easiest of the musical elements to analyze mathematically—yet they did not allow their pupils to forget the importance of timbre-quality or pitch-variation as well. If we accept their principles, we must refuse to grant that only metre matters in the sound of Greek; and we must also refuse to condone a mode of reciting Greek rhythmical phrases in a way that crucifies them on a medieval stress-pattern.

The history of classical studies in this regard resembles the history of the Christian Church. The original apostolic doctrine proclaimed three prime virtues, Faith, Hope, and Charity. Later Faith hardened into Dogma and became the dominant principle. Then in the name of Faith instruments of torture were assembled to enforce strict conformity, while Charity could only look on helplessly in tears, and Hope for many seemed dead. As a result the catholicity of Western Christendom was racked and torn.

In much the same way, overemphasis on the value of rhythm—one can see its fanaticism in the pedant's fury at a "false quantity"—has impoverished the full richness of Greek euphony by silencing the warmer virtues of melody and tone-quality.

We can take the comparison further. In recent years many religious-minded people, distressed by divisions and defections, have been trying with some success to regain "oecumenically" the richer and fuller doctrines of their early tradition. Would it not be well if those who love and cherish the ancient classics—especially in a time when Greek has to struggle hard for survival against so many challenges—should do more to revive the full music of what was once, and still could be, one of the most musical languages ever spoken?

NOTES TO CHAPTER II

[1] Dionysios, *On Composition* 11,124,20. Cf. Isocrates, *Antidosis* 46, and Krumbacher 19 f.

[2] Quintilian 1,10,9 ff.: he says that Archytas and Euenos considered "grammar subject to music" (1,10,17).

[3] On the τονάριον: see especially Quintilian 1,10,27; see also Cicero, *De or.* 3,60, 225; Plutarch, *Gracchi* 2,4; Aulus Gellius, *Attic Nights* 1,11,10–16; cf. Krumbacher 81.

[4] See H. R. Fairclough, "The Connection between Music and Poetry in Early Literature," in Gildersleeve, *Studies*, 205–227. On modern theories see William K. Wimsatt, Jr. and Cleanth Brooks, *Literary Criticism* (New York, 1957) 271–276.

[5] On music in Greek education see W. Spiegel, *Die Bedeutung der Müsik für die griechische Erziehung im klassischen Altertum* (Berlin, 1910); Marrou 134,41; Lasserre 9 ff.

[6] On the differences and similarities between song and speech see Aristoxenos, *Elements of Harmony* 1,8 ff. (cf. 1,10,9 ff., δεῖ τὴν φωνὴν ἐν τῷ μελῳδεῖν τὰς μὲν ἐπιτάσεις τε καὶ ἀνέσεις ἀφανεῖς ποιεῖσθαι . . .). See further in Johnson (*Musical Pitch* . . .), who collects the Greek definitions of musical sound.

[7] Aristides Quintilianus, *De Musica* 1,4 (pp. 5,26 ff. Winnington-Ingram). Cicero refers to a *cantus obscurior* in speech (*De oratore* 17); cf. Quintilian 1,8,2. Plutarch, *Quaest. Conviv.* 633B says that, besides actors, orators used a delivery close to singing in their epilogues. See further in C. W. L. Johnson, "The Motion of the Voice in the Theory of Ancient Music," *TAPA* XXX (1899) 42–55 and his "The Motion of the Voice in Connection with Accent," in Gildersleeve, *Studies*, 57–76; also Wilson 38 ff., De Lacy 243, Hanschke 47–49 and 107, and Grove on *Sprechgesang*. On the intermediate type of delivery called παρακαταλογή see A. Pickard-Cambridge, *The Dramatic Festivals of Athens* (London, 1953); J. W. White, *The Verse of Greek Comedy* (London, 1912) 20 and § 803; and Lasserre 29. See further in note 9 *infra*.

[8] On Gladstone's voice see Roberts on Dionysios 11,126,3 and H. C. Wyld in *Society for Pure English Tract* XXXIX 617–621; for Tennyson's see Berry 50 ff. ("deep melodious thunder," "roll of his great voice," "intoning a note, almost

chanting") and C. V. Stanford, *Studies and Memories* (London, 1908) 93 ("a voice of deep and penetrating power varied only by alteration of note and intensity of quality . . . The notes were few, and he rarely read on more than two, except at the cadence of a passage when the voice would slightly fall"). Berry suggests that the quality of Tennyson's voice affected his choice of words.

[9] Quintilian 1,8,2: cf. 11,3,57 ff. and Philostratos, *Lives of Sophists* 20,513 Isaios. Cf. Cicero's strictures on the ᾠδή orators of the Asian style who "sing with highly inflected and ululating voice" (*inclinata ululantique voce: Orator* 27); Philodemos, *Rhet.* 1,200,1 ff. (Sudhaus); Lucian, *Demonax* 12; *Guide to Rhetoric* 19; and Philostratos, *Lives* . . . 1,8,492; 1,20,513; 2,10,589 (but contrast the more favorable attitude in 1,491). Lucian, *On the Dance* 27 complains of an actor who was περιᾴδων τὰ ἰαμβεῖα. According to Chamaileon (as cited in Athenaios 14, 620c), Homer sang his poetry: cf. Fairclough as cited in n. 4 *supra*.

[10] Plutarch, *How to Listen* 7,47D.

[11] Augustine, *Confessions* 5,13; cf. Norden 1,5.

[12] Paul Valéry, *The Art of Poetry*, trans. Denise Folliot (London, 1958) 162. Cf. pp. 298–299: ". . . the finest verses in the world are trivial or senseless once their harmonic flow has been broken and their sonorous substance altered as it develops within the time peculiar to their measured movement, and once they have been replaced by an expression of no intrinsic musical necessity and no resonance.' See also pp. 165 and 295, and Francis Scarfe, *The Art of Paul Valéry* (London, 1954) 54, 80 ff.

[13] For modern views on the five qualities of sound see, e.g., Crystal chaps. ii–iii (with bibliography); Kingdon, *Groundwork* xxv ff.; and Gleason. For minute analyses of intensity, pitch, and duration in modern Greek see Pernot.

[14] See n. 7 *supra*.

[15] See Appendix.

[16] Hesychios defines βαρβαρισμός as παράτονος διάλεκτος, "wrongly accented talk." Cf. Philodemos, *Rhet.* 1,155 (Sudhaus) and the scholia on Demosthenes 18,52 (*On the Crown* 242 f.). Cf. n. 20 *infra*. Cf. Dionysios, *Excerpta ex libro xviii* (Jacoby) 292 on the "rough" accentuation of Tyrrhenius Postumius. See Gerber 1,379 ff. and 412.

[17] Chandler lists about 900 examples of words whose meaning varies with their accentuation, but does not include all possible variations in verb-forms.

[18] See LSJ at πονηρός and Wackernagel 1098.

[19] On the Chinese tones (four in Peking Mandarin, nine in Cantonese) and the tone-variations of *chu* see B. Karlgren, *Sound and Symbol in Chinese* (London, 1962) 20 ff. and Daniel Jones and Kwing Tong Woo, *A Cantonese Phonetic Reader* (London, 1913).

[20] For the mistake of Hegelochos see Aristophanes, *Frogs* 303 f. (with scholia). The lapse was notorious, for Sannyrion (fr. 8 Edmonds) and Strattis (fr. 1 Edmonds) also referred to it. According to the scholiasts on *Orestes* 279 and on Dionysios Thrax 163,22 (Hilgard), Hegelochos' mistake lay in failing to mark the elision in γαλήν' ὁρῶ. But just how elisions were heard in ancient Greek is uncertain: see further in chap. vii, n. 46. For similar alterations of accentuation cf. on μίσθωτος and Ἀσκλήπιος in the following text; cf. also δῆμος/δημός in Aristophanes,

Wasps 40 f., *Knights* 954. Some similar accentual variation between ἑταίρων and ἑταιρῶν seems to be implied in Athenaios 13,571D–E (Menander fr. 381 Edmonds) and perhaps in Aristophanes, *Ecclesiazousai* 21–23 (but for uncertainties see commentators). On the sensitivity of audiences to nuances of sound see Dionysios 11,122,18 ff., Cicero, *Orator* 173 and *De oratore* 3,50,195 f.

[21] On Οὖτις/οὔτις see p. 90 f.

[22] On μίσθωτος, -τός see the scholia on Demosthenes 18,52. Goodwin *ad loc.* calls it an absurd story and "wholly unworthy of the orator"; but see "Plutarch," *Mor.* 845B where the Ἀσκλήπιος misaccentuation is recorded. And compare Churchill's deliberate mispronunciations of words like "Nazi."

[23] *Frogs* 840.

[24] On accentual variations of the type ἑτοῖμος/ἕτοιμος see Lejeune 270 and Schwyzer 1,383.

[25] On variations like χαρίεν/χάριεν see Schwyzer 1,380.

[26] For recessive accent in vocatives and imperatives see Schwyzer 2,339, 424, 620.

[27] On the intonations of living speech see, e.g., Crystal 45 ff., Gleason 40 ff., and Kingdon, *Groundwork* and *Practice*. Kingdon says (*Practice* i): "Intonation is the soul of a language, while the pronunciation of its sounds is its 'body,' and the recording of it in writing and printing gives a very imperfect picture of the body and hardly hints at the existence of a soul" (cf. chap. iii, n. 88). See further in chap. vii, n. 49.

[28] Grube 128.

[29] Dionysios, chap. 20,120,18 and 122,11. "Word-music," μέλος, is similarly given priority over rhythm in Dionysios, *On Demosthenes* chaps. 48–50.

[30] Sextus Empiricius uses ποιότης in that sense (in *Against the Professors* 1,169) with reference to the pronunciation of Σμύρνα as Ζμύρνα. Occasionally πνεῦμα seems to be more or less a synonym for it, e.g., an Arcadios 186 as cited by Lentz xxxviii; cf. chap. i, n. 21. Varro (Goetz and Schoell 210,11–19) calls it *crassitudinem*, "thickness" (= δασύτητα): cf. Hanschke 46. For modern views on quality see Wilson, Pulgram, and the other writers cited in n. 33 *infra*. Wilson (p. 210) cites Gehring's remark that "timbre is incipient harmony, harmony developed timbre" (on account of the overtones which make every vowel a kind of chord).

[31] Dionysios 12,130,18 ff. and 15,154,11 ff.: cf. Demetrios 69,105,176. On Dionysios' metaphorical terms for sound-effects see J. F. Lockwood in *CQ* LXXXI (1937) 192–203 and LXXXII (1938) 109–115. Besides the terms quoted in my lecture Dionysios also uses ἀποτραχύνειν, ὑποτραχύνειν, ἐκμαλάττειν, πραΰνειν, διαχαράττειν, χαράττειν, διακλᾶσθαι, κατακλᾶσθαι with reference to quality (cf. chap. vii, n. 23).

[32] "The sound of *omega*," etc.: Dionysios 14,142,15 ff. The Greeks do not seem to have known about the vocal chords.

[33] On overtones (or partials or harmonics) and formants see, e.g., Crystal, Gleason, Grove (at *Acoustics*), Joos, Wood. Some reservations about the spectrographic analysis of timbre-quality are voiced by Crystal p. 33. Ancient Greeks at least recognized the octave overtone (see the Aristotelian *Problems* 19,13: possibly Plato in *Timaios* 80A–B refers to other partials). Wood 65 says that Mersenne in his *Harmonie Universelle* (Paris, 1636/7) first associated tone-quality with

overtones. Helmholtz first demonstrated this conclusively. Cf. Miller (*Anecdotal History* 84). Miller 13 says that Galileo was the first to discover their ratios (which are the same as the Pythagorean concordant intervals, i.e., $1:2:3:4$, etc.). Wood 70 f. discusses the view that pleasantness and unpleasantness in sounds depends on the degree to which the lower and higher "partials" are audible.

[34] On the importance of a "good ear" see Dionysios 23,244,23; Cicero, *Orator* 53,177; Quintilian 9,4,116; Aulus Gellius, *Attic Nights* 13,21. For a modern definition see Jones, *Outline* 3.

[35] For general remarks on synaesthesia and synaesthetic expressions in literature see S. Ullman in *The Review of English Studies* XVIII (1942) 219–228 (with bibliography) and also in *The Principles of Semantics* (2d ed.; Oxford, 1959) 266–289; Wellek 194 (with bibliography), Ogden 292–294; Stanford, *Greek Metaphor* (see index at *Synaesthesia*) and in *Comparative Literature Studies* VI–VII (1942) 26–30; and Erika von Erhardt-Siebold, *PMLA* XLVII 577–592. Robbins 107–110 cites fifty-three terms for voice-qualities, including coarse, grating, harsh, husky, raucous, shrill, metallic, strident. Crystal 37 speaks of "keen, ringing, penetrating, dull, husky, creaking, breathy." For experimental aspects see C. E. Osgood, *Method and Theory in Experimental Psychology* (New York, 1953) 642–646.

[36] See LSJ at τραχύς, λεῖος, μαλακός, ὀξύς, τόρος, διάτορος and ἀμβλύς. Cf. chap. iii, n. 44. On rough and smooth words see Demetrios 69, 105, 176. Plato uses the terms λεῖος and τραχύς to describe a word in *Cratylos* 408B–D. "Aristotle," *Problems* 11,11 explains τραχύτης of voice as being due to unevenness (ἀνωμαλία). See also Gomperz on Philodemos iv 181,20 ff. The Cyrenaic philosophers defined pleasure as a λεία κίνησις and pain as a τραχεῖα κίνησις: see, e.g., Diogenes Laertius, *Lives of Philosophers* 2,87. On metrical roughness and smoothness in Greek dactylic hexameters see L. Voltz in *Philologus* LII (1894) 385–394.

[37] οὖλον κεκλήγοντες, *Iliad* 17,756-759 (cf. 12,160; 13,441; 13,409). Cf. Stanford, *Greek Metaphor* 53.

[38] *Irsuta*: Dante, *De Vulgari Elocutione* 2,7. He also speaks of *vocabula pexa, lubrica*, and *reburra*—words that are "combed-out," "glossy," and "rumpled." For parallels in other medieval writers see Chaytor (as cited in chap. i, n. 12), 75–77. For some modern examples see Edith Sitwell, *A Poet's Notebook* (London, 1943) 18–20 and *The Pleasures of Poetry*, 1st ser. (London, 1930) 8 ff.

[39] See LSJ at λαμπρός i 4 and cf. Aristotle, *Historia Animalium* 616B 30–32. For Aristotle's views on the relationship between tactual, oral, and visual sensations see P. Kucharski, *REG* LXVII (1954) 355–390 and in general J. I. Beare *Greek Theories of Elementary Cognition* (Oxford, 1906) and Stanford, *Greek Metaphor* 48–50.

[40] Richard Crashaw, *Musick's Duel*, line 84.

[41] "Hippocrates," *On Airs, Waters, Places* 5; cf. 6 and 8 and *Epidemics* 1,19.

[42] See LSJ at λευκός i 2 (and Aristotle, *Topica* 107A 11: λευκὸν . . . ἐπὶ δὲ φωνῆς τὸ εὐήκοον) and at φαιός i 2, σομφός ii, and ξουθός i 1–4. Similar terms for voices in Latin are *candida, torva, rava, fusca*. Cf. chap. vii, n. 73.

[43] See, e.g., LSJ at μέλι i 2, μελιβόας, -βρομος, -γδοῦπος, -γηρυς, -γλωσσος, -θροος, -κομπος, -ρροθος, -σταγής, -φθογγος.

[44] Sextus Empiricus, *Against the Professors* 6,44.

[45] Aesch. *Choëph.* 386–387, πευχήεντ' ὀλολυγνόν (but Dindorf emends for metrical reasons to πυχάεντ'): see LSJ at πευχήεις, -ία, -ινος and also at ῥητινίτης.

[46] Dionysios 15,154,13. Here the verb στύφειν, which elsewhere means "to have an astringent effect," is applied to vocal sounds (cf. ἐπιστύφειν in Dionysios, *On Demosthenes* 38) and so, too, in 22,228,7. See pp. 108 f.

[47] Athenaios, *Deipnosophists* 14,626 f.

[48] See LSJ at βαρύς iii 1 (and βαρυ- compounds) and at ἀδινός (cf. Stanford, *Greek Metaphor* 54, 56).

[49] As cited by C. D. Lewis, *The Echoing Green* ii, 36.

[50] *Iliad* 3,152.

[51] *Thesmophoriazousai* 48.

[52] *Iliad* 3,363; *Odyssey* 9,71.

[53] On ancient tempo (ἀγωγή) in general see Rossi 46 ff., 55 ff., 82 ff., and the scholars cited in nn. 56 and 58 *infra*.

[54] For guesses at the speed of delivery of Homeric hexameters see, e.g., James A. Notopoulos, "Studies in Early Greek Oral Poetry," *HSCP* 68 (1964) 4 ff. (who suggests about ten 15-syllable lines per minute), and J. A. Davison, "Thucydides, Homer and the 'Achaean Wall,' " *Greek, Roman and Byzantine Studies* 6 (1965) 24 (cf. *CR* n.s. 14 [1964] 14), who suggests about eleven per minute.

[55] Maas 36: "Galen (ix 464 Kühn) following Herophilus, compares the rhythm of the human pulse with that of a metrical 'foot.' If that is a more or less correct estimate of the tempo, in terms of our timing ⌣– would occupy about one second." But Galen refers only to arsis and thesis in general, not specifically to an iamb foot, and seems to be referring to alternation of long and short syllables rather than to tempo: and two syllables to the second would be an extraordinarily slow rate of speech. Jones, *Outline* 9 says that the average rate of conversational speech in English is about 300 syllables per minute.

[56] See A. Rome, "La vitesse de parole des orateurs attiques," *Bulletin de la Classe de Lettres de l'Académie Royale de Belgique*, XXXVIII (1952) 596–609. He bases his calculations on the statements in Aristotle's *Athenaion Politeia* about the amount of water in the water clock allowed and on the capacity of a water clock (perhaps 4th century B.C.) found during the American excavations in the Agora at Athens (see S. Young in *Hesperia* 8 [1939] 274–284).

[57] *Iliad* 3,213–224.

[58] On acceleration in speech-tempo (ἐπιταχύνειν) Lockwood (as cited in n. 31 *supra*, 198) cites the scholia on *Iliad* 1,530; 17,605; 23,392 (and cf. on 20,456), as well as passages from Dionysios.

[59] The voice of the μεγαλόψυχος: Aristotle, *Nicomachean Ethics* 4,8 1125c 12.

[60] For the remarks of the physiognomists see references in General Index.

[61] The quotations are from Milton, *L'Allegro*, line 33, *Odyssey* 11,598 (see p. 106 f.), the opening line of Milton, *Lycidas*, and *Od.* 11,596.

[62] On the scientific measurement of loudness see, e.g., Pulgram 26. Some acousticians distinguish another quality of size ("fatness") in vocal sounds: against this see Fletcher 111.

[63] On the use of terms like μαχρός and μέγας to denote loudness of voice see Hanschke 18 f.

[64] Theocritos 13,58 ff. "Aristotle," *Problems* 5,2 and 11,6 (cf. 11,20; 11,51; 5,2) notes

that voices heard from far away sound shriller (ὀξύτεραι): cf. Hanschke 122 f.

⁶⁵ On ὑπόκρισις see further in chap. vii.

⁶⁶ *Characters* 4,1.

⁶⁷ *Idylls* 4,45.

⁶⁸ *On Hunting* 7,5. Cf. Denis Bingham Hall, *Hounds and Hunting in Ancient Greece* (Chicago, 1964) 51.

⁶⁹ From Z. A. B. Zeman, *Nazi Propaganda* (London, 1964) 11, by kind permission of the Oxford University Press.

⁷⁰ On the problem of stress accent in ancient Greek see Blass 132, Sturtevant 103–105, Schwyzer 392 ff. (cf. 180), Maas 4 and 56 (against the view of Eduard Fraenkel and Wilamowitz in favour of a dynamic accent on the long syllables), Pulgram, *AJP* LXXXVI (1965) 144–146, and W. S. Allen, "On Quantity and Quantitative Verse" in *Studies in Honour of Daniel Jones* (London, 1966), citing other recent studies. For older views see F. Hanssen in *RhM* XXXVII (1882) 252–260 and XXXVIII (1883) 222–244; Gilbert Murray, *The Classical Tradition in Poetry* (London, 1927) 84 f.: cf. Zielinski 148 ff. Against Murray see F. R. Dale, *CR* XLIII (1929) 165–166 (cf. XLIV [1930] 5 f.). One form, τίπτε for τίποτε, has been specially cited as suggesting loss of a vowel by strong initial stress.

⁷¹ For evidence of surviving pitch-accentuation in the dialect of Chios see Pernot 50 ff. I have observed it elsewhere in modern Greece, especially in the speech of women: cf. p. 65.

⁷² *Odes* 4,6,35 f., *servate . . . pollicis ictum.* Cf. Quintilian 9,4,51: *tempora etiam animo metiuntur et pedum et digitorum ictu.* See LSJ at κρούπεζαι and κρουπέζιον.

⁷³ See Bücher.

⁷⁴ On variation in the longness of longs and the shortness of shorts (Dionysios 17,172,20) see, e.g., Maas 37; Marguerite Durand, *Voyelles longues et voyelles brèves* (Paris, 1946); Eduard Fraenkel, "Lyrische Daktylen," *RhM* LXXII (1918/19) 161–197, 321–352; A. M. Dale, "Observations on Dactylic," *WS* LXXVII (1964) 15–36; and Rossi.

⁷⁵ See pp. 126–127. See also Szemerényi 258 f.

⁷⁶ Maas 57: "We can place a stress on the longs and on the first syllables of certain bicipitia (i.e., on the 'arsis') and pronounce without stress the brevia, ancipitia, etc. (the 'thesis')." He sees no hope of reviving the ancient quantitative scansion. We must choose, he thinks, between stressing the pitch-accent as in Byzantine or modern Greek, thereby destroying the rhythm, or else stressing the longs and the first syllables of feet beginning with two shorts. He prefers the latter method for prose as well as for verse, and welcomes the fact that "in school teaching this would give us a good excuse for not insisting on the learning of accents."

⁷⁷ *On Translations of Homer* 1–4. On attempts to imitate Greek and Latin metres in German see Maas 20 f., and on English hexameters see W. H. D. Rouse, *Matthew Arnold on Translating Homer* (2d ed.; London, 1905) 23 ff.

⁷⁸ *A Midsummer Night's Dream* iv, i, 26 f.

ADDITIONAL NOTE. For examples of a very minute analysis of poetry in terms of duration of syllables, intonation, and loudness see Grammont, *Le Vers* 86 f.

III

Theoretical Aspects of Euphony

A QUESTION postponed in the first chapter must be considered now. What makes one word or phrase more agreeable to the ear than another? Or, in abstract terms, what does the term euphony, *euphonia* (literally, "well-voicedness") mean? The Greeks certainly believed in its existence. Do we? How many, I wonder, would say that the word "lullaby" is phonetically pleasanter to the ear than "screech," or "rose-tree" than "scrub-oak," or "hullabaloo" than "caterwauling"? I imagine that if we could discuss them individually there would be wide disagreement. Some of us would probably hold that choices are unconsciously influenced by the meanings of the words, as in "lullaby" and "screech." Others might definitely prefer the sound of "scrub-oak" to that of "rose-tree."

Ultimately this is a question of taste and—to use a more pretentious term—of aesthetic values. Many scholars, perhaps wisely, accept the advice of the ancient proverb not to dispute about such matters, and prefer to keep to the solid ground of ascertainable fact. But if we want to understand Greek civilization we must not neglect Greek standards of beauty and ugliness in matters of vocal sound, any more than in the visual arts or in music. In our more scientific age the opinions and canons of the ancient critics may seem ambiguous or even ill founded. Indeed, some of their contemporaries definitely challenged them. But, all the same, full understanding of a civilization or an art can only come from a knowledge of its illusions and prejudices and errors as well as of its solid inventions and achievements. Personally I believe that the Greek views on euphony contain a great deal of wisdom and truth—though they went too far, at times, in trying to define the undefinable. But I am conscious that some who have studied the evidence consider the whole subject a mirage, "the pursuit of a phantom." For them, I hope that this kind of ghost story may at least have some psychological interest. And I remind myself that whatever modern poets and literary critics may think about ghosts and euphony, the men of Shakespeare's time paid more than a little attention to the rhetorical and psychological aspects of both.

So, mirage or no mirage, let us now look more closely at the Greek concept of euphony. The principle—though not the term *euphonia*—was familiar to the Greeks from Homer's time onward. He and his successors in the poetic art down to the early fifth century emphasized the hedonistic aspects of the sound of words and voices, using terms like "pleasant-sounding," "beautiful-sounding," or "evil-sounding." [1] This hedonism is personified in the name of the Muse of epic poetry, Calliope, "beautiful of voice," first named in Hesiod.

Homer gives us the earliest general description of euphony in Greek. Near the beginning of the *Iliad* he describes Nestor as

> Pleasant of speech . . . the clear-voiced orator of the Pylians
> from whose tongue flowed utterance sweeter than honey.

> ἡδυεπὴς . . . λιγὺς Πυλίων ἀγορητής
> τοῦ καὶ ἀπὸ γλώσσης μέλιτος γλυκίων ῥέεν αὐδή.[2]

What the poet refers to is the pleasurable effect both of the tone-quality of Nestor's words—that is, the texture and timbre of the sounds he used— and also of its rhythm, its smooth and even flow. We shall look again at these qualities later on.

The adjective *euphonos* and its cognates first emerge in the fifth century, together with other compound terms in *eu-*,[3] like εὔφθογγος "well voiced." Among the poets who use such terms the emphasis seems still to be on the aesthetic and hedonistic elements in words and voices. But once serious linguistic studies had begun with Demokritos, the *eu-* prefix acquired a more utilitarian meaning, and words like *euphonia*[4] now came to imply effectiveness rather than beauty or pleasure in speech and style. Yet the distinction must not be pressed too hard, for the most effective way of impressing and moving an ancient Greek would usually involve pleasing his ears with sensations of beauty and charm, as Dionysios often reminds us.

Another ambiguity in the use of *euphonia*, together with *eustomia* (literally, "well mouthed")[5] is that one cannot always be sure whether the emphasis is on ease of speech or on beauty of speech. Sometimes (as in Plato's *Cratylos*) the emphasis is on facility, sometimes on pleasantness (as mostly in Dionysios). Again the distinction usually need not be pressed. Ease and pleasure generally go together in speaking as in dancing—but not always, for, as will be exemplified later, cacophonous hard-to-pronounce sounds can sometimes contribute to the pleasure of literature, like mustard or curry powder skillfully used in our food.

There is another ambiguity in the Greek terms for euphony, *euphonia* and *eustomia*. Sometimes they refer primarily to the voice, sometimes to the ear—ease and pleasure in speaking or ease and pleasure in hearing. The two functions do not necessarily go together. For example, Greek tongue-twisters (χαλινοί) like κναξζβί,[6] or English ones like "I'm not copper-bottoming 'em, mum, I'm aluminiuming 'em, mum," are not particularly difficult to hear if the speaker can overcome the difficulty of pronouncing them clearly. The opposite situation, words hard to hear but easy to pronounce, can also occur, but it usually results from deficiencies in the speaker: lazy, slurred speech is an everyday example. A third variation, hard to pronounce and hard to hear, may be neglected now, since we are not concerned with the pathology of literature. The fourth, easy to hear and easy to pronounce, is the natural condition of euphony. Such distinctions, however, hardly concerned the ancient critics, because for them speaking, hearing, and reading were closely integrated.

The fullest ancient Greek discussion of euphony now extant is that in the treatise on the arrangement of words by Dionysios. Its basic principles go back to at least the fifth century. Whether any previous author had ventured to be quite so precise and so detailed in defining the euphonic properties of individual letters, we cannot now tell. Some critics in his time—especially those of the Epicurean tradition—said that people like Dionysios went too far in their speculations; and probably all modern scientific linguists would say the same. But even if Dionysios is overenthusiastic in his theories, he is also a man of judicious taste and acute critical observation, and we can learn much from him.

Dionysios finds something like a scale of euphony among the vowels, semivowels, and consonants.[7] (He does not give special attention to the diphthongs.)[8] The vowels as a class are, he believes, more euphonious than the rest. Among them the longer ones are both the pleasantest to hear and also the strongest, because their resonance lasts longer and the force of the breath is not cut short.[9] *Alpha* (in which the mouth is open widest and the breath strikes the palate) is the most euphonious (εὐφωνότατον) among the long vowels. Next in order come *eta* (with the mouth moderately open and the breath striking the base of the tongue), *omega* (with the mouth rounded, the lips contracted, and the breath striking the edge of the mouth), and *upsilon* (with more marked contraction of the lips and a narrow, strangled sound). Lowest of all is *iota*, in which the impact of the breath is on the teeth, the mouth is only a little open, and the lips do not "brighten the sound" (οὐκ ἐπιλαμπρυνόντων τῶν χειλῶν τὸν ἦχον).[10] So we have a descending order of euphonic value among the long vowels—ᾱ, η, ω, ῡ, ῑ. None of the short vowels, he thinks, has true beauty (εὔμορφον), but ŏ is less ugly than ŭ because it "parts the lips better, and receives the impact more in the region of the windpipe (ἀρτηρίαν)."

From this it looks as if Dionysios graded the vowels euphonically by the openness and roundness of the mouth and lips in pronouncing them. We have already seen that Socrates in the *Cratylos* suggested that *alpha* was apt for expressing grandeur. Perhaps an instinct toward this view is expressed in the modern tendency of some church people to say *Gawd, sawcrifice, sawcrament*. At the other extreme, *iota* was widely regarded as ugly in antiquity. Socrates (again in the *Cratylos*) said that some speakers pronounced it more like *epsilon* or *eta* for a grander effect, and Latin writers describe similar efforts to avoid its thin sound. How unfortunate then that in modern Greek *iota* has swallowed up the sounds of η, υ, ει, οι, and υι!

In discussing what he calls the half-voiced letters, *l, m, n, r*, and *s*, Dionysios first describes how they are sounded and then classifies them euphonically. Among λ, μ, ν, and ρ (the liquid letters, as Dionysios the Thracian had called them),[11] *lambda* is "pleasant to the ear and indeed sweetest (γλυκύτατον) of them all." Demetrios specially praised the sound of doubled *lambda*'s (which were truly geminated in pronunciation then, as in Italian *bella*): for example, in Καλλίστρατος.[12] They might have quoted Theocritos' description of the transparent liquidity of a pool in a line which perhaps has the greatest number of double *l*'s in Greek (if not in European literature),

λάλλαι κρυστάλλῳ ἠδ' ἀργύρῳ ἰνδάλλοντο.[13]

The Roman writers equally admired this liquid letter: we hear it babbling in Horace's lines on the Bandusian spring—

unde loquaces
lymphae desiliunt tuae,[14]

and in that lovely name *Lalage*. And one can imagine how Ovid's lips lingered on the word *meliloton* when he chose it to adorn a passage in his *Fasti*, which I shall quote later.

Lambda, then, was the sweetest letter—you can almost taste it in words like "licorice" and "syllabub." But sweetness is not enough for nobility of character, as Dionysios points out. True nobility (τὸ γενναῖον) needs, he knows, a certain element of roughness: it needs "grit," as we say. Nobility of sound needs it, too. This, says Dionysios, the letter *rho* provides, and *rho* is therefore the noblest of its class.[15] (Moralists may find significance in the fact that the fickle Alcibiades found it hard to pronounce.)[16] The Romans mostly found *r*—at least, as they pronounced it—a disagreeable sound, growling like a dog.[17] And so indeed it can be in English, too, as in Milton's

> Grate on their scrannel pipes of wretched straw.[18]

But the Greek poets often used it with pleasing musical effect, as in Homer's ἀμφηρεφέα τε φαρέτρην.[19]

Dionysios thinks that the sounds of *m* and *n* with their nasal resonance—like the musical tones of a horn, he says—have a middling amount of euphony. He does not distinguish between them at first. But in his analyses he shows a preference for *n*. Demetrios and Quintilian admired the euphony of this letter.[20] Quintilian praised its "tinkling effect" (*quasi tinniens*). Demetrios specially liked the resonant sound of double *n* as in Ἀννοῶν. He would have liked Edgar Allan Poe's "tintinnabulation of the bells" and "beautiful Annabel Lee," though in fact it is rather artificial to linger over double *l*'s and *n*'s in English. The sound of the Italian phrase *una bella donna* would have delighted him.

Some Romans disliked and regretted the frequency of the letter *m* in Latin word-endings[21] where Greek had the more elegant *n*. Certainly in a line like

> mammarum maxima mamma[22]

Martial produces a mumblification that no Greek poet could, I think, achieve. But *m*, especially when combined with *r*, gives us some of the most euphonic words in Greek—μάρμαρος, ἀμβροσία, Amaryllis, Myrmidons.

The fifth of what the Greeks called their half-voiced letters, *sigma*, had the worst notoriety among the cacophonous letters. As we have seen, its evil reputation goes back to the sixth century B.C. when Lasos of Hermione, the earliest known student of euphony in Europe, condemned it as cacophonous. Dionysios describes it as a thin and narrow whistling sound (σύριγμα) pronounced with the whole tongue lifted up to the palate while the breath passes between the tongue and palate and out round the teeth.[23] He apparently means—and other evidence confirms this—the voiceless dental sibilant *s* as in English *lesson* (though later Greek did sometimes use a voiced *s*, especially before voiced consonants, as in Σμύρνα).[24] He calls it "a graceless disagreeable (ἄχαρι . . . ἀηδές) letter which gives great pain when used in excess, for its hissing seems more akin to that of a brute beast than to that of a rational being." He goes on to say that some of the ancient writers used it sparingly and with caution. Similarly Aristoxenos had observed that musicians avoided *sigma* as being "most stiff in sound" (σκληρόστομον).[25]

Most likely what they objected to—though this is never explicitly stated —was the presence of the higher overtones (or partials) in the sibilant *s*, together with its unusual carrying power. Modern choirmasters often have to warn singers against its penetrating and unpleasant acoustic properties.[26] In speech it sometimes becomes exaggerated into what experts in speech-defects call *sigmatismus stridens*,[27] which is described as "a sharp, piercing whistling fricative"—and what could sound uglier than that?

In Greek the very name *sigma* was considered derogatory, being pop-ularly connected with σίζειν, "to sizzle," used of fish being fried, of fire being quenched, of a Cyclops' eye being burnt out, and even of the snorts or sniffs of a hungry Hercules.[28] Yet despite all its genuine faults and un-happy associations we must not be unjust to the unfortunate *sigma*. Though the early Greek language reduced its frequency in many cases, and though the new Attic dialect reduced it further,[29] and though some writers made a point of minimizing its use, it remained a common Greek letter, and many writers used it freely and fully without cacophony. When the comic poet Eubulus mocked Euripides for excessive sigmatism,[30] he was being unfair: he could have found quite as much in Sophocles and other writers.[31] Though there are seven *sigma*'s in Euripides' much-abused line in *Medea*,

ἔσωσα σ', ὡς ἴσασιν Ἑλλήνων ὅσοι,[32]

Sophocles has nine in one line of *Ajax*,

τούς τε δισσάρχας ὀλέσσας βασιλῆς,[33]

and Aeschylus has nineteen in three lines of his *Prometheus* (840–842). Similarly Homer was not afraid to speak of θάλασσα . . . ἠχήεσσα, and one of his favourite heroes is δῖος Ὀδυσσεύς, with four *sigma*'s in only six consonants.

The truth seems to have been something like this: the Greeks from early times were conscious of unusually ugly and disagreeable tone-qualities in the sibilant *s*;[34] their teachers of music and phonetics warned pupils against this; and some writers as a *tour de force*—an extreme case to prove their precept—composed *s*-less poems. On the other hand all normal writings continued to contain *sigma* as a frequent letter, and quite often authors employed it in above-the-average frequency for special ethical or mimetic effects as in Aeschylus' description of the monster Typhos:

σμερδναῖσι γαμφηλαῖσι συρίζων φόβον.[35]

(In parenthesis we may note that the Greek language owing to its lack of a symbol for the sound *sh* was unable to bring out the essential point of a curious incident in the history of the sibilants. In the twelfth chapter of the Book of Judges certain captives were only allowed to live if they could pronounce the word Shibboleth properly. The Revised Version says, "Then say they unto him 'Say Shibboleth'; and he said 'Sibboleth' for he could not frame to pronounce it right"; but the ancient Greek version uses words that mean "And they said to them 'say the password,' and they did not succeed in saying it." [36] The resources of the Greek language do not often fail in that way.)

In connexion with *sigma* Dionysios asserts that the three double letters formed from it—*zeta* (*sd*), *xi* (*ks*), and *psi* (*ps*)—are "better" than the other half-voiced letters because they are "bigger"—that is, they take more time and energy to pronounce—than λ, μ, ν, ρ, σ. Among them *zeta* is pleasantest to the hearing and because it is "quietly roughened by the breath (ἡσυχῇ τῷ πνεύματι δασύνεται), it is the noblest of its kind." [37] (Presumably he means some voicing of the *s* before the *d* sound as in English *wisdom*.) His belief in its special nobility seems to rest on the same principle as his preference for *rho* among the continuant consonants: nobility needs a touch of asperity.

Dionysios and the other writers on euphony have much less to say about the letters that he calls "voiceless" (ἄφωνα: perhaps "deficient in voice" might be nearer his meaning).[38] He grades them euphonically according to the degree of "roughness" or "smoothness" (τὸ δασύ and τὸ ψιλόν), by which he here means presence or absence of breath-quality. So the aspirated *theta, phi,* and *chi* (*t-h, p-h,* and *k-h,* dental, labial, and velar) are the strongest and best (κράτιστα). Next in the scale of euphony come the "medium" *beta, gamma, delta.* The worst (κάκιστα) are the "smooth" *kappa, pi, tau.* But opinions differed about these.[39] As we shall note again later, the Romans especially admired *phi.*[40]

That concludes Dionysios' theoretical analysis of the euphonic values of the letters. In general he gives higher rank to the sounds that are long, open, resonant, and strongly aspirated; he shows dislike for narrow, close sounds and for sibilance. And he recognizes that noble language must not be all smooth and soft; so it needs rougher letters like *rho* and *zeta.* Modern phoneticians still classify vocal sounds to some extent according to these features. They have the advantage of being able to record variations in the sound waves by means of instruments. On a spectrogram they can point to disturbances in the wave patterns which show the nature of the over-tones and formants. But as scientists they usually avoid discussing physical

phenomena in terms of beauty or ugliness. Dionysios had no oscillographs
or kymographs or phonodeiks or spectrographs to aid him, and he was
concerned with aesthetics rather than with physics. He knew that rigid
rules of euphony could not be laid down in the absence of means of precisely
measuring its constituent elements. He relied on what he calls "the non-
logical experience of the hearing" (τὸ ἄλογον τῆς ἀκοῆς πάθος),[41] by
which he means the ear of a person trained in the arts of "music" in the
wide classical sense of that word, practised in rhetorical training, and familiar with the best models of literature: in other words, the cultivated ear
which, as Quintilian says, is "disturbed by what is broken up, charmed by
what is smooth, roused by what is strained and twisted; which approves
of whatever is stable and steady, condemns whatever falters and limps,
and detests whatever is superfluous and excessive." [42] Cicero accepts the
same criterion: as he puts it, "the ear, or the mind informed by messages
from the ear, contains in itself a kind of natural measurement for all vocal
sounds." [43]

Such being the aesthetic material of literature—namely, pleasant-sounding and unpleasant-sounding letters—how should an author choose his
sounds and use them if he wants to please his audience? In his phrases he
must, as Dionysios says, either select words containing chiefly the pleasant-
sounding letters, or else—and better, since variety is an essential of good
style—he should blend the rough with the smooth,[44] the hard with the soft,
the cacophonous with the euphonious, the difficult to pronounce with the
easy to pronounce, the short with the long, so as to produce an agreeable
mixture. He must avoid using too many short words or too many long
words; he should avoid monotony in the pitch-accent or in rhythm. If he
wishes to do something finer than merely to give pleasure, if he wants to
make a beautiful composition, then he must employ the same means, but
he will choose nobler word-melodies, more dignified rhythms, and mellower
variations of sound.[45] No cut-and-dried rules and techniques can be taught
for effectively achieving verbal pleasantness or beauty: the only guide
Dionysios thinks, is a sense of timeliness and fittingness (τὸν καιρὸν ὁρᾶν).[46]

When Dionysios goes on to illustrate what he means by pleasant or
beautiful composition he concentrates mostly on rhythms and letter-group-
ings. The second factor is illustrated by his remarks on the sound of Sappho's
lovely ode to Aphrodite beginning (with a beautiful melody of α's and o's
among τ's and π's):

ποικιλόθρον' ἀθανάτ' Ἀφροδίτα

Immortal Aphrodita of the dappled throne . . .

This is what he says of the whole poem:

The euphony (εὐέπεια) and gracefulness (χάρις) of the language arise from the continuity and smoothness of the joinings (ἁρμονιῶν, which also suggests "melodies"). The words lie close to one another and are woven together according to certain affinities and natural alliances of the letters. Almost right through the whole ode those vowels are joined to mutes and semivowels which are naturally prefixed or affixed to one another when pronounced together in a syllable of one word. There are extremely few collisions of semivowels with semivowels or mutes such as would disrupt the regular wave of the sounds (διασαλεύσουσαι τοὺς ἤχους).[47]

At the end of this analysis of Sappho's ode Dionysios refers to a principle which pervades all classical rhetoric. Sappho, he says, avoids clashes of vowels against directly following vowels:

as for juxtapositions of vowels, I find that those which occur in the clauses themselves are still fewer [than those of semivowels], while those which join the clauses to one another are only a little more numerous. The result is, as one would expect, that the language has a certain easy flow and softness, as the joinings of the words do not ruffle the surface of the sound (μηδὲν ἀποκυματιζούσης τὸν ἦχον).

Here we have the familiar rhetorical principle of the avoidance of what the Romans called *hiatus* (itself a good expressive word as it contains in itself a hiatus between *i* and *a*).[48] Two aspects of euphony are involved in this principle. Two successive vowels, if they are to be clearly enunciated—as in τὰ ἄλλα or τὸ ὄνομα—demand a break in vocal continuity, a stoppage in the emission of breath (the glottal stop, as it is now called)[49] which makes the vocal effort a little harder than if a consonant intervenes. (In fact, English often introduces an unwritten glide-sound, saying *hiyatus* or "the idear of it," and there is some evidence for this occasionally in Greek.) In this way successive vowels could reduce ease of pronunciation.

Secondly, from the aesthetic point of view hiatus infringed a fundamental canon of Greek art which is well expressed in Plato's *Philebos*:

By beauty of form I do not mean, as is commonly meant, namely the beauty of living creatures or of pictorial art . . . I mean straight things and curved things and all that a lathe, rule, or square may produce from them in plane or solid form. . . . Smooth, clear reverberations of sound, emitting a single melody which is tonally pure, are beautiful absolutely and not in virtue of any external relationship: and the pleasure which attends such beauty enjoys the same kind of independence.[50]

Here Plato with his emphasis on the beauty of linear continuity says in philosophic language what Homer implied in his praise of Nestor's eloquence as already quoted—"from his mouth *flowed* utterance sweeter than honey."

So, too, many metaphorical terms for poetry and oratory in Greek and English reflect this sense of "the flow," that steady, clear, unfaltering diction of an accomplished bard or orator, as a source of aesthetic delight. Later Greek writers use the term εὔροια for this.[51]

As will be exemplified soon, the Greek language had various devices for minimizing vowel clashes. But in practice hiatus, internal and external, was quite often admitted in Greek verse and prose. Indeed, internal hiatus, as in γοόωσα or Αἰαίη, was regarded as a delightful feature of Homer's speech, and the terminal kind, as in ἄλγε' ἔχοντα is not uncommon. Demetrios praised the euphonic effect of such successions of vowels, citing Homeric forms like ἠέλιος and ὀρέων in which, as he tells us, the successive vowels have a special melody of their own. To illustrate this he mentions a curious fact:

In Egypt the priests hymn the gods by means of the seven vowels which they utter in due order; and the sound of these letters is so euphonious that men listen to it in preference to pipe and lyre. So if we do away with this clashing of vowels we simply take away the melody and music of speech.[52]

In this Chant of the Seven Vowels we are on the border of magic and mysticism, but we must not cross it until the next chapter. In sober fact, modern phoneticians have found a firm scientific basis for the belief that the vowels do have an inherent melodic scale of their own.

Hiatus between vowels in successive words was generally avoided after the early epic. In prose from the fifth century downward fashions varied, though the tendency was to minimize it. Isocrates never allowed it, thereby making his style rather too smooth, as ancient critics noted. Plato as he grew older grew stricter about hiatus. Demosthenes used it occasionally, but with restraint. Aristotle shunned it in the works he intended for more popular reading, but was less careful about it in his esoteric studies. The avoidance continues in Polybios, Plutarch, and Diodoros. Others, like Lucian and Arrian, were laxer. In the case of the works attributed to the rhetorician Libanios one can distinguish between the genuine and the spurious by the fact that the forgers are stricter in avoiding hiatus than the master himself.[53]

Meanwhile sensible teachers allowed reasonable freedom. Indeed, they admired it at times. Demetrios finds a mark of the grand style (τῷ μεγαλοπρεπεῖ χαρακτῆρι)[54] in the collisions of identical long vowels and diphthongs in phrases of Thucydides like μὴ ἤπειρος εἶναι and Κερκυραῖοι οἰκιστής.[55] In the case of short vowels he finds such a phrase as πάντα μὲν τὰ νέα καὶ καλά ἐστιν pleasanter with the hiatus καλά ἐστιν than καλά 'στιν, which he claims is both less euphonious and less distinguished.[56] (I think his ear liked the continuing chime of the *alpha*'s and *epsilon*'s in the whole phrase.) Similarly Dionysios admires cases of hiatus in Thucydides[57] and also thinks that Demosthenes deliberately and effectively used the jarring hiatus μᾶλλον δὲ ὅλον in an attack on Philip—but this example has been questioned.[58]

At the same time considerations of meaning had to be kept in mind. Important words were not usually run together by elision. So, for example, a form like ἐκτήσατ' Ἀριστοτέλης was avoided in contrast with regular uses like ἀλλ' αὐτός or δηλώσαιμ' ἄν.[59] On the whole, then, rhetoricians, except Isocrates and his followers, wisely set no absolute ban on hiatus. As Demetrios observes, the prudent author will use discretion, avoiding jerkiness and disintegration of sound on the one hand and over-smoothness on the other, for, as he adds, "much euphony results from the concurrence of vowels." [60]

This ideal continuity of line in speech can also be broken by clashes of consonants,[61] as in a hideous example quoted by Cicero, *rex Xerxes*.[62] Almost as bad is Francis Thompson's nearly unpronounceable phrase in *The Hound of Heaven*, "foist'st us off." Rhetoricians recommended that except for deliberately austere or cacophonous effects, such combinations of consonants as do not normally occur inside single words should be used sparingly. When Homer joins sounds like μὲν σκηριπτόμενος he intends, Dionysios believes, the awkward νσκ collocation to give an effect of hard effort.[63] If such cacophonies occur inappropriately they are, of course, a blemish on style.

Another important negative principle for maintaining euphony was the avoidance of acoustic monotony. The regular classical term for deliberate variation in style is μεταβολή, "change of state." [64] To quote Dionysios, "I do not think many words are needed on this aspect. Everybody, I believe, is aware that in narrative and in speeches (ἐν λόγοις)"—Rhys Roberts translates "prose," but Dionysios specifically cites Herodotos, Plato, Isocrates, and Demosthenes—"variety is most pleasant and most beautiful." [65] Here I shall look at only one aspect of it which classical students have tended to neglect.

Our word "monotony" comes from the Greek word μονοτονία,[66] whose basic meaning was "similarity in pitch-variation" or, in other words, a lack of variety in the voice-melody as prescribed by the pitch-accent on every important Greek word. Dionysios in describing the finest kind of style specifically mentions the various pitch-accents which, as he says, "by their variegation steal away satiety" (αἱ καλούμεναι προσῳδίαι διάφοροι κλέπτουσι τῇ ποικιλίᾳ τὸν κόρον).[67] Unfortunately nowadays few writers on Greek style or commentators on Greek authors take any notice of variations in the pitch accent. For example, complaints have been made about the monotony of a phrase in the *Philoctetes* of Sophocles[68] which if pronounced in the traditional Anglicizing way sounds like

legg-ŏh, segg-ŏh, doll-ŏh.

No one will deny that such a jingle is unworthy of Sophocles. But what did Sophocles in fact intend us to say and hear? To know this we must pronounce the pitch-accent as well as use the correct classical tone-qualities and make the right syllable divisions.[69] Then we hear something quite different: λέγω σ' ἐγὼ δόλῳ. The two addled "eggs" of the traditional pronunciation disappear, and instead we have the varying λέ and σε, -γω and -γὼ (and we notice that the tone-quality of the vowels changes slightly with the pitch-variation), while the monotony of a twice-repeated and stressed *oh* disappears in the variation of ω and ωι (with the *iota* properly pronounced).

To take one other example out of innumerable possibilities: contrast what in the traditional English pronunciation is approximately

Ah-teem-y-as men ow, prom-eeth-y-as de sow

with the full melodic and tone-textural effect of

ἀτιμίας μὲν οὔ· προμηθίας δὲ σοῦ,[70]

where the only entirely identical sounds are the endings -ίας. In fact, a properly trained Greek ear would probably find charm and delight in pitch-variations like μὲν οὔ and δὲ σοῦ.

I turn now from rhetorical views on euphony to the nature of the language in which the Greek authors themselves wrote and the Greek critics theorized. To what extent did the established sounds of Greek affect the theory and practice of euphony among the Greeks? In practice, clearly, the alphabetical sounds had an absolute and complete control over an author's diction except insofar as a man of genius could impose his own originality on the language by coining new words or introducing new forms or prescribing new pronunciations, as when, to take an extreme example from English, Lewis Carroll wrote his unforgettable lines,

'Twas brillig, and the slithy toves
Did gyre and gimble in the wabe;
All mimsy were the borogroves,
And the mome raths outgrabe.[71]

I hope to show later that Greek authors sometimes—though in a more restrained way—took similar liberties for the sake of sound-effects. But as the bricks and mortar, so to speak, of their work, classical authors had to use the language as it came to them. Similarly the ancient critics seem to have derived most, if not all, of their theories of euphony from the nature of Greek itself. They were not interested enough in the phonology of non-Greek languages to derive any euphonic principles from them,[72] unlike the Latins with their reverence for Greek.

When the Greeks thought about the origins of their own language they seem to have assumed, as Plato certainly did in the *Cratylos*, that euphony had been a guiding principle in its evolution. Linguists in our time generally reject any aesthetic motive in linguistic development, though ease in pronunciation, which is sometimes a synonym for mere laziness, is recognized as an influential factor. The Greeks apparently were the victims of a complex chauvinistic fallacy: they believed that their language was euphonious; therefore they assumed that those "name-givers"—to use Plato's fallacious term—who controlled the early development of the language were guided by euphonic principles. Yet, fallacious or not, this was what the Greeks were generally satisfied to believe. So, since our primary interest here is to understand their point of view on euphony, I propose now to look at some features of Greek in terms of the euphonic principles already cited from the ancient critics.[73]

To begin with, Greek was well endowed with devices for avoiding hiatus. The chief of these, elision,[74] was widely permitted, and so, too, were many forms of vowel coalescence.[75] For the same reason consonants sometimes were inserted—I must apologize to scientific linguists for following Plato in using terms that imply a purposive process in the making of language—between words as in λέγουσι-ν ἄνδρες, οὐ-κ ὤν, οὕτω-s ἐστίν.[76] We find the same feature, of course, in other European languages, as in French *a-t-il*, and in some dialects of English an unwritten consonantal *y* or *r* sound is generally used as in "my eye" (*my-y-eye*) and "idea of" (*idea-r-of*).[77] For clarity this insertion of a non-semantic letter was often a better technique than elision or coalescence.

Awkward clashes of consonants were also avoided in several ways.[78] The simplest was to drop out letters as in πέπεικα for *πέπειθ-κα, λάσκω for *λάκσκω. Or a vowel could be inserted as in πινυτός, for *πνυτός (but the place name Πνύξ existed as the only common Greek word beginning in πνυ-). The name given to this process was *anaptyxis*. Or else a grouping could be made easier to pronounce by means of an intermediate consonant: so we have κύλινδ-ρ-ος from κυλίνδω, μεσημβρία from *μεσημρία, ἄνδρα from a root *nr (whence *Nero*).[79] We see the same phenomenon in our "chamber" from French *chambre* from *camram (cameram), and we hear something like it when a child says *chimbley* for *chimney*.

As another expedient, one of the adjoining consonants may be assimilated as in ὄμμα for *ὄπμα or ζευκτός for *ζευγτός,[80] and similarly at word endings, as is perhaps fossilized in the form Stamboul ('s τὰμ πόλιν) for Istanbul (εἰς τὰν πόλιν). There is some evidence in older manuscripts that assimilation of that kind was more frequent in classical times than the orthography of our modern editions suggests.

Ancient Greek words generally contained a higher proportion of vowels than Latin or modern English. This partly resulted from the transformation of Indo-European consonants. Vocalic *m* and *n* generally became *a*. Two consonants almost completely disappeared, *digamma* and consonantal *y*: so we find οἶκος where Latin has *vicus*, ἔργον where English has *work*, and ἧπαρ where Latin has *iecur*. Initial consonants sometimes had vowels prefixed ("prothesis"),[81] as in ἐλεύθερος compared with *liber* and ἄστρον compared with *stella* (*sterla) and *star*. All final consonants except *nu*, *rho*, and *sigma* were eliminated, so we find nothing like the heavy Latin endings in *-m*, *-st*, *-nt*, *-lt*, and *-nc*, which give a Roman weightiness to Latin. Latin *domum* is δόμον, *decem* δέκα. (Modern Greek has gone further by often eliminating final *nu*, just as Italian dropped the final *-m* of Latin.)

The treatment of sibilant *s* is the outstanding example of parallelism between early Greek linguistic development and classical Greek theory of euphony.[82] In early Greek there is a marked inclination to reduce the sibilant element of Indo-European, especially at the beginning of words, between vowels, and after liquid letters, so we have ἵστημι for *σίστημι, γένεος for *γένεσος, ἤγγειλα for *ἤγγελσα and ἡδύς (Latin *suavis* from *suad-vis). So, too, the Attic ττ for σσ and ζ indicates reduced sibilance in a large number of words, though poets may have regretted the loss of the sea-sound from θάλασσα and the whispering z from συρίζω. We also have Attic use of ρρ for ρσ, as in θάρρος for θάρσος, giving reduced sibilance. (In contrast with the Greek, the Phoenician alphabet had no less than four different sibilants. Early Semitic also had several rough "gutturals" not found in Greek. Instead of *cheth*, for example, we find the palatal *chi*, which was pronounced as *k-h*, not as in German *ich* or *Nacht*.)

In other features of Greek we find what looks almost like a deliberate striving to avoid monotony of sound, which is the negative aspect of a fondness for variety. Repetitive syllables are dropped from words so that what should etymologically have been *κελαινονεφής appears as κελαινεφής, *ἀμφιφορεύς as ἀμφορεύς. If two successive syllables began with aspirates, the first was usually modified to its unaspirated form, as in τίθημι for *θίθημι, πέφηνα for *φέφηνα. Noteworthy, too, are the lengthenings adopted to avoid the rhythmical monotony of more than two successive short syllables, as in forms like σοφώτερος (for -ότερος),[83] ἀθάνατος (always so in poetry for ἀθ-), ἑτέρωθι (for -οθι), and ὁδοίπορος (for ὁδο-). In these an alternative would have been to eliminate one of the short vowels: but ancient Greek was usually zealous to preserve its vowels.

The absence of strong word-stress[84] in Greek had the effect of keeping a smoother line of sound in Greek speech. It also preserved the variety of the Greek vowel sounds in notable contrast with some other European languages. The effect of stress in Latin was to reduce many of the unstressed vowels to the indeterminate neutral vowel, the *schwa indo-germanicum*,[85] as in English "the syllable" (-*thŭ syllubl*); and in other cases the unstressed vowel was lost. The Greek pitch-accent did not have that effect: for example, the Greek form Σικελός retains three distinct full-toned vowels while Latin *Siculus* reduces the last two to the indeterminate vowel, and δεξιτερός loses two vowels entirely in *dexter*. Modern Greek shows the effect of strong stress even more drastically: classical ὑγίεια has become little more than *ya*, ἐξηῦρον has shrunk to ξέρω, and the borrowed Latin *hospitium* to σπίτι.

The result of such linguistic developments (all of which are not, of course, unique to Greek)—whether prompted by any conscious striving toward beauty and pleasure in diction or not—was to evolve a language rich in vowels, largely free from awkward consonantal clusters and offensive sibilance, and capable of clear articulation together with a flowing continuity. At times the proportion of vowels in a phrase is astonishingly high. Homer's line, for example,

> υἱέες υἱωνοί τε βίης Ἡρακληείης

has eighteen vowels to nine consonants. So, too, the vocalism of names like Laocoön, Pasiphaë, Agesilaos, Nausicaä, make early Greek seem rather like North American Indian with its Minnehaha and Niagara, or even like the Polynesian languages where English Smith becomes *He-mi-té* and Wilcox *Gilikukusu*—a fine example of what the Greeks called *anaptyxis*.[87] If, as an ancient commentator remarks, the vowels are like the soul of speech and the consonants like the body,[88] then what name could be less soulful than Wilcox or Smith and what more soulful than Gilikukusu or Nausicaä?

But there is always a risk, as Dionysios of Halicarnassos saw, that a language may become too melodious and vocalic and euphonic. A language, like an orchestra, needs clashing, clanging, and thundering instruments as

well as a lighter wood-wind group; and a versatile author will need cacophonous sounds at times to express the harsher aspects of what he wants to
say. Ancient Greek retained ample powers to express heavier-harsher things
with suitable sounds. Not all rough groups of consonants were smoothed
away, nor was hiatus always avoided. I hope to illustrate its powers of
cacophony as well as euphony more fully in later chapters. Here I shall
just quote one example of deliberate harshness in

$$\text{ἐφεψαλώθη κἀξεβροντήθη σθένος}^{89}$$

in contrast with a line that ancient and modern commentators have considered one of the most euphonious in Greek,

$$\text{πὰρ ποταμὸν κελάδοντα παρὰ ῥοδανὸν δονακῆα.}^{90}$$

Admiration for the euphony of Greek was not confined to the Greeks
themselves. The Romans, so endearingly modest about the limitations of
Latin, frequently expressed their admiration for the euphony of Greek.
They contrasted the euphony of *phi* (pronounced *p-h* as in "shepherd"),
a *littera iucundissima*,[91] with the cacophony of their own *f* (a harsh labio-
dental fricative like ours), which they considered a *littera insuavissima*.
Unhappily we now pronounce it as the rough *f*. Quintilian also considered
upsilon a most pleasing letter[92]—unlike the Latin *u*, which was a back
vowel, as in our "fool" and "put," and often sank into the indeterminate
schwa. The Romans in their classical period also paid Greek the compliment
of adopting two letters from the Greek alphabet which they had not thought
worth taking over in their more primitive period, namely, *zeta* and *upsilon*,
writing the second as *y* (*i-grec*, as the French call it).

The Latin poets delighted to use Greek words, especially those with
pleasing alternations of light consonants and vowels like Lalage, Helicon,
Melicerta. Sometimes they composed whole lines almost entirely out of
Greek names. Listen to the play of the Greek vowels in these lines from
Virgil and Ovid:

Phyllirides Chiron Amythaoniusque Melampus[93]

and

Has, hyacinthe, tenes, illas, amaranthe, moraris;
pars thyma, pars casiam, pars meliloton amant.[94]

To return to the euphonic evolution of Greek. The generalizations and
assumptions already offered here would demand many reservations and
qualifications in a longer discussion. Two of these I must mention. First,
Greek was never homogeneous and static. It varied from region to region
and from era to era. Each major region had its differences in dialect; each

generation made linguistic changes. When was Greek at its best? Some scholars think—and I agree with them—that the supremely euphonious period is preserved in the Homeric poems. One scholar puts it like this:

In the Homeric language . . . side by side with contracted forms, forms yet un-contracted are delightfully abundant. In these the consonantal dams [e.g., inter-vocalic *s* and *i* and digamma] have been washed away but the vowels have not yet run together—and there is a liquid, continuous vocal flow, a slow free gliding of the voice from vowel to vowel. This is a glorious and passing moment in the history of Greek. For precisely that which constitutes the charm of Homeric vocalism is also the germ of its future decay. And the decay is already apparent in the contracted forms.[95]

Besides this post-Homeric loss of vowels through contraction, another tendency gathered impetus: the substituting of close front-vowels for open back-vowels[96]—most clearly seen in the early use of -η- for -ᾱ- in Ionic and Attic. By the Byzantine era Greek had lost four of its vowel sounds and most of its diphthongs. Also during the postclassical periods other finer shades of tone-variation, as in ᾰ/ᾱ, ε/η, ο/ω, tended to disappear under the hammer blows of emergent stress. Some consonantal sounds also were changed—*beta, theta, phi, chi*—while other new ones emerged, including that *f* sound whose ugliness Quintilian deplored. Modern Greek has many virtues, but one deficiency is incontestable: its phonetic range is far less varied than that of ancient Greek, mainly owing to iotacism, as when ὑγίεια becomes *ee-éeya*, and the recently quoted line

υἱέες υἱωνοί τε βίης Ἡρακληείης

becomes something like

x   x   x   x
ee-ee-eys ee-aw-nee tey vee-ees E-ra-klee-ee-ees.

Yet one can still hear the authentic classical clarity and euphony in words like παρακαλῶ, with its rippling and superbly articulated flow; and ancient Greek has no words so lovely for a butterfly as πεταλοῦδα or for a flower as λουλοῦδι, where the probably non-classical *dh*-sound has a charm all of its own. And my ear still delights to remember how a Greek waitress at Olympia pronounced the pitch accent and all the crystal-clear consonants in κολοκύνθια.

Besides a superbly varied range of phonemes ancient Greek had two other serviceable features for writers eager to exploit sound-effects. The existence of four major literary dialects, with many cross-mixtures, provided a lavish variety of timbre-quality.[97] In fact, one ancient critic compared their effect to that of the chief modes in Greek music.[98] Another suggested that they had different "feels." [99] Though in theory each literary genre was limited to a particular dialect, in fact there was a good deal of freedom to choose. Theocritos uses Doric forms in hexameters with brilliant effect and even with humour in the incident with the Syracusan women.[100] Several Doric and a few Aeolic forms are found in the dialogue of Attic tragedy. Homer's dialect seems to have been highly eclectic apart from his strict avoidance of Doric. Pindar's choral lyrics blend Aeolic forms with the conventional Doric. This freedom, though often severely restricted, gave poets a greater choice of sound-effects than obtains in most European languages, in which one dialect is usually standard for serious literature. In modern English, for example, Burns is the only major poet who wrote in a dialect.

The second feature was partly a result of this dialectical variety, but also partly a result of poetic innovation. I mean the extraordinary number of variant forms of the same word that were available for a poet's choice. If Homer, for example, wanted to use the present infinitive of the verb "to be," he could use any one of five forms, ἔμεναι, ἔμμεναι, ἔμεν, ἔμμεν, and εἶναι. For the third person plural of the imperfect of κεῖμαι he also had five choices, κέατο, κέατ᾿, κείατο, κείατ᾿, and κεῖντο. In the Attic tragedy the name of Athena is sometimes Ἀθηναία, sometimes the Doric Ἀθάνα, while in ordinary speech the Athenians said Ἀθηνᾶ. Attic inscriptions occasionally even have Ἀθηνάα, which (with its delightful echoing *alpha*'s) Theocritos uses once in an Aeolic poem.[101] Greek poets also had considerable liberty in omitting the augment, in using uncontracted forms, and in choosing variations in case endings. Commentators generally explain these in terms of metrical convenience. But such forms also provided useful variations in timbre-quality and pitch-accent. Some, in fact, do not offer a metrical variation at all: for example, νεφεληγερέτα Ζεύς, or μητίετα Ζεύς; or the three examples of the dative feminine plural in -αις instead of -ῃς. These last, if genuine, may well have been chosen for assonance with the other α or αι sounds in the rest of the lines, while the forms νεφεληγερέτης Ζεύς, or μητιέτης Ζεύς, properly pronounced, would obviously be cacophonous in their clashes of consonants and monotonous in their successive *eta*'s and *epsilon*'s.

From what has been said in this chapter it is clear, I hope, that the Greek language had rich potentialities for euphonic exploitation. In the next two chapters I shall try to illustrate how variously and subtly the Greek poets and orators exploited these advantages both for expressing their meaning and for giving pleasure to the ear of their hearers.

NOTES TO CHAPTER III

[1] On classical euphony in general see especially Norden, Wilkinson, Marouzeau, and Herescu. Licymnios, according to Aristotle, *Rhetoric* 3,2 (1405B 6), defined beauty in words as being partly in their sounds as well as in their meaning. Alexander on Aristotle, *Topica* B, 6,112B 22, says the Stoics asserted that pleasure (τέρψιν) in words came from the ears, delight (εὐφροσύνη) from the meaning.

[2] *Iliad* 1,248 f. As well as ἡδυεπής, Homer uses γλυκερός, κάλλιμος, καλός, and ἡδύς of sounds: also δυσκέλαδος of the noise of a rout (*Il.* 16,357).

[3] The earliest compounds in εὐ- referring to sounds are εὐηχής (Pindar) and εὔφωνος (Pindar and Aeschylus): see LSJ for references to words cited here and below. εὔφωνος and δύσφωνος first occur in the title to Demokritos' study (see p. 9). Sophocles uses εὐέπεια in *O.T.* 932: see Rhys Roberts, in *CR* XVIII (1904) 19, who translates it as "elegant diction" against Jebb's "fair greeting." See LSJ for the many compounds (referring to music, speech, or style) in εὐ- (there are fifty-eight of these), ἡδυ-, καλλι-, γλυκυ- (all late), and δυσ- (αἰσχρο- and πικρο- compounds refer to content, not form).

[4] εὐφωνία occurs first in Xenophon, *Memorabilia* 3,3,13 with reference to goodness of voice and does not seem to have been used specifically for euphony before Demetrios (70 and 155) and Dionysios.

[5] εὐστομία appears first in the *Cratylos* (Plato does not use εὐφωνία). It occurs there three times: in 404D it refers to the alleged substitution of Φερρέφαττα for Φερέπαφα; in 412E it refers to the alleged insertion of κ in διαϊόν to form δίκαιον; in 414C it refers to "those who wished to give a spectacular appearance to words [literally, 'dress them up like tragic actors' (τραγῳδεῖν: cf. 418D)], putting on and taking off letters for the sake of εὐστομία and distorting words in every way for the sake of ornamentation (καλλωπισμοῦ)." In the first two of these cases εὐστομία could be simply "ease of pronunciation"; in the third it more probably means "fine diction." But he goes on there to ask contemptuously: "Do you not think it outlandish (ἄτοπον) to put the *rho* into κατόπτρον? I think that's the kind of thing people do who care nothing for the truth but only for the shaping of their mouths" (like Pericles, perhaps, as mentioned on p. 10), which rather suggests a meaning of "elegance of enunciation." If Peipers' emendation στόματος (for ὀνόματος) is correct in 398D we have another reference to ease of pronunciation there (referring to the alleged change from ἔρως to ἥρως). Terms implying beauty or beautification of words occur seven times: namely, ἐπὶ τὸ κάλλιον with reference to the alleged change to Ἀθηνάα from Ἡθονόη in 407C; and καλλωπισμός or καλλωπίζειν in 408B (Ἑρμῆν for Εἰρέμην); 409C (ἀστραπή for ἀναστρωπή); 414C (distortion of words in general), 417E (βλαβερόν for βουλαπτεροῦν), 426D (στάσις for something like στάεισις). Socrates uses two other aesthetic terms for variations in pronunciation: εὐπρεπεία, "handsomeness" or perhaps in a derogatory sense "speciousness" (cf. LSJ s.v. II: they do not list the *Cratylos* use), referring to the alleged insertion of ε in Ποσειδῶν (402E); secondly μεγαλοπρεπέστερα, "more mag-

nificent" (see chap. i, n. 52), but Socrates seems to be mocking here, too, for he uses the term "dressed up like a tragic actor" for the same changes soon afterwards (418D).

[6] For Greek tongue-twisters see Quintilian 1,1,37: also L. J. D. Richardson in *Hermathena*, LII (1938) 108 f.; Dornseiff, *Alph.* 69; Krumbacher 57, n. 2; and C. Wessely, *Studien zür Paläographie und Papyruskunde* (Leipzig, 1912) xliii–xlv.

[7] Dionysios 14. Aristides Quintilianus, *De Musica* 2,11–14 (cf. 1,20 f.), gives a similar survey of the euphonic qualities of the letters.

[8] On Greek views about the diphthongs see especially Blass 21 ff. He discusses their classification into three types by Theodosios and Choiroboskos and Aristides Quintilianus 1,21, namely: δίφθογγοι κατὰ διέξοδον (or κατὰ συμπλοκήν), in which the voice passes successively between both vowel sounds; δ. κατ' ἐπικρατείαν, in which one sound prevails over the other; and δ. κατὰ κρᾶσιν, in which there is complete fusion. These are late writers and they may not have had the classical pronunciation clearly in mind, as is plainly the case with Sextus Empiricus (c. 200 A.D.) in his remarks in *Adv. Mathem.* 100 ff. and 625 f. Some scholia on Dionysios Thrax (Uhlig ii 39, 332, 500) classify αι, αυ, ει, ευ, οι, ου (the only six diphthongs recognized by Dionysios) as εὔφωνοι; ην, ωυ, and υι as κακόφωνοι, and ᾱι, ῃι, and ωι as ἄφωνοι.

[9] On the superior euphony of the long vowels cf. Demetrios, 72 ff.; Aristides Quintilianus, *De Musica* 2,13; Eustathios 12,6 ff. (on *Il.* 1,1); and Hermogenes, Περὶ ἰδέων 1,224 (Spengel 2,291,11 ff.), who emphasizes the importance of the widely opened mouth for ᾱ and ω. Cf. McKay, *Poet* . . . , 83–87.

[10] Hermogenes, Περὶ ἰδέων 1,225 (Spengel 2,291,30–32) also condemned *iota* as rendering style least dignified because it causes the mouth to grow narrow and to grin. Cicero (*De Oratore* 3,46) says that Cotta and his imitators tried to avoid the *i* sound. Quintilian (1,4,17) cites *Menerva* (for *Minerva*) and *magester* (for *magister*) as examples of its avoidance. Aulus Gellius (*Noctes Atticae* 13,21) notes that Virgil and other elegant writers employed the alternative endings *-es* and *-is* for the accusative plural of the third declension with clever effect: see p. 77.

[11] "Liquid letters": Dionysios Thrax 632,9.

[12] On *lambda* (or *labda*): Demetrios 174; Philodemos, *On poems* iv 199,15, on which see Regina Schächer, *Eos* XXIX (1926) 24 f. and Aristides Quintilianus 2,11.

[13] *Idylls* 22,39.

[14] *Odes* 1,22.

[15] Athenaios 11, 467A refers to *rho* as εὔκολον, "agile," "adaptable" (like Sophocles in *Frogs* 82). Socrates (*Cratylos* 426D) connects it with the idea of movement, as in ῥεῖν, τρέχειν, τρόμος, presumably because of the tongue's vibration in sounding it. Cf. LSJ at ῥοῖζος and Eustathios on *Od.* 5,402.

[16] See pp. 141 ff.

[17] Persius 1,109, calls it the "dog letter": cf. Lucilius frs. 3–4 and 389–392 (Warmington).

[18] *Lycidas* 124.

[19] *Iliad* 1,45.

[20] Admiration for *n*: see Quintilian 12,10,31; Demetrios 174. Demetrios 175 thinks that the addition of ν to accusatives of the third declension, as in Δημοσθένην,

Σωκράτην, was for the sake of euphony. The frequency of the *n* sound was enhanced in Greek by the frequent use of the paragogic *nu* after final -ε and -ι. (It is wrongly called νῦ ἐφελκυστικόν by a mistranslation: see Hedde Maassen, "De litera ν Graecorum paragogica quaestiones epigraphicae," *Leipziger Studien* IV 1 ff., cited by Blass 88 n. 1.) Blass also observes: "Our custom of placing the ν ἐφελκυστικόν in prose to prevent hiatus and in all cases where there is a definite pause, but elsewhere of leaving it out, has no foundation whatsoever."

[21] Quintilian 12,10,31.

[22] Martial 1,101, cited by Herescu 234, who quotes other examples.

[23] Cf. Plato, *Theaitetos* 203B, where *sigma* is described as οἶον συριττούσης τῆς γλώττης. Herodotos 1,139 may be evidence that Greek ears were more sensitive to sibilance than Persian ears were.

[24] On the pronunciation of *sigma* see Sturtevant 73–76; Blass 91 f. (who notes that the *sh* sound is "unknown even in modern cultivated Greek"); Lejeune, chap. iii; Schwyzer 140 and 216 ff.; Jeffery 25 ff.; and (for Mycenaean and epic Greek) Strunk 162 ff. For Latin *s* see Sturtevant 160–162, Allen 35 f. (he describes it as a "voiceless alveolar fricative," Sturtevant as a "voiceless dental sibilant": both mean approximately *s* as in "lesson"). Cicero (*Orator* 161) endorses the view that *s* is uneuphonious and notes with approval the elision of final *s* (see Allen 37). According to Quintilian 12,10,23, M. Valerius Messala wrote a book on the letter *s*. See further in notes 26–28 *infra*. In Lucian's *Judgement* Sigma complains that he has been evicted by ξ in words like ξυγγενής, by ρ in words like μύρρινος, as well as by ζ in words like σμάραγδος and Σμύρνα (which, however, were not normally spelt with *zeta*'s) and by τ in words like μέλιττα, γλῶττα.

[25] Aristoxenos on *sigma*: see Athenaios 11,467A.

[26] On the penetrating power of *s* (as in "sink") see, e.g., Joos 88 f., who notes that its power is distributed continuously over the higher frequencies, while *sh* (as in "shoe") contains even higher frequencies. The *sh* form is often used to overpower other vocal sounds, as when we call "shssh" or "hush": cf. Gleason 372 and Muller 54 f. on the similar "white noise" which is most effective in masking other sounds.

[27] On *sigmatismus stridens* see Robbins.

[28] See LSJ on σίζω.

[29] See p. 62.

[30] Scholia on *Medea* 476 (= Eubulus frs. 26 f. Edmonds).

[31] For the belief—unfounded—that Euripides' language was excessively sigmatic see Eustathios 813,44 ff. (on *Iliad* 10,409), who cites Aelius Dionysius as saying that the Greek comic writers avoided sigmatic words, and cites a parody of *Medea* 476 (ἔσωσας ἡμᾶς ἐκ τῶν σιγμάτων Εὐριπίδου); 1170,54 (on *Il.* 19,49), where he calls Euripides ὁ φιλοσίγματος; and 1379,55 ff. (Proemium to the *Odyssey*), where he says that the epic poet Tryphiodoros wrote a λειπογράμματον (asigmatic) version of the *Odyssey* because he was a lisper (cf. chap. i, n. 27). For the absence of any statistical basis (at least, in extant Greek tragedy) for the belief that Euripides was more sigmatic than his rivals see John A. Scott, *AJP* XXIX (1908) 69–77 and Todd. For sigmatism in Homer see Scott *AJP* XXX (1909) 72–77.

[32] *Medea* 476.

³³ *Ajax* 39.

³⁴ See n. 26 *supra*.

³⁵ *Prometheus* 357.

³⁶ The Greek of the LXX version of Judges 12:6 is καὶ εἶπαν αὐτοῖς Εἴπατε δὴ Σύνθημα (v. 1. Στάχυς)· καὶ οὐ κατηύθυναν τοῦ λαλῆσαι οὕτως.

³⁷ In describing *zeta*'s "quiet roughening by the breath" Dionysios seems to be characterizing something like the fully voiced *zeta*, as in our "amazed," which was probably already prevalent in Hellenistic times (see Sturtevant 91–93), but (probably on traditional grounds) he classes it as a double letter, with *xi* and *psi*. On *xi* and *zeta* cf. Philodemos, *On poems* vi 182 (Jensen).

³⁸ Aristides Quintilianus 1,20 uses the term ἄφωνα in this sense: τὰ δὲ μικρὸν καὶ ἀμαυρὸν ἠχοῦντα παντάπασιν ἄφωνα.

³⁹ Aristides Quintilianus 2,11 considers the dentals the most euphonious, especially *tau* (*ibid.* 2,14), and the gutturals roughest. See nn. 44 and 78 *infra*.

⁴⁰ Roman admiration for *phi*: see note 91 *infra*.

⁴¹ The "non-logical experience of the hearing": Dionysios 23,244,23.

⁴² *Inst.* 9,4,116.

⁴³ *Orator* 53,177. See also Aulus Gellius 13,21.

⁴⁴ Demetrios 176 defines a smooth word (λεῖον ὄνομα) as one containing a high proportion of vowels (e.g., Αἴας). As an example of a rough (τραχὺ ὄνομα) he cites βέβρωκεν. The anonymous rhetorician in Walz, *Rhetores Graeci* 3,588 f. cites ἀναρριχῶμαι, ἀτραπός, σμαραγή as "rough" (σκληρά), and κύριε ἐλέησον as "slender" or "delicate" (λεπτή). See chap. ii, n. 36.

⁴⁵ Dionysios, 12,130,23 ff.; 12,134,7 ff.; 16,160,8 ff.

⁴⁶ τὸν καιρὸν ὁρᾶν: Dionysios 12,132,20.

⁴⁷ Analysis of Sappho's poem: Dionysios 23,240,5 ff. Cf. 22,230,19 f.: τὸ δ' εὐεπὲς οἱ συνεχεῖς τε καὶ οἱ συλλεαινόμενοι ποιοῦσιν ἦχοι.

⁴⁸ Hiatus: the earlier Greek rhetoricians used the same terms for vowel-clashes as for consonant-clashes, namely, σύγκρουσις, σύμπληξις, σύμπτωσις, συμβολή. The equivalent terms to the Latin *hiatus* are τὸ χασμῷδες, which first occurs in Apollonios Dyskolos, *Pron.* 50,11 (Schneider); χασμῳδία (first found in the scholia on Aristophanes, *Ploutos* 696; the anonymous rhetorician in Walz 3,589,22–25; and in Eustathios 11,32 ff., 12,1 and 12,8)); and χάσμησις (Eustathios 12,4).

The whole of the passage in Eustathios 11,20 to 12,35 is valuable for the euphonic implications of such vowel-clashes as are found in Πηληϊάδεω Ἀχιλλῆος—a remarkable piece of vocal gymnastics for the first line of a poem. Hermogenes uses χαίνειν in this sense (Schwyzer 399).

On hiatus in Homer see A. Shewan, *CQ* XVII (1923) 13 ff. On hiatus in general see Schwyzer 1,240 ff. and 399 ff., Maas 89–91, Gerber 387. Cf. nn. 76 and 77 *infra*.

⁴⁹ Possibly the term ψῦγμα in Dionysios 20 means a glottal stop.

⁵⁰ *Philebos* 51c. Cf. the definition of τὸ στιλβόν in "Aristotle," *On Colors* 3,793A.

⁵¹ See, e.g., Philostratos, *Lives of Sophists* 2,25,612 and 27,620.

⁵² Demetrios 68.

⁵³ For the use of hiatus by the authors mentioned in this paragraph see Maas 90 f.

⁵⁴ Demetrios 72.

⁵⁵ Thucydides 6,1 and 1,24.

[56] Demetrios 72 notes that concurrence of different long vowels as in ἠώς or of diphthongs as in οἴην gives variety as well as elevation of style. Cf. Aulus Gellius 6,20.
Demetrios 207 observes that such types of hiatus should be avoided in the "plain
style," but that hiatus between short vowels or between long and short (as in
ἠέλιος) is permissible in it. Cf. Eustathios 11,42 ff. (on the hiatus in *Iliad* 1,1).

[57] Dionysios 22,230,24 ff.

[58] Dionysios, *Demosthenes* 42 (on *Olynthiacs* 2,22). Blass 129 thinks that Dionysios
projected the rhetorical usage of his own time onto Demosthenes here.

[59] Blass 128.

[60] Demetrios 68.

[61] On the avoidance of awkward clashes of consonants see Schwyzer 1,399 ff. and
n. 78 *infra*.

[62] *De Oratore* 3,43.

[63] See p. 107.

[64] On μεταβολή (Latin *variatio*) see Dionysios 19.

[65] Dionysios 20,202,16 ff. Cf. *On Demosthenes* 48.

[66] The noun μονοτονία occurs only in Quintilian 11,3,45 and is used there in a wide
sense. For the difficult use of μονότονος by Athenodorus as cited by Varro see
Hanschke 124–126. For monotony in the pitch-accent (cf. p. 146) Dionysios uses
ὁμοιότονος (12,132,6); ὁμοιοτόνως occurs in Eustathios 1400,20. For the principle
of variation in accentuation cf. Walz, *Rhetores Graeci* 3,589,22 and 5,599,5;
Tiberianus 111,75, and Maximus Planudes in Bachmann, *Anecdota* 2,100,30. An
important piece of evidence for sensitivity to pitch-accent patterns in ancient
Greek is in Philodemos (Hausrath 246 f., fr. 18), where Demetrios of Byzantium
is cited as saying that Homer used τείχεος ἐκτός (and not ἔξω) in *Il.* 9,67 and 20,49
and ἁλὸς ἔξω (not ἐκτός) in 17,265 in order not to trouble the hearing (ὀχλεῖσθαι
τὴν ἀκοήν) by monotony in accent-pattern: cf. Hanschke 8 n. 2 and 115 f. and
Wackernagel 1190. Possibly something similar is implied by the anonymous
rhetorician in Walz 3,589,22–25, but this is a late source.

[67] Dionysios 19,196,16 ff.

[68] *Philoctetes* 101.

[69] On Greek syllable-divisions see Sturtevant in *AJP* LIII (1922) 35–51.

[70] Sophocles *Electra* 1036.

[71] Lewis Carroll, *Through the Looking Glass* chaps. i and vi.

[72] But for an early example of Greek interest in the phonetics of a foreign language
see Herodotos as cited in n. 23 *supra*.

[73] On euphonic aspects of the development of the Greek sound-system see Schwyzer
169–371 (with bibliography to 1938), Lejeune, Thomson, and the good summary
in Goodwin and Gulick 11–26.

[74] On elision and aphaeresis ("prodelision") see Schwyzer 402 f. and Goodwin and
Gulick 16 f.

[75] On the various types of vowel coalescence (contractions, crasis, synizesis) see
Schwyzer 401 and Goodwin and Gulick 12–16.

[76] Avoidance of hiatus: Schwyzer 288 f., 399 f.; Goodwin and Gulick 12 and 25 f.; and
pp. 57 ff.

[77] The Greeks sometimes used glide-sounds after ῐ and ῠ followed by a vowel: see

J. M. Toland, *HSCP* XLVI (1935) 212–216, and Schwyzer 224. Schwyzer 289 cites, without conviction, Meillet's suggestion that the *tau* in words like βω-τ-ι-άνειρα and βο-τ-άνη was euphonic (as in *cafétier, bijoutier, cloutier*). On the consonantalization of ι before a vowel see Schwyzer 244 f. and Maas § 120.

[78] For avoidance of awkward consonantal clusters ("prophylaxis") see Schwyzer 276 ff.; Goodwin and Gulick 18 ff.; Kourmoules; and n. 87 *infra*. In contrast Eustathios 1273,41 and 1350,24 notes a device called στομφασμός in which consonants were added, as in ἀμφασία (which only occurs as ἀμφασίη) for ἀφασία and γνάμπτω for γνάπτω (but the latter is only found elsewhere in Hesychios). Dionysios uses the term σπαδονισμός of the effect of harsh vowel-clusters on sounds (*On Demosthenes* 40). Philodemos (iv 181,20 ff. Gomperz) finds τραχύτης in πολυγράμματον εἶναι καὶ πολὺ τὸ ἄφωνον ἔχειν.

[79] On the insertion of a "euphonic" *rho* cf. Plato's remarks on κάτοπτρον in *Cratylos* 414c. In general see Schwyzer 277.

[80] On assimilation (and dissimilation) see Schwyzer 213 f., 254 ff., and Goodwin and Gulick 18 ff.

[81] On "prothesis" see Schwyzer 411 ff. The "deictic iota" (see Schwyzer 611) could serve a similar function at the end of a word: cf. Dionysios 6,108,13.

[82] Treatment of *s*: see Schwyzer 306–308, and Goodwin and Gulick 21 f. But occasionally Greek has *s* where Indo-European had not, e.g., in μέσος.

[83] On "the keen sensitivity to syllabic quantity" implied by this "loi σοφώτερος" (first enunciated by Saussure) see Galton 281, who cites other discussions.

[84] On stress see chap. ii, n. 70.

[85] On the neutral or indeterminate vowel *schwa* see Sturtevant 119–122 and Allen 4 and 56 f. (Possibly something like it was heard in such variants as κάναστρον, κάνιστρον, κάνυστρον.) For Claudius' effort to introduce a sign for it in the Latin alphabet see Tacitus, *Annals* 11,14.

[86] *Iliad* 2,666.

[87] On "anaptyxis" (e.g., δολιχός for *δολχός, πινυτός for *πνυτός) see Schwyzer 277–279 and n. 78 *supra*. See also Szemerényi 73–75.

[88] On the vowels as the "soul" of speech and the consonants as its "body" see the London Scholia on Dionysios Thrax (Hilgard 497,12) and Priscian, *Inst. Gramm*, 1,17 (pp. 13, 22 Hertz).

[89] Aeschylus, *Prometheus* 364.

[90] *Iliad* 18,576.

[91] On the euphony of *ph* see Quintilian 12,10,27 f. and Cicero, *Orator* 160.

[92] On *upsilon:* Quintilian 12,10,27 f.; cf. Sturtevant 115–119 and Allen 48–50. In the same passage Quintilian possibly (the reading is uncertain) praises the Greek *zeta* (but against this see E. A. Hahn, *Language* 17 [1941] 24 ff.). The favourite word *Zephyrus* contained these three admired sounds.

[93] Virgil, *Georgics* 3,550.

[94] Ovid, *Fasti* 4,439 f. See Herescu 243 f. for other examples. He cites Quintilian's remark (12,10,33), "by so much is Greek speech pleasanter (*iucundior*) than the Latin that our poets whenever they want their song to be sweet (*dulce*) adorn it with words of theirs."

[95] Bachtin 32. This was written before the deciphering of Linear B, which seems to

record an even higher vocalism that we find in Homer's Greek, but the script was less phonetically suitable for expressing the sounds of Greek than the later alphabet: on this see Mario Doria, *Atti dell' Istituto Veneto di Scienze, Lettere ed Arti* CXIX (1961) 709–743 and CXX (1962) 643–675, and Strunk. (I am indebted to Mr. J. T. Hooker for guiding me to these articles.)

[96] Bachtin 30 suggests that the "fronting-raising-closing" tendency in Greek resulted from the influence of the pre-Hellenic populations of Greece on the Indo-European invaders. On the tendency see, e.g., Schwyzer 233; M. S. Ruipérez. *Word* XII (1956) 67–81; and I. Fischer in *Studii Clasici* III (1961) 29–32.

[97] See C. D. Buck, *The Greek Dialects* (rev. ed.; Chicago, 1955) and Schwyzer I, 75 ff. On Doric see G. Björck, "Das Alpha Impurum . . ." *Acta Soc. Litt. Hum. Regiae Upsaliensis 39,*L (Uppsala, 1952). For examples of the avoidance by Greek poets of successions of ᾱ's or η's see Tucker. On "dialect sonority" see McKay, *Poet* . . . 76–90, 122 f. Cf. chap. iv, n. 15.

[98] Metrodoros (cited by Iamblichos, *Life of Pythagoras* 34) compared Ionic and Aeolic with the chromatic genus of music and Doric with the enharmonic.

[99] Demetrios 177 says that Attic has a sharp effect, πικρῶς (but this might also refer to taste), compared with Doric. Aristides Quintilianus 2,13 considers the Dorian dialect masculine, the Ionian feminine in quality.

[100] *Idylls* 15,87–95.

[101] *Idylls* 28,1. See LSJ at Ἀθήνη.

IV
Euphony in Practice

UP TO the present I have touched mainly upon the classical theories of speech-sounds and euphony. Now I turn to consider the actual practice of the ancient Greek authors. Here the ground is less firm for reaching general agreement. Artists and creative writers rarely tell us explicitly how they propose to achieve their artistic effects. They prefer to hide their art, leaving it to us to discover its secrets if we can. A painter like Titian doesn't attach labels to his paintings telling us just why he used red here or blue there or yellow there, and Sophocles, though he wrote a book on the chorus and made some sharp remarks about his rivals in tragedy, never, so far as we know, explained details of his choice of sound-effects in his poetry, nor did any other famous classical author. What I shall try to do here and in the next chapter is to discuss some of these techniques which make the music of Greek literature. I shall confine my examples chiefly to poetry, not because it would be impossible or very difficult to find them in prose, but because poetry by its nature is more obviously euphonic and musical.

Let us begin with an example from modern poetry. Here is the first verse of "The Lake Isle of Innisfree" by W. B. Yeats:

> I will arise and go now, and go to Innisfree,
> And a small cabin build there, of clay and wattles made:
> Nine bean-rows will I have there, a hive for the honey-bee,
> And live alone in the bee-loud glade.

Why did the poet choose those special words to express his meaning? Why, in particular, did he use the two unusual compounds "honey-bee" and "bee-loud"? The first obviously provides the necessary rhyme for "Innisfree" as well as a parallel rhythm to it. The second—"bee-loud"—repeats this rhyme and gives a broadening assonance to the *o*-sounds in "bean-rows" and "alone." But even the simpler words are to some extent chosen for euphony. The second line is a melody on the vowel *a*—"And a small cabin . . . clay and wattles made." But why "*nine* bean-rows"? Why not twelve or six, or those symbolical numbers three or seven? For anyone who has ears to hear the answer is obvious. The poet wanted a word containing an *i*-sound to chime with the long and short *i*'s in "I will arise," "Innisfree," "cabin," "build," "will I," "hive," "live," and "in," and also containing *n*-sounds to echo those in "now," "Innisfree," "cabin," "bean," "honey," and "alone," as well as the *n*'s in the five unobtrusive but not insignificant *and*'s. That, I am sure, is primarily why he chose "nine"— not because he thought nine rows would look best in his garden, or were about as much as he could cultivate by himself (poets are seldom energetic gardeners), or because nine is three times three and therefore revered by Pythagoreans. No: he was making music, and "nine" gave the quality and quantity and pitch-value that his melody needed.

We can, I believe, hear Homer doing the same kind of thing. In the last book of the *Odyssey* Odysseus is trying to prove his identity to his father: he describes how his father gave him when he was a boy various fruit trees to be his own personal possessions:

> ὄγχνας μοι δῶκας τρισκαίδεκα καὶ δέκα μηλέας
> συκέας τεσσαράκοντ'· ὄρχους δέ μοι ὧδ' ὀνόμηνας
> δώσειν πεντήκοντα. . . .[1]

The numbers are chosen for their sound-patterns: τρισκαίδεκα with καὶ δέκα (note the skillful variation in the pitch-accent), and τεσσαράκοντ' with πεντήκοντα. Similarly when the poet wants to give a name to the Phaeacian who won the long jump at the games in Scheria he chooses "Amphialos." Why? It is obvious if one listens to the Greek

> ἅλματι δ' Ἀμφίαλος πάντων προφερέστατος ἦεν.[2]

The anagrammatic assonance of α, λ, μ, α, and ι, gives a euphonic appropriateness to the choice of name.

In cases of this kind a writer of fiction has a great advantage over a recorder of facts. Herodotos was not at liberty to choose a more euphonious name than Xerxes for the loser at Salamis, if he had wanted to; nor could Thucydides have given a less euphonious name than Cleon to the demagogue he so much disliked. But a poet, except when he is handling strictly historical material, can choose his names or his numbers to suit his melodies whenever he likes. And even when he is using an established name like Achilles, he can vary it with synonyms like Pēleïdes or Pēleïon or Aiakides—each with a different euphonic quality of its own. Usually in cases of this kind when classical scholars attempt to explain why a poet uses several different-sounding words for the same person or thing they say it is for the sake of metrical flexibility. But I hope that I have already established that metre is not necessarily the supremely important consideration in euphony. Alliteration and assonance, and sometimes pitch-variation, also influence the poet's choice of words, just as a painter's choice of colours is influenced by structural considerations as well as by considerations of hue and intensity.[3]

When I say that writers choose certain words for their sound-effects, I do not mean to suggest that a Homer or a Yeats necessarily paused and consciously said to himself, "I need a word with such-and-such vowels and consonants to express such-and-such a meaning." As Dionysios saw long ago, the process of selecting the most effective embodiment for thought doubtless becomes largely unconscious and instinctive for any fully accomplished writer. As he puts it:

When we are being taught to read the letters, first we learn off their names, then their shapes and values, then in due course the syllables and their modifications, and after that words and their properties, such as lengthenings and shortenings and their pitch-accents and suchlike. Then when we have acquired the knowledge of these things, we begin to write and to read by syllables and slowly at first. And when the lapse of a considerable time has implanted the forms of words firmly in our minds, then we deal with them with the greatest ease, and whenever anyone gives us a book we go through it by habit and with incredible speed. Now this is what we must assume happens in the case of the trained athletes of the literary profession with regard to the arrangement of words and the euphony of clauses.[4]

That is, to develop the metaphor suggested by Dionysios in his last sentence, a skilled author is like an expert tennis player who, thanks to his trained mental and muscular reactions, can play each shot in the most effective way without any conscious thought about the mechanics of the process; so his conscious mind can be absorbed in deciding how to direct each shot toward a win. Similarly the expert writer concentrates mainly on his conceptual meaning, leaving the choice of the most effective word-sounds to an unconscious process. This was especially necessary in the early stages of Greek literature when oral composition prevailed.

But we can sometimes see a writer consciously and deliberately choosing his words or rearranging them for euphonic effect. Dionysios cites the well-known case of Plato, who took great care with the opening sentence of his *Republic*. So, too, in Paul Valéry's description of how a poet may ponder the choice of a word:

I seek a word (says the poet) which should be feminine, of two syllables, containing *p* or *f*, ending in a mute, a synonym for breaking, separation, and not erudite or uncommon. . . .[5]

In matters of this kind a single syllable, even a single letter, can make or mar a line. An eminent Roman scholar is recorded as having discussed when a writer should use either of the two variant case-endings of the Latin third declension, *-im* or *-em*, *-īs* or *-es*.[6] He cited two phrases from Virgil to illustrate their different effects. In

>   urbisne invisere Caesar
>   terrarumque velis curam

the poet effectively employs the brighter and lighter *-i-* form in *urbisne*, while in

>   centum urbes habitant magnas

he uses the broader and more full-blooded *-e-* form.

Now let us think for a few moments about the materials that an author has at his disposal for producing whatever sound-effects he wants. He has a definite keyboard of sounds to choose from—namely, the speech-sounds of the language he is using. In Greek the alphabet of twenty-four letters seems to have provided a fairly good notation for all its basic sounds, with one exception—the nasalized *gamma* in words like ἄγγελος (which ought to have been given a special symbol but was not, though some grammarians gave it a special name *agma*).[7] What each letter indicated was chiefly timbre-quality. But the other two main factors in speech—namely, rhythm and pitch-variation—were also inherent in every group of syllables in Greek.

With these resources at his disposal a Greek author interested in the sound-effects of his words could choose his tones like a musician. He had a sensitive and subtle instrument, the human voice, for the performance of his compositions, and a fairly flexible notation—the alphabet—for indicating what he wanted played on that instrument. Unlike a modern writer, who may write for the eye and the brain alone, the ancient Greek poet always had to choose *some* kind of sound-group for his compositions, since the silent enjoyment of literature was out of the question in his time. His problem was what kind of sound-effects he should select within the limits imposed by the other function of literature—to convey conceptual meaning.[8]

Faced with the necessity of imposing some kind of sounds on his audience, the ancient Greek author could adopt any one of three different ways of using this compulsory material. He could choose sounds which supported and strengthened his conceptual meaning, or sounds that were neutral to his meaning, or sounds that were contrary to it. In what follows I shall consider only the first choice. I shall not consider cases where an author for the sake of irony, or in order to express some kind of irrationality or mental disorder or even schizophrenia, deliberately chooses schizophrenic sounds that clash with the nature of the statements they convey—ugly sounds to express a beautiful idea, for example, or slow sounds for a notion of quickness. Nor shall I delay over the authors who prefer to use neutral sound-effects in their compositions, except to remark that in contemporary literature this choosing of words with little or no regard for their sounds is the general rule: writers write mainly for the eye and brain not for the ear. What I am going to confine myself to is the choice of words for the sake of their suitability in rhythm, voice-melody, timbre-quality, tempo, and volume-variation, as well as for their meaning. This is what the ancient teachers of rhetoric recommended, and it is just what Plato and Demosthenes and probably almost every surviving Greek author from Homer to Nonnus generally did; their aim was not simply to find words with the meanings they wished to convey but the words whose sounds embodied those meanings most effectively.

When I say "most effectively" here I mean "effectively" in three different ways. Speech-sounds can either stir the emotions; or they can give an audial pleasure akin to music; or they can reinforce the conceptual meaning of words by certain kinds of patterns and repetitions. These three—often combined with one another—are the effects that I propose to consider now, leaving a fourth kind of euphonic effectiveness, onomatopoeia, for the next chapter.

Let us first consider the power of words to stir the emotions by their sounds as well as by their meanings. This power was widely recognized in antiquity. I shall quote two passages to illustrate the prevailing belief. The first is from the treatise once commonly called *On the Sublime*:

Harmonious arrangement of words is not only a natural source of persuasion and pleasure among men but also a marvelous instrument of lofty eloquence and of emotion. For does not the music of the pipe put certain emotions into its hearers and as it were drive them out of their mind and make them full of the dancing frenzy (κορυβαντιασμοῦ) and by supplying a certain rhythmical movement compel the hearer to move in it and to identify himself with the tune even if he is entirely ignorant of music? Yes by Zeus and so, too, the sounds of the lyre, though in themselves they mean nothing, yet by the variations in their sounds and by the clashing and blending of the notes in concert (συμφωνίαις) they often cast a marvellous spell (θαυμαστὸν ἐπάγουσι . . . θελγητρον), as you know. And yet this music of instruments is only a semblance and spurious imitation of persuasion, and not, as I have said, a genuine activity of man's nature. Are we not then to think that the arrangement of words which is a kind of harmony of the language implanted by nature in man and which touches not merely the hearing but the soul itself, since it evokes many variegated shapes of words, thoughts, actions, beauty, melody—all of them born with us and bred in us—, and since by the combined effect of the blending and variety of its own sounds it introduces into the souls of those who are nearby the emotion that affects the speaker, and since it always brings the audience to share in it, and *by the architecture of the words it makes a unity of great elements* [I emphasize those words because they are important for the conclusion of this chapter]—are we not to think that this arrangement of words by these very means bewitches us and disposes us on every occasion to a sense of stateliness and dignity and height (ὄγκον . . . ἀξίωμα . . . ὕψos) and every other emotion it embraces, gaining an absolute mastery over our minds? But it is lunacy to dispute about things that are widely admitted, since experience is sufficient proof.[9]

Similarly Dionysios describes his emotions while reading Demosthenes. He has just said that when he reads Isocrates he gets a feeling of seriousness and steadiness as from the sound of pipes being played at a ceremony of pouring libations or from Dorian and enharmonic tunes. He goes on:

But whenever I take up any of the speeches of Demosthenes, I get possessed with a kind of ecstasy [ἐνθουσιῶ] and I am led this way and that, changing one emotion for another, doubt, agony, fear, scorn, hate, pity, benevolence, anger, spite, taking in turn all the emotions that have the natural power to master the human mind. And it seems to me that there is no difference between me in this condition and the people who are being initiated into the rites of the Great Mother and the Korybantes and other rites of that kind.[10]

He goes on to say that if such can be the effect of Demosthenes' words on a reader long after their delivery, their power to move contemporaries must have been amazing.

There is nothing original in these passages except their eloquence. The doctrine of the emotional power of *mousiké* goes back to the Homeric poems. Plato had said much about it in his *Republic* and elsewhere. Various attempts had been made to explain its cause. One of the Aristotelian problems[11] asks why should only the sense of hearing have an ethical quality, and answers that it alone of the senses depends on perceptible movements and rhythms: these, it is assumed, are akin to emotional perturbations. Similarly Aristotle's nephew and pupil Theophrastos defended the view that hearing was the most emotional (or passionate, παθη τικωτάτη) of all five senses because it can cause ecstasies, disturbances, and flutterings (ἐκστάσεις, ταραχάς, πτοίας) of the spirit.[12]

What must be insisted on in the present context is that these emotional effects are primarily attributed to the sound of the words, not to their meaning. An orator could also, of course, move his audience by the content of his speeches, or he could win tears and sobs by displaying objects of pity before their eyes—

> Show you sweet Caesar's wounds, poor, poor dumb mouths,
> And bid them speak for me.[13]

But his subtlest method was through the ear. "Ah, but the authors you have just quoted were primarily concerned with style and so they were inclined to exaggerate stylistic effects." Yes, they did exaggerate at times: but even when we make full allowances for overenthusiasm, the fundamental fact remains that the Greeks in general—even the least volatile of them, like Aristotle—recognized the emotional force of the sound of words, their rhythms, their timbre-qualities, and their pitch-variations, whether they liked it or not.

This is what so many teachers of the classics now, including writers on rhetoric and style, tend to ignore. They concentrate on the logical and intellectual aspects of ancient literature and criticism. They fully discuss the emotional, imaginative, and sensuous elements in the content of literature, but they neglect these same qualities in the substance of words, except with regard to metre and prose rhythm, and even these are more often taught mathematically than aesthetically. I know that words like "aesthetically" often antagonize scholars. But, whatever terms we use, unless we try to educate our students to understand and enjoy the experience which "Longinus" and Dionysios were so enthusiastically describing in the passages quoted we are impoverishing their understanding of classical literature.

I shall not try to give large-scale examples of this power of euphony to affect the emotions, by quoting any long passages. Several examples are offered by Dionysios. In our present state of insensitivity to the sound of Greek it would take many years of teaching and training before we could experience it aurally as fully as Dionysios could. Instead I shall mention one simple type of emotional song-poem—the lullaby where the power of song is used to calm and not to excite emotions.[14] Unhappily, the simple songs of the old-time Greek mothers to their children have not been preserved. But Thecritos in his idyll on Hercules as a baby gives us some inkling of what a Greek lullaby was like. Thecritos describes how the hero's mother, while she caressed her twin boys as they lay in their cradle made from a great shield, sang these words:

εὕδετ' ἐμὰ βρέφεα γλυκερὸν καὶ ἐγέρσιμον ὕπνον,
εὕδετ' ἐμὰ ψυχά, δύ' ἀδελφεοί, εὔσοα τέκνα.
ὄλβιοι εὐνάζοισθε καὶ ὄλβιοι ἀῶ ἵκοισθε.[15]

The carefully constructed euphonies must be clear to every listening ear—repeated sounds, repeated words, repeated phrases, monotony of pitch-accent, and a notable double rhyme in the last line. If the reader fails to feel something of the soothing hypnotic effect that Theocritos intends, he loses both the sensuous charm of the lullaby sounds and also the intellectual pleasure and enlightenment of observing how skillfully the poet has created a lullaby effect inside so formal a metre as the hexameter, and how brilliantly here as elsewhere he has exploited the broad Doric *alpha*'s in a genre where they were previously exceptional. But we shall miss some of that last sound-quality if we are not careful about our text, for the two best modern editors have deliberately reduced the Doric quality of the poem against the testimony of the manuscripts.

(In parenthesis perhaps I may remark that the hypnotic effect of poetry is not confined to lullabies and children. Music has charms to soothe any savage breast. I could tell how a wildly intoxicated professor was once calmed and put asleep by a friend who recited to him some of his own most monotonous poems in a most monotonous voice. As I witnessed the scene, it was positively orphic to see those wild eyes glaze and close, those wild words sink into incoherent mumblings and silence, and how that flushed face relaxed into slumber. Explain it as you please, the operative element there was certainly the sound of words.)

Some of the ancient critics would have had no qualms about explaining such a scene. It would be taken simply as an illustration of the magical power of poetry. They would cite legends of magician-poets like Orpheus and Arion who could control even animals and fishes by their songs. They could recall the Binding Spell in the *Eumenides* of Aeschylus.[16] They would remember the song of the Sirens in the *Odyssey*[17] and that strange incident when Odysseus was bleeding to death on the slopes of Parnassos and his uncles staunched the flow by singing an incantation (ἐπαοιδή) over him.[18] I have heard an account of a similar case of blood-staunching in Russia from an officer of the Imperial Guard who saw it himself.

In spells of that kind the magical effect was thought to depend either on the referential meaning of the words—invocations of aweful daimons or elemental powers—or else on the sound of the words, or on both together. The papyri have preserved many magical spells in which the sound seems to matter most.[19] I shall venture to print three of these formulas, despite the risk that some fearsome demon might be immediately evoked if a reader should rehearse them aloud and pronounce the sounds correctly. Here they are:

$$\alpha\ \epsilon\ \eta\ \iota\ o\ \upsilon\ \omega\ \omega\ \omega$$
$$\iota\eta\omega\ \ ov\epsilon\ \ \omega\eta\iota\ \ v\epsilon\ \ \epsilon\iota\omega v\ \ \alpha o\eta\ \ ov\eta$$
$$\iota\iota\iota\iota\ \ ooooo\ \ vvvvvv\ \ \omega\omega\omega\omega\omega\omega\omega$$

(We may note in passing that the third formula with its four *iota*'s, five *omicron*'s, six *upsilon*'s, and seven *omega*'s, embodies the "law of increasing members" [20] as in

Friends, Romans, countrymen,

or in Euripides, *Hippolytos* 621

$$\mathring{\eta}\ \chi\alpha\lambda\varkappa\grave{o}v\ \mathring{\eta}\ \sigma\acute{\iota}\delta\eta\rho ov\ \mathring{\eta}\ \chi\rho\upsilon\sigma o\tilde{\upsilon}\ \beta\acute{\alpha}\rho os$$

or in the "rhopalic" hexameter.) Another papyrus recommends the devotee to say *alpha* to the east, *epsilon* to the north, *eta* to the west, *iota* to the south, *omicron* to the earth, *upsilon* to the air, and *omega* to the sky. Sometimes the actual tone of voice to be used in uttering the magical vowels is prescribed; e.g., *alpha* is to be spoken "with a swelling tone and an open mouth." Probably the Chant of the Seven Vowels sung by the priests of Egypt referred to in chapter iii was a magical formula of this kind.[21] It is even possible that when Christ in the Book of the Revelation says "I am Alpha and Omega" [22] he is referring to this Chant of the Seven Vowels as used by the Gnostics and others, and not to the full alphabet.

I must not linger in this fearful and fascinating field where certain sound-patterns were believed to command supernatural powers. But we may note in passing that when Greek authors from Homer onward used metaphors that described poetry or music as being able to "enchant" or "bewitch" or "charm" or "cast a spell over" people, these terms were more highly charged for ancient readers than for us with so few seriously believing in magic.

As has just been shown, the basis of magical spells sometimes consisted in repetitions of the vowels alone. But apart from any supernatural effects, such successions of vowels in poetry can (as Demetrios was exemplifying when he cited the Egyptian Chant of the Seven Vowels) have a specially melodious effect. That is probably why when Homer wants to find speech-sounds to embody the beautiful qualities of Calypso's voice as she sits weaving cloth in her cave, the words he chooses are ἀοιδίαουσ' ὀπὶ καλῇ.[23] They are full of tuneful vowels and diphthongs—ἄ, οι, ῐ, ᾰ, ου, o, ῐ, ᾱ, ηι—almost an incantation in themselves. Then when the poet wants us to hear Circe singing—a sharper type than kind Calypso, and the contrast in the sound of the names Κίρχη and Καλυψώ hints at this—Homer mod-

ulates the same vowel-melody into a heavier, slower key in ἀειδούσης ὀπὶ
καλῇ.[24] (But a few lines later her singing is described with the more tuneful
form of the verb, καλὸν ἀοιδιάει.) The song of the Sirens sounds shriller—
λιγυρῇ θέλγουσιν ἀοιδῇ.[25] In phrases like this[26] we are on the borderland
between pure euphony and onomatopoeic euphony. But there is no sound-
for-sound mimesis; so in general these sound-effects may be best regarded
as special examples of Homer's love for vocalic richness, as in single words
like ἠέλιος or Αἰαίη or ἐώϊα or the extraordinary ἄαστος, or the word for
song itself ἀοιδή, for which an Attic author would use contracted forms.

In view of this Greek delight in vowel patterns I am sure it is not a
mere chance that Pindar begins his first Olympian and Pythian odes with
syllables containing five different vowels in succession, ἄριστον μὲν ὕδωρ
and χρυσέα φόρμιγξ.[27] It sounds almost as though the master-poet was
announcing the theme of some great fugue in these sequences of the five
main tones of his vowel-scale at the beginning of two major works. Something similar can be found at the beginning of the third Isthmian and the
fourth Nemean, εἴ τις ἀνδρῶν εὐ- and ἄριστος εὐ-. The mathematical
chances against such a series of vowels occurring in a random selection are
139 to one. But the chances against any major Greek poet's leaving the
euphony of the opening words of any poem to mere chance are, I would
say, something more like 10,000 to one.

Consonants can also, of course, be used to give acoustic pleasure by their
intrinsic tone-qualities. Dionysios, as we have seen, discusses this in detail
and we need not delay over it here. As Dionysios exemplifies, many Greek
writers both in poetry and prose use a high proportion of the pleasanter
consonants δ, λ, ν, ρ,[28] and avoid awkward letter-clusters in describing
pleasant things or in trying to win the good will of their hearers, while
they exploit the rougher letters and letter-clusters in the opposite conditions, as, for example, Demosthenes does in denouncing the iniquities of
Philip the Second of Macedon.[29]

A widely recognized technique for pleasing the listener's ear was the use
of repetitions and patterns of repeated letters and syllables. Such sound-
patterns are enjoyed because design has in itself a pleasing effect apart
from its constituent elements. The classical and postclassical Greek rhetoricians studied this technique carefully and produced an elaborate ter-
minology for it. They coined terms like *homoiokatarkton*[30] (similarity of
sound at the beginning of words or phrases), *homoioteleuton* (similarity at
the endings of words or phrases), *parechesis* (general similarity in tone-
qualities), *paromoiosis* (similarity in both rhythm and tone-quality), and
paronomasia (a general similarity between two words of different meanings,

but here considerations of meaning rather than of sound are dominant). These refer primarily to timbre-quality and pitch-variation rather than to rhythm (for which there were terms like *parisosis* and *isocolon*). Our commonest modern terms for similar features are alliteration, assonance, and rhyme. But the term alliteration has no exact equivalent in classical rhetoric.[31] Probably the reason why the ancient critics did not isolate it was that they thought of euphony in terms of letter-groups rather than of letters in isolation, although they did attribute specific euphonic qualities to single letters. In a line like

$$\tau\nu\varphi\lambda\grave{o}\varsigma \ \tau\acute{\alpha} \ \tau' \ \tilde{\omega}\tau\alpha \ \tau\acute{o}\nu \ \tau\epsilon \ \nu o\tilde{\nu}\nu \ \tau\acute{\alpha} \ \tau' \ \acute{o}\mu\mu\alpha\tau' \ \epsilon\tilde{i}^{32}$$

what seemed significant to their ears probably was the variety of syllables beginning with *tau* rather than the recurrence of *tau* by itself.

The Greeks used rhyme[33]—*homoioteleuton* as they called it—much more sparingly than Western European poets, probably because the frequent similarities of the case-endings made rhymes in the end-syllables of words less noticeable to them than to us. Double or triple rhymes do seem to be employed with deliberate stylistic intention at times. The drunken Hercules in the *Alcestis* speaks a series of four lines ending in double rhymes or near-rhymes:

$$\beta\rho o\tau o\tilde{i}\varsigma \ \ddot{\alpha}\pi\alpha\sigma\iota \ \kappa\alpha\tau\theta\alpha\nu\epsilon\tilde{i}\nu \ \dot{o}\varphi\epsilon\acute{i}\lambda\epsilon\tau\alpha\iota,$$
$$\kappa o\grave{\upsilon}\kappa \ \ddot{\epsilon}\sigma\tau\iota \ \theta\nu\eta\tau\tilde{\omega}\nu \ \ddot{o}\sigma\tau\iota\varsigma \ \dot{\epsilon}\xi\epsilon\pi\acute{i}\sigma\tau\alpha\tau\alpha\iota$$
$$\tau\grave{\eta}\nu \ \alpha\ddot{\upsilon}\rho\iota o\nu \ \mu\acute{\epsilon}\lambda\lambda o\upsilon\sigma\alpha\nu \ \epsilon\grave{i} \ \beta\iota\acute{\omega}\sigma\epsilon\tau\alpha\iota\cdot$$
$$\tau\grave{o} \ \tau\tilde{\eta}\varsigma \ \tau\acute{\upsilon}\chi\eta\varsigma \ \gamma\grave{\alpha}\rho \ \dot{\alpha}\varphi\alpha\nu\grave{\epsilon}\varsigma \ o\tilde{i} \ \pi\rho o\beta\acute{\eta}\sigma\epsilon\tau\alpha\iota,$$

(and the next line ends in $\dot{\alpha}\lambda\acute{i}\sigma\kappa\epsilon\tau\alpha\iota \ \tau\acute{\epsilon}\chi\nu\eta$). Here Euripides apparently intends to embody the sententious and monotonous speech of an inebriated simpleton—the singsong cadences of the kind of sermon that nice-minded but unoriginal persons tend to deliver when alcohol has removed their sense of intellectual inferiority.[34] Rhyme was also used in proverbs for similar sententious emphasis, but here without any association with drunkenness, as in Homer's

$$\chi\rho\grave{\eta} \ \xi\epsilon\tilde{i}\nu o\nu \ \pi\alpha\rho\epsilon\acute{o}\nu\tau\alpha \ \varphi\iota\lambda\epsilon\tilde{i}\nu, \ \dot{\epsilon}\theta\acute{\epsilon}\lambda o\nu\tau\alpha \ \delta\grave{\epsilon} \ \pi\acute{\epsilon}\mu\pi\epsilon\iota\nu.^{35}$$

We find the same technique in proverbs of our own—"a stitch in time saves nine," "finders keepers, losers seekers."

In sound-patterns of this kind there is utility as well as pleasant hearing. Phrases that have end-rhymes are easy to remember. So, too, phrases with initial assonances such as "waste not, want not," "look before you leap," "penny wise, pound foolish." Obviously, too, equivalence of rhythm helps the mnemonic effect, as in the examples cited, and equivalence of pitch-accent is often enlisted as a memory-aid. Here we can see very simply and clearly how the three main factors in euphony—timbre-quality, pitch-accent, and rhythm—combine to arrest and impress the mind of any hearer.

This technique is not, of course, confined to proverbs and aphorisms. We hear the same kind of memorable assonance in Homeric formulas like Ζεῦ κύδιστε μέγιστε, 'Αχαιῶν χαλκοχιτώνων, χεῖρα βαρεῖαν—with less straightforward variations like ἄναξ ἀνδρῶν 'Αγαμέμνων, δολιχόσχιον ἔγχος. These are all formulaic; but we also hear assonances in unique phrases like Λυχάονος ἀγλαὸς υἱός. Sometimes the assonances become full puns or etymologies as in Εὐπείθει πείθοντο or ἅλματι δ' 'Αμφίαλος. Most elaborate of all examples of this is, perhaps, the epigram

ἄκρον ἰατρὸν "Ακρων 'Ακραγαντῖνον πατρὸς "Ακρου
κρύπτει κρημνὸς ἄκρος πατρίδος ἀκροτάτης.[36]

Apart from their stylistic usefulness for supporting and emphasizing the conceptual meaning, rhymes and assonances seem to have tickled the ears of the Greeks agreeably with little or no reference to their sense. Sounds which we might find rather too jingly for serious literature—κῦμα μάχης, for example, and ἔργα γάμοιο—are freely used by the best epic and tragic writers, though Isocrates objected to them.[37] But we, when we read them, generally overdo the jingle by ignoring variations in the pitch-accent: if in these phrases we read -μα μά- or -γα γά- rightly, the variation in timbre-quality caused by the variation in the pitch-accent is something like what we have in music when a sharp comes after a natural. But complete jingles like the English "hoity toity" or "argy bargy" do also occur in Greek.

Shakespeare's metaphor of "tickling the ears" may perhaps explain the Greek's fondness for other varieties of sound-patterning. They apparently enjoyed hearing anagrammatic sound-effects in juxtapositions of words like ἀρετή and ἐρατη, ὄχλος and χόλος, or more elaborately in phrasal anagrams like 'Αρσινόη, "Ηρας ἴον or Πτολεμαῖος, ἀπὸ μέλιτος.[38] We, addicted as we are to silent reading, can hardly, I think, *hear* the redistribution of the same letters of 'Αρσινόη in "Ηρας ἴον, but very likely the Greeks did (though when they came to more elaborate acrostics, palindromes, and conundrums based on the ingenious manipulation of letters like mathematical symbols they presumably had to see them written out before they could follow them).

But to return to the simpler types, clearly a Greek audience must have been amused by letter-jumblings, or else Aristophanes would hardly have used phrases like ὁ πλοῦς πολύς, or more elaborately

χαῖρ' ὦ Χάρων, χαῖρ' ὦ Χάρων, χαῖρ' ὦ Χάρων,[39]

for which a phonetic rendering could be "Cheerio, cherub, cheerio, cherub, cheerio, cherub."

But assonance and syllable-patterning are not exclusively humorous. Many poets use them in serious contexts. We can hear something very close to it in Homer's ἀμφηρεφέα τε φαρέτρην or Pindar's πολὺν ὗσε χρυσόν and ἕλε βελλεροφόντας. I personally find solemnity and pathos in the assonance of a phrase that Sophocles gives Ajax in the speech before his death—στένοντα πόντον, as in Virgil's *suadentque cadentia sidera somnum*.[40]

A simple kind of sound-patterning for euphonic effect is the repetition of whole words within a phrase or succession of phrases.[41] The Greek rhetoricians recognized several distinct types. They gave the name *anaphora* (or *epanaphora*) to repetition of a word at the beginning of successive clauses, as, for example, in the triple mention of Nireus at the beginning of three lines in the second book of the *Iliad*—he is not mentioned again by Homer—

Νιρεὺς αὖ Σύμηθεν ἄγε τρεῖς νῆας ἔΐσας
Νιρεὺς Ἀγλαΐης υἱὸς Χαρόποιό τ᾽ ἄνακτος
Νιρεὺς ὃς κάλλιστος ἀνὴρ ὑπὸ Ἴλιον ἦλθε.[42]

This carefully spaced *epanaphora*, as Demetrios notes, gives an impression of extended activity so that (to quote)

though Nireus is only named on one occasion in the course of the action yet we remember him no less than Achilles and Odysseus who are spoken of in every line. The reason for this lies in the powerful effect of the epanaphora. . . . Writing can be like a banquet; a few dishes can be arranged so as, somehow, to seem many.[43]

If we ask why Homer should have exercised such skillful technique on a minor character never to be used again, the answer is easy: it is a characteristic Greek tribute to sheer beauty.

Repetition, as Demetrios goes on to say, can be effective even with the simplest words. When a writer—we do not know his name—writes "To the war flocked both Greeks and Carians and Pamphylians and Phrygians," the triple repetition of the conjunction gives, Demetrios claims, something of the impression of an endless crowd (ἐμφαίνει τι ἄπειρον πλῆθος). Shakespeare uses the same device in

Tomorrow and tomorrow and tomorrow,

where the rhythm emphasizes the "ands." Similarly Homer in a description of a series of uninterrupted routine actions begins four successive lines with ἐκ δ᾽ εὐ-, ἐκ δὲ, ἐκ δ᾽ ἐ- and ἐκ δὲ.[44] More elaborately, when he wants to show how quick and eager several heroes were to volunteer for a dangerous enterprise he begins four successive lines with ἠθελέτην, ἤθελε,

ἤθελε, ἤθελε.⁴⁵ When we speak and hear these repetitions (and not merely see them), the sense of sameness and succession is much more vivid.

A few other examples will show the wide scope of this device. In the nightmarish scene in the *Bacchai* of Euripides just before the terrible rending asunder of Pentheus by his mother and the other maenads, Dionysos exerting his divine strength slowly drags down the top of a fir tree so as to place Pentheus on it:

$$\kappa \alpha \tau \tilde{\eta} \gamma \epsilon \nu \ \ \tilde{\eta} \gamma \epsilon \nu \ \ \tilde{\eta} \gamma \epsilon \nu \ \ \dot{\epsilon} \varsigma \ \ \mu \dot{\epsilon} \lambda \alpha \nu \ \ \pi \dot{\epsilon} \delta o \nu.^{46}$$

How vividly that repeated verb with its bending circumflex accent and its tapering-off vowels renders the slow, ominous bending of the fatal wood. Euripides could easily have expressed the same idea in conceptually descriptive terms by using adverbs or adjectives meaning slow, relentless, sinister, or doomfraught. Instead he makes the very sound of the words embody his message. There are English parallels in Dryden's *Alexander's Feast:*

> Fallen, fallen, fallen, fallen
> Fallen from his high estate,

and in Tennyson's song in *The Princess:*

> Blow, bugle, blow, set the wild echoes flying,
> Blow, bugle; answer, echoes, dying, dying, dying.

Rather simpler but no less memorable is the effect of Sappho's heartbreaking lines, quoted by Demetrios⁴⁷ to illustrate another variety of repetition called *anadiplosis,*

> Maidenhood, maidenhood, where have you gone and left me?
> Never again shall I come to you, never again.

> παρθενία, παρθενία, ποῖ με λίποισ' ἀποίχῃ
> †οὔκετι ἤξω πρὸς σέ, οὔκετι ἤξω†.

Demetrios also commends the type of repetition called *anaphora* in Sappho's happier lines to Hesperos, the evening star (the text unfortunately is corrupt in the second line):

> Ἔσπερε πάντα φέρων ὄσα φαίνολις ἐσκέδασ' Αὔως
> †φέρεις ὄιν, φέρεις αἶγα, φέρεις ἄπυ μάτερι παῖδα†.

The opening word Ἔσπερε is followed three times by the echoing word φέρεις (almost its anagram). In contrast with the despairing note of the other fragment, this gives a calm steady confidence: indeed, here in terms of meaning as well as of sound is the answer of mature wisdom to a girl's anxiety.

Euripides was a master of these more poignant repetitions. But some of us may agree with Aristophanes in thinking that he occasionally overdid them, lapsing from pathos into sentimentality, as suggested in the parody:

δάκρυα δάκρυά τ' ἀπ' ὀμμάτων
ἔβαλον ἔβαλον ἀ τλάμων,[48]

where as well as the double repetition the sustained alpha-omega pattern piles on the pity. Yet when the occasion is worthy of highly formalized language these repetitions can have a solemn liturgical effect. Aeschylus finely uses this device at the end of *Seven against Thebes*, where the two sisters of the dead champions repeat in turn

δορὶ δ' ἔκανες
δορὶ δ' ἔθανες[49]

and similar phrases, all of them rhythmically identical, some of them almost totally identical. The repetition stirs our emotions, and the parallelism symbolizes the unanimity of the two sisters' grief.

Repetition in its many forms can be used for a wide variety of purposes. Contrast the fierce cry of the Erinnyes in the *Eumenides* of Aeschylus (preceded by a shrill prolonged moaning sound as a stage direction demands —μυγμὸς διπλοῦς ὀξύς),

λαβὲ λαβὲ λαβὲ λαβὲ φράζου,[50]

and the

ἔα ἔα· βάλλε, βάλλε, βάλλε, βάλλε
θένε, θένε[51]

of the startled chorus in *Rhesos*, with the melancholy, momentary recollection of a lost happiness when Hector reminds himself that his fight with Achilles is no amorous dalliance between a youth and a maid, a youth and a maid (he repeats), dallying with each other

τῷ ὀαριζέμεναι ἅ τε παρθένος ἠΐθεός τε
παρθένος ἠΐθεός τ' ὀαρίζετον ἀλλήλοιιν[52]

(and we may also note how Homer, as is his custom, fills the lines with vowels and avoids all ugly consonantal clashes, to express the implicit pleasure of the scene).

We can hear similar varied effects in Lear's despairing

Never, never, never, never, never,[53]

in Tennyson's admiring

Elaine the fair, Elaine the loveable,
Elaine the lily maid of Astolat,[54]

and in the drinking song's inexorable

> Down, down, down, down,
> Down among the dead men let him lie.

Most emphatic of all types of repetition is the full refrain, that is, a whole line repeated at calculated intervals like the haunting

$$αἴλινον \ αἴλινον \ εἰπέ·\ τὸ \ δ' \ εὖ \ νικάτω^{55}$$

in the *Agamemnon* of Aeschylus or in the "Down among the dead men" refrain just quoted. At times the effect of these is spread over a wide area, sometimes running through a long poem, as in Theokritos' witchcraft idyll with its

$$ἴυγξ, \ ἕλκε \ τὺ \ τῆνον \ ἐμὸν \ ποτὶ \ δῶμα \ τὸν \ ἄνδρα,$$

and

$$φράζεό \ μευ \ τὸν \ ἔρωθ' \ ὅθεν \ ἵκετο, \ πότνα \ Σελάνα.^{56}$$

Refrains are especially effective in solemn supplications, lamentations, imprecations, and incantations.

The significant fact about all these types of repetition is that they are all essentially effects of sound, not of logical statement. Since the repeated words are the same, the repetition adds no new conceptual meaning. In fact, if an author wishes to clarify or emphasize his conceptual meaning he normally uses different words, synonyms or paraphrases or amplifications. Repetition is more like a repeated note or group of notes in music, and in its most solemn moments it is like the tolling of a bell—

> Toll for the brave!
> The brave that are no more.

One can appreciate its effect more in terms of being hit several times by a stick than of observing an abstract mathematical series. We feel the effect of repetition rather than think it, as we feel an increase in the temperature of the air or in the weight of a bundle of books.

These are only small-scale uses of a technique that can be deployed on a far larger scale. Sometimes the key words in an extensive passage are set in a subtle scheme of assonances which may extend through a dozen lines or more. One remarkable example (whose euphony has already been analyzed)[57] comes at the opening of the twenty-first book of the *Iliad*, the introduction to the fight in the river:

> $ἀλλ'ὅτε \ δὴ \ πόρον \ ἷξον \ ἐϋρρεῖος \ ποταμοῖο,$
> $Ξάνθου \ δινήεντος, \ ὃν \ ἀθάνατος \ τέκετο \ Ζεύς,$
> $ἔνθα \ διατμήξας \ τοὺς \ μὲν \ πεδίονδε \ δίωκε$
> $πρὸς \ πόλιν, \ ᾗ \ περ \ Ἀχαιοὶ \ ἀτυζόμενοι \ φοβέοντο$

ἤματι τῷ προτέρῳ, ὅτε μαίνετο φαίδιμος Ἕκτωρ·
τῇ ῥ'οἵ γε προχέοντο πεφυζότες, ἠέρα δ'Ἥρη
πίτνα πρόσθε βαθεῖαν ἐρυκέμεν · ἡμίσεες δὲ
ἐς ποταμὸν εἰλεῦντο βαθύρροον ἀργυροδίνην,
ἐν δ'ἔπεσον μεγάλῳ πατάγῳ, βράχε δ'αἰπὰ ῥέεθρα,
ὄχθαι δ'ἀμφὶ περὶ μεγάλ'ἴαχον · οἱ δ'ἀλαλητῷ
ἔννεον ἔνθα καὶ ἔνθα, ἑλισσόμενοι περὶ δίνας.
ὡς δ'ὅθ'ὑπὸ ῥιπῆς πυρὸς ἀκρίδες ἠερέθονται
φευγέμεναι ποταμόνδε · τὸ δὲ φλέγει ἀκάματον πῦρ
ὅρμενον ἐξαίφνης, ταὶ δὲ πτώσσουσι καθ' ὕδωρ·
ὡς ὑπ' Ἀχιλλῆος Ξάνθου βαθυδινήεντος
πλῆτο ῥόος κελάδων ἐπιμὶξ ἵππων τε καὶ ἀνδρῶν.

The key words, ποταμός and Ξάνθος are introduced in the first two lines
and then their syllables ξα, τα (or θα), πο (or φο, with a variant προ) are
repeated with skillful modulations in the following thirteen lines, blending
into the noise of the routed Trojans as they struggle in the stream μεγάλῳ
πατάγῳ . . . ἀλαλητῷ. The intervention of Hera with her mist is thrust
in with the emphatic, almost punning phrase ἠέρα δ' Ἥρη and its effect
soon becomes audible, mixed with the sounds of the rushing river and the
dying Trojans in a series of r syllables which come to a climax in phrases
like βράχε δ' αἰπὰ ἐέεθρα and ὑπὸ ἐιπῆς πυρὸς ἀκρίδες ἠερέθονται where a
sensitive ear can still hear the echo of Hera's eerie mist in the word
ἠερέθονται. In line eleven the ν, θ, and α sounds of Ξάνθος are given another
brief but effective innings. The last phrase of the passage returns mainly
to the consonants and vowels of Ξάνθος and ποταμός with an added bitter
i sound in ἐπιμὶξ ἵππων.

Another example of such ingenious use of sound-echoes has been famous
since Homer's time. It is the incident in the ninth book of the *Odyssey*
when Odysseus deceives the Cyclops by giving his name as "No-Man" [58]—
a nice choice of nomanclature, as a modern scholar has homerically remarked. The basis of the whole elaborate play on sounds lies in a double
variation—one in accent between the coined name Οὖτις with a circumflex
intonation on the first syllable (the poet repeats this unusual form three
times within four lines so that all his hearers would get it right) and the
ordinary word for "no-one" οὔτις with an acute accentuation on the same
syllable. The other variation is between the alternative form of the word
for "no-one" which is used in hypothetical clauses, namely, μήτις with
paroxytone accent, and the noun μῆτις with a properispomenon accent,
meaning "prudence, forethought." Let us hear how Homer plays conjuring
tricks with these two pairs—Οὖτις, οὔτις; μῆτις, μήτις.

When Polyphemos has been blinded he roars for help to the neighboring

Cyclopes. They crowd round the blocked door of the cave and ask rather peevishly why he has disturbed their sleep. Can it be that someone is robbing his cattle or trying to kill him? They use the phrase ἤ μή τις[59]—two acute accents here owing to a following enclitic—twice in the emphatic position at the beginning of two successive lines. Polyphemos replies from inside the cave that Οὖτις is trying to kill him. But the intonations of furious ogres are likely to be hard to hear, especially from outside a resonant cave blocked by a huge boulder. So we can hardly blame his fellow Cyclopes when they mistake, or neglect, the nature of the pitch accent and think he is saying οὔτις, not Οὖτις—in terms of English stress-accent "no man" (with equal stress and divided as no-man) instead of "Noman" (stressed on the first syllable and divided more like "nom-an"). So with a kind of perverse nominalism—I almost wrote noman-alism—they sententiously reply, "Well, if no-one (μή τίς) is doing violence to you, then your affliction must come from Zeus, so the best thing for you is to say some prayers."

Clearly the poet is very pleased with this paronomasia, whether he invented it himself or not. So, like any comic writer, he decides to make the most of it. Two lines later he says that Odysseus rejoiced in his μῆτις ἀμύμων, "his faultless foresight," and soon he uses this word μῆτις again.[60] Then he repeats Οὖτις.[61] Then shortly afterward he expands it into οὐτιδανὸς Οὖτις.[62] Finally he repeats οὐτιδανός fifty-five lines later.[63] Each of these echoes and variations οὖτ-, οὔτ-, οὐτ-, μῆτ-, and μῆτ- would no doubt win a smile from his audiences. Even eleven books later the paronomasia might still be humorously recognized when Odysseus, in a moment of despondency rallied his sinking heart by reminding himself how he escaped even from the cannibalistic Cyclops by using his μῆτις.[64]

Obviously the validity of this kind of analysis may be questioned on two grounds: first, that the sound effects are too widely spaced out to be perceptible to the average listener; secondly, that the so-called significant sounds may be nothing more than the result of random choice. In answer to the first I suggest that in a world of oral literature listeners are likely to have been quicker to notice sound repetitions and patterns than we are in our world of silent reading; and, in fact, any sensitive listener to music can appreciate themes and variations fully as subtle as that. In ideal conditions one could make an experimental test by reading the river passage for the first time to hearers as sensitive as Homer's own audience. But where in our present state of pronunciation and listening would we find such an audience? The only way of finally answering the second objection is to make a full survey of all sound-patterns in the *Iliad* (a gigantic task which would be greatly complicated if allowances were made for differences in authorship) to determine whether the features said to be significant in this passage are in fact significantly above the possibility of random occurrence. This is beyond my present scope.[65] So in the absence of conclusive proof or disproof I follow Dionysios and other ancient critics in accepting the view that effects of that kind were often deliberately contrived.

Now I shall venture to go even further before I end. The passage about the river Xanthos lasts for merely sixteen lines. In it the poet has exploited the musical elements of speech—besides the assonances noted, I could also have pointed out effective uses of metre and the pitch-accent—to convey his meaning in terms of sound as well as of ideas. The total effect is one of superb integration between the material used and the conceptual contents, which is a sure mark of supreme artistry. But on a far greater scale, a whole long poem if it is to give complete aesthetic and emotional satisfaction to a cultivated audience should have this integrity of formal structure— an architectonic euphony, we might call it, remembering "Longinus'" reference (quoted earlier in this chapter) to "the architecture of the words" which "makes a unity of great elements."[66] This would be something akin to the total effect of a symphony or concerto. Much of value could, I believe, be learned from fuller investigation of large-scale poetic euphony. With tone-quality and pitch-accent as well as metre to consider, the complexity of such studies would be great, but not, perhaps, beyond analysis with the help of computers. If the difficulties of calculating how to send a rocket to Mars can be mastered, presumably the complexities of Homer's total euphonic technique could be mastered, too.

Much more than mere matters of form are, I believe, involved in this architectonic euphony. We all know how Aristotle, probably in answer to Plato's strictures on the emotionalism of Greek drama, asserted that the supreme power of tragedy was to effect a *katharsis* of pity and fear and suchlike emotions. Aristotle also maintained that one could experience the force of a play by reading it—and he meant, of course, reading it aloud. So clearly the katharsis did not depend on the visual experience of a dramatic performance. (This is what one would expect in view of the fact that the supreme tragic incidents were almost always expressed in terms of words, by the death-shrieks of the victim or in a vividly recounted description, and not visually.) Would it be unreasonable, then, to suppose that the katharsis was partly at least produced through euphonic means?

A rather neglected theory of katharsis[67] has suggested that essentially it is not a purgation or a purification, but a re-establishment of emotional harmony in the listener, and that this harmony is achieved through a harmony of form which authors impose on their material. The proposer of this theory cited two classical analogies: first, the fact cited by Plato—and, indeed, known to every mother without any enlightenment from Plato— that the psychological disorders of a fractious infant are calmed when it is rocked rhythmically; secondly, the belief common in the ancient world that certain types of madness were cured by music and dancing. (This belief in the therapeutic power of music and dancing is also found in the folklore of the tarantella in southern Italy).[68] In these analogies the chief controlling element which brings psychological harmony to the disturbed personalities of the infant or the corybantic madman is rhythm. But rhythm in the wider sense is not just a matter of beat: it depends to some extent also on timbre-quality and pitch-variation. I suggest, then, that in those great kathartic tribal dances of the Athenians, the tragedies that were produced annually at the city dramatic festivals in honour of Dionysos, the tone-qualities and the pitch-variations of the poets' words may have shared with their metres in achieving the final katharsis.

To sum up this last suggestion on the power of architectonic euphony: as we have noted earlier in this chapter, the Greeks were conscious of the power of great literature to rouse the emotions to a kind of frenzy. But, as Plato saw, such frenzies are the enemies of the balanced personality. So Plato condemned them. But Aristotle answered him: great literature both rouses our passions and brings them back to a healthy equilibrium. As a mother by the rhythm of her rocking calms the passions of an infant too young to know the meanings of words, so when we are older an author of genius first stirs our emotions profoundly and then by the rhythm of his words brings them back to a haven of harmony and peace, turning chaos into cosmos.

Just how this can happen is perhaps one of the unexplainable mysteries of great art. But I believe that the total effect of word-music masterfully employed throughout a whole *magnum opus*—or at least in each part of it capable of being aurally appreciated in a single hearing—may help more than is generally realized in that supreme artistic achievement. In other words, although in every great poetic recitation what matters primarily is its meaning and message, yet the total effect of its sound-patterns should be like the effect of a musical composition, first stirring our emotions, then swaying our emotions, and finally creating a harmony and balance in our emotions.

NOTES TO CHAPTER IV

[1] *Odyssey* 24,340–342.

[2] *Odyssey* 8,128 ff. (cf. 8,114). Simpler examples of this euphonic choice of names are in *Il.* 2,758; *Od.* 24,465 f. (but *Il.* 5,472 f. and *Od.* 1,60–62 are etymological puns on established names).

[3] See, e.g., O. Skutsch, in *RhM* XCIX (1956) 200, on Theocritos' choice of the rare word φωλάδες for its *omega*-sound in *Idylls* 1,115; J. A. Scott, *AJP* L (1929) 71–75, who suggests that Homer uses plural verbs with neuter plural subjects for euphonic reasons; and J-A. de Foucault, *RPh* XXXVIII (1964) 68, who suggests euphonic reasons for some cases of hyperbaton of the verb. Perhaps the reason why Herodotos never has σύν σφι (but has σύν δέ σφι seven times) is euphonic: cf. J. E. Powell in *CR* LII (1938) 163 f.

[4] Dionysios 25,268,16 ff.

[5] Paul Valéry, *The Art of Poetry* (see chap. ii, n. 12).

[6] Aulus Gellius, *Attic Nights* 13,21 (his quotations are from Virgil, *Georgics* 1,25 and *Aeneid* 3,106). In the subsequent discussion he makes some comments on the euphony of Homer. It is noteworthy that he assumes translators will try to render the sounds as well as the meaning of the original poem.

[7] On the nasalized *gamma* in words like ἄγγελος see L. J. D. Richardson in *Hermathena* LVIII (1941) 57–69.

[8] Cf. van Groningen 9 ff.

[9] "Longinus" 39.

[10] Dionysios, *On Demosthenes* 22.

[11] *Problems* 19, 27, and 29.

[12] Theophrastos as cited (and objected to) by Plutarch, *On Right Hearing* . . . 2,38A. Cf. Diogenes Laertius, *Lives* 10,76. See p. 115.

[13] Shakespeare, *Julius Caesar* III,ii, 229 f.

[14] See I. Waern, "Greek Lullabies," *Eranos* LVIII (1960) 1–8. See also Bücher.

[15] Theocritos 24,7–9. It is characteristic of contemporary neglect of sound-effects in editions of classical texts that neither Gow nor Legrand refers to the euphony here (but Cholmeley did); they also diminish the effect of the Doric *alpha*'s here by adopting in l.10 Wilamowitz's δίνησε for the MSS δίνασε. On p. 416 Gow notes that if Papyrus 3 were followed the poem would have a broader Doric appearance. Cf. chap. iii, n. 97–99, and K. Strunk in *Glotta* XLII (1964) 165 ff.

[16] Aeschylus, *Eumenides* 306 ff.

[17] *Odyssey* 12,181 ff.

[18] *Odyssey* 19,457 f. For a modern parallel similar to the Russian example cited by me see A. B. Lord as cited in n. 57 *infra*.

[19] For the vowels in magical formulas see F. Cabrol, *Dictionnaire de l'archéologie chrétienne et de liturgie* (Paris, 1907), I, Cols. 1268–88, and III 264–268, and Dornseiff, *Alph.* 35 ff.

[20] On the "law of increasing members" cf. Wilkinson 175. A special type is the

"rhopalic" line (e.g., *Il.* 3,182), in which each word is longer by one syllable than its predecessor: cf. Aulus Gellius, *Attic Nights* 14,6,4 and Gerber 366.

[21] See p. 58.

[22] Rev. 1:8. See *Hermathena* XCVIII (1964) 43 f., where I suggest that if this interpretation is adopted it adds another symbolism of seven to those already explicit in the Revelation. It also fits in with the references to music and to the planets. The seven vowels were also associated with the seven stars of the Pleiades, the seven strings of the heptachord, the music of the spheres, the Hebrew tetragrammaton for God, and the seven archangels: see *PW* at *Hebdomas*;[2] Cabrol (as cited in n. 19 *supra*) I, Cols. 56–58. See also A. A. Barb, "The Survival of the Magical Arts," in *The Conflict between Paganism and Christianity in the Fourth Century*, ed. A. Momigliano (Oxford, 1963) 111; Dornseiff, *Alph.* 11 ff., 35 ff., 82 f.; and the London Papyrus 46 (Kenyon 66,24) cited by Dornseiff, *Alph.* 47 f.

[23] *Odyssey* 5,61. Cf. McKay, *Poet* . . . 88.

[24] *Odyssey* 10,221, 227. Homer uses the more vocalic form of the verb (ἀοιδιάειν) only in *Od.* 5,61 and 10,227.

[25] *Odyssey* 12, 44, 183.

[26] Cf. Agathias' use of ἐνδιάουσα of the ὀλολυγών in *Anthology* 5,291,6.

[27] See Fr. Pfister, "Die fünf Vokale als Anfang," *Würzburger Jahrbücher für die Altertumswissenschaft* III (1948) 196 f., and L. Alfonsi, "Le cinque vocali come inizio" in the same journal IV (1949) 381–383 and cf. Gomperz 63. The mathematical chances given in my text are those against α, ε, ι, ο, and υ all occurring in any group of five vowels picked at random from the whole seven.

[28] Dionysios 17,168,5 ff.

[29] Dionysios, *On Demosthenes* 43.

[30] On such "figures of speech" as *homoiokatarkton*, etc., see especially John C. Robertson, *The Gorgianic Figures in Early Greek Prose* (Baltimore, 1893); Norden; and Wilkinson, 25 ff. See also LSJ at ὁμοιολεξία, παρόμοιον, παρομοίωσις, ὁμοιοπρόφορον, ὁμοιόπρωτον, παραγραμματεύω (and -ιζω). Dionysios 22,212,8 observes that the "austere" style avoids such devices.

[31] On uses of alliteration in Greek see Ilona Opelt, "Alliteration im Grichischen" *Glotta* XXXVII (1958) 205–232 (with a review of earlier studies); P. Ferrarino, "L'Allitterazione," *Rendioconti delle sessione della Reale Accademia delle Scienze dell' Istituto di Bologna* ser. iv, 2, (1938/9), 93–168, Classe di scienze morali; and Norden 1,59. Ferrarino attributes the coinage of the term to Pontano. For alliteration in specific Greek authors see especially Shewan; G. Bernhardt, *Die allitterationis usu apud Homerum* (diss. Jena, 1905); Ch. Rideel, *Alliteration bei dem drei grossen griechischen Tragikern* (diss. Erlangen, 1900); and Seymour (as cited in n. 33 *infra*). On assonance see J. D. Denniston, "Some Observations on Assonance in Greek Prose," *Proceedings of the Cambridge Philological Association*, CLVII (1936) 8 ff. Macdermott 14 notes that alliteration appeals more to the eye than assonance (especially in English, where assonantal vowel-sounds are often spelled differently). B. F. Skinner in *Verbal Behaviour* (London, 1957) 246 ff. discusses the statistical approach to alliteration, assonance, and rhyme, and offers evidence that Shakespeare sometimes took trouble to reduce alliteration in his sonnets. David L. Masson gives a detailed classification of types of alliteration in "Sound-

Repetiton Terms," *Poetics* (Publication of International Conference on Phonetics in Warsaw) (Warsaw, 1961). Cf. Fraenkel on *Agamemnon* 268.

[32] Sophocles, *O.T.* 371: see Jebb's note.

[33] On rhyme see O. Dingeldein, *Der Reim bei dem Griechen und Romern* (Leipzig, 1892); G. Amsel, "De vi atque indole rhythmorum," *Breslau phil. Abh.* 1 (1887); Norden 2, 810 ff.; Shewan; Verrall 245 ff., and McKay, *Poet* . . . 85. For the importance of considerations of rhyme in textual criticism see O. Skutsch, "Rhyme in Horace," *Bulletin of the Institute of Classical Studies* 11 (1964) 73–78. A. Platt, *CR* XXXV (1921) 141–143 considers examples of rhyme in the Homeric poems, finding, for example, a feeling of "senseless ineffectuality" in νεκύων ἀμένημα κάρηνα (*Od.* 11,49). Thomas D. Seymour, *Introduction to the Language of Homer* (Boston, 1902) 15 f. gives useful lists of parecheses, etc., but remarks: "The poet seems to have looked with indifference on the similarity of sound in neighbouring words" and, later, "most examples of parechesis . . . are probably accidental." As one example he cites the close proximity of ποσὶν and πόσιν in *Od.* 4,136 f. (but there the pitch accent makes an agreeable variation: see p. 59). On euphony in Homer in general see Victor Bérard, *Introduction à l'Odyssée* (Paris, 1924) I 381–412 and II 11–28 (where he objects to several parecheses); he gives a bibliography.

[34] *Alcestis* 782–785. Cf. Verrall 245 ff.

[35] *Od.* 15,74. For similar internal rhyme see *Il.* 2,484.

[36] See Diogenes Laertius, *Lives of Philosophers* 8,65: cf. *ibid.* 3,26 for another example.

[37] On jingles see Jebb on *Ajax* 807 f.; G. B. A. Fletcher, *CR* LII (1938) 164 f.; A. Biese; and Shewan. For Isocrates' objection to forms like εἰποῦσα σαφῆ, ἡλίκα καλά, ἔνθα θαλής: see Maximus Planudes' notes on Hermogenes, Walz, *Rhet. Gr.* 5,469; and Benseler-Blass on Isocrates 2,275.

[38] On anagrammatic assonance see Eustathios 45,43 ff. (on *Il.* 1,54) and 488,12 ff. Plato, *Cratylos* 404c, suggests an anagrammatical etymology of Ἥρα from ἀήρ. See also Dornseiff, *Alph.* 63 on anagrams in general.

[39] Aristophanes, *Frogs* 136, 184: cf. *Ploutos* 278, where a pun on Χάρων and ἄρχων is implied. Platt, *Essays* 178 notes the pleasure of similar effects in phrases like "the lake-reflected sun," and "and like a skylit water." Cf. Milton's "Jousted in Aspramont or Montalban." Van Groningen cites Aratos fr. 334, ῥεῖα γὰρ οὖν ἔκρινε διὰ στίχας ὀξὺς ἀείρας.

[40] *Iliad* 1,45; Pindar, *Olympians* 7,9 and 4,13. Sophocles, *Ajax* 675; Virgil, *Aeneid* 2,9. Contrast the gaiety of τὴν δ᾽ ἐθέλων ἐθέλουσαν ἀνήγαγεν ὅνδε δόμονδε in *Od.* 3,272 with *Od.* 9,414,422,455,460,515; 20,19–21.

[41] On repetitions see Robertson (as cited in n. 30 *supra*) 20 and 26 ff., and for Homer's uses of them see Shewan 202 f., and cf. Wackernagel 1234 f.

[42] *Iliad* 2,671–673, cited by Demetrios 61 f.

[43] Demetrios 63.

[44] *Iliad* 1,436–439: cf. 2,382–384. Cf. Wilkinson 66 ff.

[45] *Iliad* 10,228–231.

[46] *Bacchai* 1065.

[47] Demetrios 140 f.

[48] Aristophanes, *Frogs* 1354 f.

[49] Aeschylus, *Seven* 962.

[50] Aeschylus, *Eumenides* 130.

[51] Euripides, *Rhesos* 674–676. For other quadruple repetitions see Sophocles fr. 314 (Pearson) and Aristophanes, *Acharnians* 281.

[52] *Iliad* 22,127 f.

[53] *King Lear* V,iii,310; cf. IV,vi,192, "Then, kill, kill, kill, kill, kill."

[54] *Lancelot and Elaine* 1 f.

[55] Aeschylus, *Agamemnon* 121, 139, 159.

[56] *Idyll* 2, 17, 22, 27, etc., and 69, etc. Cf. *Id.* 1,64, etc., 94, etc., and 127 etc.

[57] A. B. Lord in Wace, *Companion* 200–202. I have added some suggestions. For similar anticipatory and retrospective phonetic emphasis on key words in Aeschylus (e.g., *Supp.* 40–56; *Ag.* 281–283, 489–492) see W. Porzig, *Aischylos* (Leipzig, 1926). For the same technique in English poetry see Wilson 304 ff.; in French, P. Guiraud, *Langage et versification d'après l'œuvre de Paul Valéry* (Paris, 1953) 91. See additional note to this chapter.

[58] *Od.* 9,366 ff.

[59] *Od.* 9,405 f.

[60] *Od.* 9,414, 422.

[61] *Od.* 9,455.

[62] *Od.* 9,460.

[63] *Od.* 9,515.

[64] *Od.* 20,19–21. See on this final echo and the preceding repetitions A. J. Podlecki, *Phoenix* XV (1961) 125–133.

[65] See Additional Note *infra*.

[66] For Greek recognition of the ability to perceive order in a complex whole (ἡ ἐπιστημονικὴ αἴσθησις) see De Lacy 246 ff.

[67] See W. F. Trench, "The Place of Katharsis in Aristotle's Aesthetics," *Hermathena* LI (1937) 110–134, and cf. *Hermathena* LXXXV (1955) 52–56.

[68] See Walter Starkie, *The Waveless Plain* (London, 1938), chap. 12.

ADDITIONAL NOTE TO CHAPTER 4

After my analysis of the euphonic qualities of *Iliad* 21, 1-16, was finished, Mr. Louis Roberts of the University of California, Berkeley, using a computer, kindly provided me with figures for letter frequencies in this and eight other passages chosen at random from the *Iliad* and *Odyssey*. It emerged that the frequencies of π, τ, ξ, and θ in this passage are distinctly above the average thus:

π in *Il.* 21, 1-16, average 1.8 per line; in the eight other passages (amounting to 441 lines in all), average 1.3 per line.

Similar figures for τ: 2.1, 1.9.

Similar figures for θ: .9, .5.

Similar figures for ξ: .38, .09.

Obviously much fuller and more detailed analysis of the phonetic constituents of any such passage would be necessary before one could conclusively establish a clear idiosyncrasy. Comparative statistics for single letters, as given above, would have to be supplemented with statistics of consonant groups and phonemes. Ultimately what would be needed is a complete analysis of the phonetics of the whole *Iliad*. Valuable conclusions might be derived from such a survey, but it is beyond my scope. It is to be hoped that some scholar trained in statistical method may undertake it. Meanwhile I am grateful to Mr. Roberts for his ready and effective help in this minor foray into an unconquered area of classical studies.

V

Mimesis in Words

In this chapter I shall avoid using the term "onomatopoeia," for two reasons. First, it is usually confined to simple sound-for-sound imitations, and I hope to show later that there are several other kinds of word-mimicry besides this direct mimicry. Secondly, for anyone who knows any Greek the term "onomatopoeia" (ὀνοματοποιΐα)[1] is unsatisfactory because it etymologically means simply "word making." So instead I shall use the broader (and a more etymologically tolerable) term *mimesis*, a favourite word in classical Greek criticism for describing the relationship between a work of art and its object.

The deeper meanings of *mimesis* have been much discussed elsewhere,[2] and I must not pursue them in detail here. It meant much more than mere "imitation." In fact, its meanings in Greek range from "copying, facsimile making" to "re-presentation" and even "re-embodiment." When Pythagoras spoke of things as existing by *mimesis* of numbers, he certainly did not mean mere "imitations";[3] nor could Aristotle have meant simply "copying" when he said that in tragedy the plot was the *mimesis* of the action.[4] Similarly Socrates, according to Xenophon,[5] insisted that a sculptor in creating his *mimesis* of a beautiful object can improve it by adding features from other similar objects, and that he is not confined to imitating external appearances, but can suggest character and emotion by facial expressions, gestures, and postures. So in what follows, when I speak of *mimesis* in words I shall not restrict my illustrations to mere imitations of sound as in "boom" or "tick-tock."

There is a risk, however, that if we look and listen for subtler effects, we may go too far and strain credulity. An influential critic of our time has remarked on such efforts to detect subtler examples of sound-mimesis in literature:

It is sad to have to discourage so harmless a pastime. Most alleged instances of onomatopoeia are imaginary. . . . The mysterious glory which seems to inhere in the sound of certain lines is a projection of the thought and emotion they evoke, and the peculiar satisfaction they seem to give *to the ear* is a reflecting of the adjustment *of our feelings* which has been momentarily achieved.[6]

There is much to argue about in these assertions. For my present purpose it must suffice to say that the ancient Greeks, at any rate, were clearly addicted to this harmless pastime and to that mysterious glory, and if we want to understand their attitudes to poetry we must bear with—or better still, perhaps share—their foibles for a while.

Before exploring some of the subtler forms of verbal mimesis it may be well to glance for a few moments at some sources of antipathy to such explorations. First: sensible critics have been antagonized by ridiculously farfetched suggestions about verbal mimesis.[7] Secondly: there is no agreed scientific basis for argument about adequacy or inadequacy in verbal mimicry. Thirdly: poets rarely state their intentions in matters of this kind, leaving it uncertain whether sound-effects are deliberately calculated or not. Fourthly: silent reading reduces our sensitivity to sound-effects, and many, perhaps the majority, of present-day readers are naturally more sensitive to visual impressions than to auditory impressions[8]—for example, they think of telephone numbers as visual data, not as a series of sounds—remembering "83329" as a row of shapes, not as a choriambic and spondaic phrase "eight–double-three–two–nine."

Another reason why a good many scholars and critics rather despise studies in sound-mimesis is the fact that what matters supremely in our study of literature is its contents, not its form. But in every true work of art the form is part of the substance, and the substance part of the form, and the two are no more separable in a work of art than body and spirit in a living person.[9] Sometimes the form creates the substance, sometimes the substance the form. If Keats had not been compelled by the structure of his verse in his *Ode to a Nightingale* to find rhymes for "path," "home," and "corn," he might never have created the wonderful romantic evocation that follows:

> The same that oft-times hath
> Charm'd magic casements, opening on the foam
> Of perilous seas, in faery lands forlorn.

All these motives for antipathy add up to this practical difficulty in what follows here: probably the majority of my readers are on the visualizing side of this psychological dichotomy. If so, I ask for their patience.

If some of what I have to say seems farfetched, even incredible, to them, may I offer three pleas in mitigation of sentence? First, what I am trying to do is to hear Greek poetry as the ancient Greeks themselves intended it to be heard. Secondly, it is natural that anyone who makes the effort to listen as keenly as possible to complex sounds will hear, or think he hears, more than those who have been accustomed—even advised—to ignore them. And finally, is it not true that the palace of literature, like the Kingdom of Heaven, has many mansions in it, with room for ear-philologists and eye-philologists to live together in both visual and acoustic harmony? As St. Paul says on the unity of the body:

The body is not one member, but many. . . . If the whole body were an eye, where were the hearing? If the whole were hearing, where were the smelling? But now hath God set the members every one of them in the body, as it hath pleased him. And if they were all one member, where were the body? But now are they many members, yet but one body. And the eye cannot say unto the hand, I have no need of thee: nor again the head to the feet, I have no need of you. Nay, much more those members of the body, which seem to be more feeble, are necessary: And those members of the body, which we think to be less honourable, upon these we bestow more abundant honour. . . . And if one member suffer, all the members suffer with it; or if one member be honoured, all the members rejoice with it.[10]

This, I believe, is also true of the many facets of a great literary composition, especially in oral literature.

Before I quote examples of verbal mimesis in both its simpler and its subtler forms in Greek literature, one further question needs to be answered. Why did the ancient Greeks believe sounds to be the best medium for *mimesis?*[11] We would hardly agree that the products of musical instruments and the human voice are more effectively mimetic than, say, paintings or sculptures. The reason for the Greek view was partly, I think, technological, partly psychological. Technologically it was impossible for the ancient Greeks to produce the extraordinarily faithful copies of visual objects that we are used to in everyday life—photographs, imitation jewellery, or fake coins. How many men today—I do not say women for obvious reasons—can tell at a distance the difference between a fake leopard-skin coat and a real one, or between false pearls and true pearls? Much of our physical world consists of deceptive copies and reproductions—our furniture, our clothes, our pictures. Most of it was impossible for the Greeks in the absence of machines and chemical science. They had no standardized paints or dyes, no finely graded instruments for measuring or weighing, and they could not make any photographic reproductions. One has only to remember the wide range of colour produced under the name of Tyrian purple—varying from sepia to crimson, it seems—to recognize how variable were the materials, as well as the processes, of the ancient visual arts and crafts. In Greek sculpture alone—and perhaps in some of the lost paintings—it was possible to come close to a deceptive likeness. But even there the naturalism was far less deceptive than what can be achieved by modern techniques.

Technologically, then, exact visual *mimesis* was much harder for the ancient Greeks than for us, and our modern chemical reproductions of tastes, smells, and textures were impossible. No Greek in fifth-century Athens would, or could, mistake a sculpture or a painting for a living person in the same way as we are deceived by one of Madame Tussaud's wax-works or by a *trompe l'œil* wall painting. But it was different with vocal *mimesis* at all its levels from simple mimicry to the expression of profound emotions. Even the cleverest of modern actors is unlikely to be able to surpass the actors of the ancient world in reproducing a tone of voice or in harrowing our feelings with sheer pathos of sound. Though modern science has enabled us to understand and analyze the mechanics of sound in ways unknown to any ancient Greek, yet, voice for voice, there is no reason to believe that we are better equipped than they to exploit the resources of vocal mimesis to the full, that is, the power of the sound of words to entertain, delight, and move.

Let us now consider some examples of both the simpler and the subtler types of verbal mimesis in Greek literature. The more obvious kinds need only be briefly mentioned. Greek with its rich variety of clear vowels and diphthongs and its open, well-articulated syllables was well equipped to provide imitations of sounds in nature. We hardly need to be told what animals are being mimicked in βαῦ βαῦ or βῆ βῆ or γρῦ γρῦ:[12] the English words are similar, "bow-wow," "baa-baa," and "grunt." More elaborately, the croaking of frogs becomes a whole phrase in the famous

βρεκεκεκὲξ κοὰξ κοάξ[13]

(where the lower pitch of the two grave accents in the first two words and the final acute accent help in the effect). Specially elaborate are the cries of the birds in Aristophanes' play, such as

ἐποποῖ ποό, ποό, ποό, ποό, ποό, ποό, ποῖ
ἰώ, ἰώ, ἰτώ, ἰτώ, ἰτώ

and

τριοτό, τριοτό, τοτοβρίξ

and

τοροτοροτοροτοροτίξ
κικκαβαῦ κικκαβαῦ
τοροτοροτοροτορολιλιλίξ.[14]

How flat-footed in comparison are Nash's attempts at imitating bird-cries in his poem on spring:

Cuckoo, jug-jug, pu-we, to-witta-woo

—worst of all "jug-jug" for the divine voice of the nightingale! Two other amusing mimicries come from the political machinery of Athens—βλόψ for the plop of the water falling in a water clock, and κύξ for the sound of a voting-pebble dropping into the urn.[15]

Mimicries of this kind are all non-language in the sense that the mimetic words are not declined or conjugated, but many of the simpler forms were turned into normal parts of speech. So we have regularly declined nouns like κόκκυξ, the cuckoo; κρέξ, the corncrake; κόραξ, the croaking raven; and βομβύλιος, the bumblebee—contrast with its lazy, bumbling name the sharp sibilance of the name for the aggressive wasp or hornet, σφήξ, whose initial *sp(h)* we can also hear in English "wasp" and Latin *vespa*. So, too, we have semi-mimetic nouns like ψιθυρισμός, "a whispering," and μῦκηθμός, "mooing," and verbs like τιττυβίζειν, πιππίζειν, and μινυρίζειν. There are many verbs and nouns like ἀλαλάζειν, ἀλαλαγή, and ὀλολύζειν, ὀλολυγμός, formed from such human cries as ἀλαλαί, ἐλελεῦ, ὀτοτοτοῖ, αἰαῖ.[16] Sometimes proper names are derived from mimetic terms of this kind: Chremes, for example, in New Comedy is so called from χρέμπτεσθαι, "to clear one's throat," the ugly sound heard mostly from curmudgeonly old men which modern novelists sometimes render as "hrrrmph" (a nastier variety of "hem, hem"). The pretty name of Lalage similarly comes from a mimetic verb.

Sometimes mimetic words in Greek are modified to express special nuances of sound. We can hear the giggling of girls in κιχλίζειν, loud guffaws in καχάζειν, and exultant jubilant laughter in καγχαλᾶν. (Cf. the word for the plashing of water on pebbles in καχλάζειν, and κάχληξ, "pebble, shingle.") The differences in the vowels of ἀλαλάζειν, ἐλελίζειν, and ὀλολύζειν can imply differences of sex as well as of emotion. Emotionally, too, it would mean very different things if you should shout ἰαί, or ἰαύ, or ἰέ, or ἰή, or ἰοῦ, or ἰύ, or ἰώ, or that wonderful exclamation quoted in the *Frogs*, ἰαυοῖ,[17] though in all cases you would be uttering a species of ἰωή.

In less comic and less emotional kinds of literature the sound-mimicries are generally more subtly contrived than those, and we need more alert ears to hear them. We can hear, for example, the bleating of goats clearly enough in Homer's phrase μηκάδας αἶγας. But not so many have noticed the effect intended in his description of the high-pitched cry of girls in ἀμφήλυθε θῆλυς ἀϋτή.[18] There the narrow *u*-vowel, though not emphasized by the tonic accent, seems to be intended to make us hear the very sound of their voices (a similar phrase is, however, used to describe a smell later).[19] Similarly when Homer tells us that one of the rivers in Hades is called Κώκυτος we are probably meant to hear in its ω/υ sounds and its rough *kappa*'s the harsh wailing from which the river took its name. And when Theocritos begins his first idyll with

$$\dot{\alpha}\delta\acute{υ} \;\; τι \;\; τ\grave{\text{ο}} \;\; \psi\iota\theta\acute{υ}ρισμα \;\; καὶ \;\; ἀ \;\; πίτυς^{20}$$

are we not meant to hear the very sound of the syrinx in those recurrent *upsilon*'s and in the *sigma*'s and labial and dental consonants?

These kinds of sound-effects are generally lost in translation. Take, for instance, the phrase in St. Paul's discourse on charity[21] which is rendered in the Authorized Version "a tinkling cymbal" and in the Vulgate *cymbalum tinniens*. The Greek phrase, κύμβαλον ἀλαλάζον, has a remarkable triple occurrence of *alpha* before *lambda* and, unlike the Latin and English versions, contains no thin *i*-sounds. St. Paul, I think, intended a contemptuous parody of the resonant, plangent sounds of the cymbals of the votaries of Cybele or Dionysos which he probably had encountered in Asia Minor.[22] The nearest English sounds with the required sense would perhaps be "ululating cymbals" or "reverberating tambourines." To translate the broad and sonorous Greek as "tinkling cymbals" defrauds the ear and trivializes the implications. Those seventeenth-century translators had never heard the orgiastic sounds of frenzied Asiatic fanatics. But we today can hear something like them when the Beatles or the Rolling Stones rouse their audiences.

One other example of inadequate translation: Aeschylus in the *Agamemnon* has just made his chorus describe how the prophet Calchas interpreted the omen of the two eagles killing a pregnant hare. The incident is rounded off with the sentence

$$τοιάδε \;\; Κάλχας \;\; ξὺν \;\; μεγάλοις \;\; ἀγαθοῖς \;\; ἀπέκλαγξε.^{23}$$

The sound of Κάλχας . . . ἀπέκλαγξε (combined with the high proportion of *alpha*'s in the line) would have a double force for Greek hearers· First, the assonance between the proper name and the verb would give an etymological solemnity to the interpretation of the omen, as if to say "the clangor of the voice of Calchas was true to his name, nature, and destiny," as when Shakespeare's John of Gaunt says of himself:

Old John of Gaunt and gaunt in being old.[24]

Secondly, the unprecedented use of the resonant first aorist of κλάζω with reference to articulate human utterance—the noun κλαγγή is used of

Cassandra's wild prophecies later in the play—would probably suggest to the listeners both a significant analogy between the voice of Calchas and the cry of the birds in the omen—for the verb is frequently used of bird-cries elsewhere—and also its clangorous sound would suggest the particular timbre of the prophet's doom-fraught utterance. Yet some translators are content to render it with phrases like "Thus did the prophet declare," or "Calchas cried." One could add many other inadequacies of this kind where the fault lies in neglecting or misvaluing the sound of Greek.

The examples that I have given of verbal mimesis have chiefly been based on sound-effects produced by timbre-qualities. But other elements in vocal sound can also be exploited, especially rhythm.[25] It is mostly the rhythm, reinforced with internal rhyme, that so clearly imitates the trotting of mules in Homer's celebrated line

πολλὰ δ'ἄναντα κάταντα πάραντά τε δόχμιά τ'ἦλθον,[26]

as in Browning's

> I sprang to the stirrup, and Joris, and he;
> I galloped, Dirck galloped, we galloped all three,[27]

but here the coincidence of word-ending and rhythm suggests a steadier movement. Similarly slowness can, of course, be expressed by a series of long syllables—especially syllables of the longer type of longs—and swiftness by shorts; so, too, large size by long words,[28] weight by heavy syllables, and so on. Tennyson, for example, gives a feeling of lightness, and height, as well as of sharpness in a line like

> A cry that shivered to the tingling stars.[29]

Contrast the slow, heavy effect in Cowper's

> Toll for the brave—
> The brave! that are no more.[30]

and Milton's

> Yet once more, O ye laurels, and once more.[31]

But in these examples timbre- counts as well as rhythm.

Sometimes the mimesis does not depend on a sound-for-sound similarity between words and meanings. It may consist in a direct imitation of movements of the vocal organs, as we have already noticed in connexion with the so-called gesture-words.[32] For example, in pronouncing the syllable χα- the mouth is opened to its maximum extent in order to sound the aspiration of the palatal in front of the following open vowel. So we find words in Greek meaning yawn, gape, and guffaw beginning with that syllable.

And Homer when he wants a name for a monster that opens her vast mouth wide and swallows down ships calls her Charybdis (Χά-ρυβδις),[33] where also the second half of the name suggests a rushing vortex. So, too, if you pronounce the name of Scylla (Σκύλλη) correctly, the movements of your mouth suggest those of a dog gnawing and worrying a bone (cf. σκύλλω, σκύλος, σκύλαξ, etc.) as she gnawed Odysseus' unfortunate companions. Similarly in the *Iliad*,[34] after a sharp speech from Zeus to Hera and Athene, when Homer says that the goddesses ἐπέμυξαν he is using a harsh form of the gesture-word μύζειν, "to thrust out the lips" (as if saying *mu*), to indicate how they pouted and mumbled and muttered at his remarks. Simpler examples of gesture-words are πτύειν, where the *pi* and *tau* make the tongue and lips of a speaker behave much as in the action of spitting itself (the Doric aspirated form ἐπιφθύσδω is even more expectorant), and ἔθιγε (Latin *tetĭgi*, English "tig"), which makes the tongue tip the palate as lightly as fingertips touch an object. And in κνυζεῖσθαι the initial movements of the lip and nose closely resemble those of a whimpering dog or child, which is what the word means.[35] And if one properly pronounces Aeschylus' tremendous line

σμερδναῖσι γαμφηλαῖσι συρίζων φόβον,[36]

one can feel the champing of the dreadful jaws of Typhon as well as hear his fearsome hissing.[37]

To illustrate how a master poet can exploit many of these acoustic and kinaesthetic types of mimesis in a single passage I shall quote in detail one out of the many subtle analyses of sound-effects offered by Dionysios.[38] In the eleventh book of the *Odyssey* Homer describes the efforts of Sisyphos, how he pushes the great rock up the steep hillside and then, time and time again, feels it slip from his grip and roll bumping down again to the level ground. Here are Homer's words:

καὶ μὴν Σίσυφον ἐσεῖδον κρατέρ' ἄλγε' ἔχοντα,
λᾶαν βαστάζοντα πελώριον ἀμφοτέρῃσιν.
ἦ τοι ὁ μὲν σκηριπτόμενος χερσίν τε ποσίν τε
λᾶαν ἄνω ὤθεσκε ποτὶ λόφον· ἀλλ' ὅτε μέλλοι
ἄκρον ὑπερβαλέειν, τότ' ἀποστρέψασκε κραταιΐς·
αὖτις ἔπειτα πέδονδε κυλίνδετο λᾶας ἀναιδής.

Dionysios analyzes the sound-effects minutely. In the first five lines he finds a physical impression of the weight of the stone, the strain of moving it from the ground, the thrust of the man's limbs, his ascent up the hill and the difficulty of pushing the rock upward. He attributes this effect partly to the timbre-qualities and placings of the syllables, partly to their quantities, and partly to the rhythms. (Some details of his analysis are puzzling, but the main principles are clear, and I follow them in what follows.) There are several cumbersome groups of consonants like νκρ, λγ, μφ, νσκ, σχ, σκ, containing many of the rougher letters. The proportion of long syllables in the first three lines is above the average for Homer (Dionysios seems to have counted the τοι as long, or else perhaps read ἤ τοι μὲν), and he also seems to have regarded many of these longs as being longer than the normal,[39] presumably because they are closed (or "heavy") syllables. Then the gaps between the words are, he thinks, made specially perceptible by the repetition of vowels in hiatus, like ἄλγε' ἔχοντα, λᾶαν (twice), and ἄνω ὤθεσκε, or else by clashes of semivowels and mutes like μὴν Σι-, -ον κρ-, -αν βα-, -ν σκ-, -σ χ-. Also, the fact that almost all the words in the third and fourth lines are monosyllables or disyllables increases the frequency of breaks between words (though it is remarkable that Dionysios does not notice the trochaic caesuras).[40] These gaps, he says, express the duration of Sisyphos' effort, while the long syllables suggest the resistance and the heaviness of the rock and the difficulty of moving it, while the intake of breath between the words and the contiguity of the rough letters suggest the efforts and the delays and the vastness of the work. Finally, the long-drawn-out rhythms indicate the straining of the limbs and the thrusting and the dragging as Sisyphos rolls the rock upward. One feature Dionysios does not pick out—the echoing effects in λᾶαν ἄνω ὤθεσκε (a favourite device of Homer), which may express the repeated and protracted efforts, and possibly might even hint at the inner agony—"Ah! Ah! Ah! Oh! Oh!"

With this sense of slow strain Dionysios contrasts the later line which describes how the rock, released from Sisyphos' control, tumbles bumping down the slope

αὖτις ἔπειτα πέδονδε κυλίνδετο λᾶας ἀναιδής.

Here there are no monosyllabic words and only two disyllables: ten out of the seventeen syllables in the line are short, and several of the longs, being in open syllables, are less long than those in the previous lines. Further, the line is not delayed by clashes of vowels or harsh consonants: the only two groups of consonants are formed from the euphonious *nu* and *delta*. So smooth are the transitions between the words, says Dionysios, that the whole line is like one long single word—in other words, the line contains no collocations of letters unusual within a normal Greek compound word, in contrast with such collocations in the previous lines as νς, νκρ, νβ, νσκ. Metrically all the free feet are dactyls, and the fact that some of the longs are of the shorter type of long makes the rhythm almost trochaic. (He ignores the trochaic caesura because caesura was not, it seems, identified by critics until later.) The total effect, he concludes, is one of swiftness, revolving movement, and downward flow. He does not draw attention to the near-repetition of the earlier λᾶαν ἄνω in λᾶας ἀναιδής at the end of the last line. Was it intended to suggest that the long agonizing effort must now start all over again?

Perhaps many may think that these interpretations go far beyond belief. But at any rate the fact remains that in this passage the poet has produced some unusual sound-patterns, and presumably he intends specific, relevant sound-effects.

Let us now consider the question whether words can convey a mimesis of other sensations besides those of sound, movement, effort, height, heaviness, and so on as already illustrated. What about mimesis of the so-called lower senses, touch, taste, and smell? Mimesis of touch we may readily concede in theory, at any rate, if we agree with the ancient critics that syllables can be rough like τραχύς and κάρχαρος, or smooth like λεῖος and μαλακός, as in the contrast in English between "harsh" and "rugged" and "mellow" and "level." If it is also granted that certain vowels give a greater feeling of sharpness than others, we can find examples of this in πικρός ("sharp") against ἀμβλύς ("blunt"), or "pin" against "ball." Similarly "tip," ἔθιγε, and *tetigi*, by their sounds as well as by their muscular movements, suggest a lighter impact than "touch," θιγγάνω, and *tango*.

But what about taste? Both the Greeks and we ourselves accept metaphorical analogies between sound and taste in expressions like "honey-sweet voices" and "sugary sonnets." Lucretius introduces his fourth book with an elaborate comparison between the charms of poetry and the sweetening smeared on a cup of medicine to make it palatable. But can we have direct mimesis based on some physical identity? Some modern critics think we can. Listen to Keats' description of delicious liquors in his *Eve of St. Agnes*:

> And lucent syrops, tinct with cinnamon.

It has been suggested that in pronouncing these words fully and delicately the tongue and mouth go through the movements of savouring delectable liquids.

Dionysios seems to have meant something like this when he wrote about words that, as he says, "make us pull a wry face (στύφουσαι), or cause our mouths to water (διαχέουσαι), or bring about any of the countless other physical conditions that are possible." [42] He does not give any examples from the sensation of taste. But I think we can find some in Homer. He describes fig-trees and their succulent, luscious fruit as συκέαι τε γλυκεραί, anticipating in practice the theory outlined in Plato's *Cratylos* that in pronouncing the γλ- in a word like γλυκύς the tongue moves as if tasting a pleasant, sticky liquid. Further, in συκέαι τε γλυκεραί the two *upsilon*'s flatten the tongue while the two *kappa*'s raise it to the palate as in our word "succulent." It is hardly just a coincidence that similar sounds were used both by Keats in his "lucent syrops, tinct" as quoted and also by Lucretius when he described the tasting of honey in the words

contingunt mellis dulci flavoque liquore.[43]

The mention of honey—so important a foodstuff in ancient Greece—prompts another example of what looks like taste-mimesis. Our Germanic word "honey" is rich and euphonious, but hardly mimetic in any obvious way. Contrast the sound of Greek μέλι, Latin *mel*, French *miel*, Irish *mil*: the lips close on the *m*: the tongue rises with the *l*: we are going through the actions of tasting something deliciously sweet. In fact this is another gesture-word such as Plato and Aulus Gellius identified.

But such mimicries as these are often much more than empty gestures. Modern psychologists have suggested that the process of adopting a particular physical posture or performing a particular action—as when one holds out one's hands in a gesture of welcome or turns up the corners of one's mouth in the shape of a smile—are capable of producing the habitually corresponding emotion and mood.[44] The Greeks probably knew this by intuition and experience; and I imagine that a search, among the dramatic authors especially, would find evidence for such an awareness—that smiling may make us feel happier, as well as feeling happier may make us smile, or that sometimes we feel sad because we sigh, not sigh because we feel sad. At any rate I believe that when the Greeks said μέλι they consciously or unconsciously experienced the sensation of tasting honey, because their mouths had gone through the movements of tasting it,[45] though in this case it is a specific physical sensation that is imaginatively induced, not a mood.

We can go further on this assumption. Suppose an author wants to give an impression of sweetness and delight about something outside the natural range of tasting, will he exploit this kind of kinaesthetic mimesis? Homer certainly seems to. Early in the *Iliad* when he first introduces Nestor, he wants to make us realize the very flavour and savour of his sweet flowing eloquence. For this purpose the poet exploits both word-music and mimesis like this:

λιγὺς Πυλίων ἀγορητής
τοῦ καὶ ἀπὸ γλώσσης μέλιτος γλυκίων ῥέεν αὐδή.[46]

There we can hear all the familiar taste-sounds with subtle variations built round what is semantically the key word λιγύς, whose consonants and vowels anticipate in timbre-quality, as well as meaning, the physical effect of γλώσσης μέλιτος γλυκίων. So, too, in a later book when Homer wants to emphasize the seductive delight of being really angry, he says "anger is far sweeter than honey dripping down":

πολὺ γλυκίων μέλιτος καταλειβομένοιο.[47]

Could words also convey a mimesis of smell? If they could, then we would expect to find many examples in Greek literature, for the Greeks revelled in the smells of perfumes and unguents and incense, in the odours of cooking and in the bitter-sweet aromas of hillside shrubs in the summer heat. But I have not yet found any very likely examples. It is true that both the commonest word for a smell, ὀσμή, and also σμύρνα, the word for a favourite ingredient in voluptuous smells, myrrh, contain the initial *sm*-sound found in our word "smell"; but it also occurs in many other kinds of Greek and English words. Incidentally, Greek has not, and could not within its phonetic conventions have had, any exact single-word equivalent to that remarkable English group of "nosy" words beginning in *sn*-: sniff, snuff, snuffle, sniffle, snivel, snore, snort, snooty, snot, snout, and others. But a skillful writer could easily arrange his words to produce junctures of final *sigma* and initial *nu*. Also to express the idea of breathing in general Greek has a group in *pn*-, including πνέω, πνεῦμα.

To some extent, at least, these *sm*- and *pn*- words are gesture-words: in pronouncing the nasal the nostrils are moved as in the process of smelling. Swinburne uses not merely *sm*- but *msm*- in a phrase evocative of the rich odours of summer,

the warm smell grew,[48]

in which the most sceptical critic will, I hope, admit that there is more of a sense of smelling than in, say, "there was an increase in olfactory perception." But I know of nothing quite like it in Greek.

A distinction must be made between this kind of mimesis and simpler kinds mentioned earlier, like μυγμός, ἀλαλάζον, or even τραχύς and μαλακός. In them the mimesis was directly audible. But here there is no directly perceptible equivalence between the sound of μέλι and the taste of honey. Instead they are linked by a common non-acoustic and non-gustatory feature, namely, identical movements of the vocal organs. These movements are perceptible to anyone speaking the words. But are they perceptible to mere listeners? The answer is yes, if we admit the existence of a kinaesthetic sense in listening to words, a sense by which the brain receives from the listening ear not only an awareness of sounds but also a feeling of the vocal actions causing those sounds. This is in fact what happens when anyone reproduces a new sound while learning a language by ear. It is seen even more remarkably in the workings of our power to store in the mind records of sound that enable us to reproduce these exact sounds after an interval. (That was how Helen of Troy was able so deceptively to mimic the voices of the wives of the Greek heroes inside the Wooden Horse, and how the Delian women could "imitate the tongues of all men and the babble of their speech," and how Cleopatra could "tune her tongue to any dialect she liked.")[49]

If we accept the view that word-movements are in fact used by the Greek poets for mimesis, we can occasionally understand some curious poetic word-forms better. Take for example the strange new (and afterwards very rare) word γλάγος, which Homer substitutes for the common term for milk, γάλα, in a simile describing the mustering of the Greek army in the *Iliad*.[50] Why? Let us consider the context. The poet wants us to be keenly aware of the appearance and movements of the gathering Greeks. Visually and dynamically, he tells us, they are like a flaming forest fire. The sound of their voices is like the loud cries of flocks of geese or cranes or swans in the rich meadows of Asia. Then he tells us that their movements are like those of the dense swarms of flies that gather round pails of rich milk in the springtime. But the poet also wants to excite some of our other senses besides our visual imagination. So he fills the simile of the birds with word-mimicry of sound and movement. In the simile of the flies he goes further. He wants us to realize that these are unusually thick swarms of flies. He could easily have made his words hum and hover—as Handel when he was composing music about the plague of flies in Egypt filled his staves with demisemiquavers. Instead he goes to the psychological root of the matter—the richness of the springtime milk that attracts such an exceptionally large number of flies. He wants us to taste that milk for ourselves. The normal word γάλα was not quite expressive enough; the *g* and the *l* were too far apart; he needs a word more like our "glug, glug, glug" as we gluttonously gulp down the creamy richness; so he makes a new form γλάγος and says ὅτε γλάγος ἄγγεα δεύει[51] (and we note the nasal -γγ- with γλ- too). Thus, if we have sensitive ears, we experience, rather than just know, what he means.

Linguistically in substituting a form γλάγος for simple γάλα, "milk," Homer has used much the same technique as Lewis Carroll in *Through the*

Looking Glass when he makes the White Queen just before she turns into a sheep say "better, be-etter, b-e-e-etter . . . . . be-e-ehh." And this in turn is only a variation on the way in which Aristophanes parodies Euripides in *Frogs* with the word εἰ-ει-ει-ει-ει-ει-λίσσετε, "wi-i-i-i-i-ind." All are distortions of common words for mimetic effect. But Homer's is much the subtlest.

In a similar way poets invent new words to express sound effects. Probably this is the case with the form τετραχθά, which only occurs twice in Greek literature. In the *Iliad* it is used in a description of the shattering of a sword on a helmet:

τριχθά τε καὶ τετραχθὰ διατρυφὲν ἔκπεσε χειρός.[52]

In the *Odyssey* it occurs when the sail of a ship is ripped open by a blast of wind:

τριχθά τε καὶ τετραχθὰ διέσχισεν ἲς ἀνέμοιο.[53]

In each it provides a repetition of the harsh τρ- and -χθ- sounds. In the Iliadic passage the τ, ρ, and χ sounds are continued to the end, while in the other εσ and ισ sounds are introduced to suggest the whistling of the wind through the ripped sail.

Two other types of mimesis deserve more attention than can be given within our present scope. The first, the exploitation of cacophony,[54] is illustrated by an experiment I made with a Greekless class. Students were asked to say what the first word in the Homeric phrase κεκακωμένος ἄλμῃ[55] suggested to them. One of them suggested that it sounded to him like something ugly and foul, and others agreed. That, of course, was what Homer intended with those repeated *kappa*'s, since he was describing the hideous appearance of Odysseus after a long voyage and a shipwreck. Questioned further, however, the student said that he had been guided by a similar sound meaning "filthy" in an African language he knew. So his response was not necessarily a proof of effective mimesis in the word κεκακωμένος. (He also knew Latin, so perhaps the Latin word *cacare*, "to defecate," or specifically Catullus' powerful phrase "*cacata charta*," [56] may have unconsciously prompted him.) But from another point of view these parallels in other languages suggest that there is something intrinsically ugly to the human ear in words containing repetitions of the syllable *ka*. There are many examples of its use in Greek abusive phrases, as when Helen depreciates herself as κυνὸς κακομηχάνου ὀκρυοέσσης,[57] or when Oedipus[58] describes himself as κακός τ' ὢν κἀκ κακῶν.[59]

In such phrases an author represents ugly images or ideas by ugly sounds. More commonly—since his intention is usually to please—he represents beautiful and pleasant images or ideas by beautiful or pleasant sounds. So Homer frequently uses a higher proportion of the more agreeable vowels and consonants when he is describing something elegant or lovely, as for example in his reference to the palm-tree at Delos,

Δήλῳ δή ποτε τοῖον Ἀπόλλωνος παρὰ βωμῷ
φοίνικος νέον ἔρνος ἀνερχόμενον ἐνόησα,[60]

where the proportion of *nu*'s is especially high. And in contrast we hear the ugly consonant-clusters in his reference to Scylla and her rock—

ἦλθον ἐπὶ Σκύλλης σκόπελον.[61]

But to get the full force of such deliberate uses of euphony or cacophony one must listen to longer passages.

Such mimeses of images or ideas by sounds of a correspondingly ugly or beautiful nature is not the same as those illustrated in a previous chapter,[62] where, for example, Calypso's delightful song is embodied in the delightful vowel-filled phrase ἀοιδιάουσ' ὀπὶ καλῇ, for there the primary process is to express sound by sound. But the two types have much in common.

One further kind of mimesis remains to be considered. Theophrastos believed that hearing is the most emotive (παθη τικωτάτη) of the five senses.[63] We may not agree with his absolute superlative. But obviously no one will deny that things heard can be extremely moving. And if the belief is true that the Greeks were more sensitive to nuances of sound than we in our era of silent reading and clamorous noises, then Theophrastos may have been fully justified. Certainly in the Greek theatre, for example, dramatists of the golden age relied more on the effect of things heard than of things seen. The moment of death was almost always conveyed to the audience audibly, not visually. The Greeks in the crowded Theatre of Dionysos at the spring festival in 458 B.C. heard the death-agony of Agamemnon in his two terrible cries,

ὤμοι, πέπληγμαι καιρίαν πληγὴν ἔσω[64]

and

ὤμοι μάλ' αὖθις δευτέραν πεπληγμένος,[65]

before they actually saw his corpse revealed on the *ekkuklema*—and how appallingly heart-piercing those cries must have been as they rang out in the voice of some great actor, echoing back from the cliffs of the Acropolis high above the theatre! So, too, with the other death-cries in Greek tragedy.

But this is not *mimesis* in the sense that concerns us here. Such cries so far as their phonetic verbal elements are concerned, as distinct from the tones of voice that the actors used, are expressions rather than mimeses. They are extensions of simple exclamations like αἰαῖ, ἐέ, οἰοῖ, or ὤ ὤ. The rich variety of these expressive exclamations in ancient Greek deserves more sympathetic study than it has yet received from scholars. Editorial comments and translators' versions of lines like Philoctetes'

$$\dot{α}παππαῖ \quad παπαππαπαππαπαππαπαῖ^{66}$$

and Cassandra's

$$ὀτοτοτοτοῖ \quad ποποῖ \quad δᾶ^{67}$$

are often evasive or perfunctory. Yet an important emotional climax may be embodied in them.

A question we must specially ask in connection with the power of words to express emotion is: can the mere sound of words give a mimesis of an emotion or of a mood by means of the phonetic elements discussed in a previous chapter—rhythm, pitch-variation, tone-quality, intensity, and tempo? Is it illusory, for example, to find in Matthew Arnold's lines

> Coldly, sadly descends
> The autumn evening,[68]

where the vowel-sequences impose a falling cadence on almost every word (including, against normal usage, the word "descends"), a sense of sinking despondency and melancholy? The conceptual meaning of the lines, of course, suggests such a mood. But is part of the effect not in the sound?[69] Dryden presumably aims at the same effect in his memorable

> Fallen, fallen, fallen, fallen,
> Fallen from his high estate.[70]

I personally find a similar mood-mimesis in a climactic line in Ajax's majestic speech before he goes out to die—

$$ἡμεῖς \quad δὲ \quad πῶς \quad οὐ \quad γνωσόμεσθα \quad σωφρονεῖν.$$

There to my ear the three rising-falling circumflex accents combined with the limited vowel range ($η$, $ε$, $ει$, and $ω$, $ου$, o with only one weak variant in $ᾰ$) convey a feeling of melancholy resignation, while the three *omega*'s strongly placed in the second half of the second, third, and fifth feet may have been intended to suggest a concealed groan.[72]

There are other, more elaborate examples of this technique of embodying echoes of an exclamation inside ordinary words to be found elsewhere. For example, in Bion's *Lament for Adonis* and in Moschos' *Lament for Bion* the -αι- sounds of the opening words αἰάζω and αἴλινα reecho with unusual frequency in the rest of the poems.

Can we go even further and say that the sound of words could give a mimesis of character as well as of emotion, of *ethos* as well as of *pathos*?[73] A writer on Shakespeare's *King Lear* finds the texture of Goneril's language "thick, fat, cumbrous and heavy" while Lear's is "lighter and brighter" in a certain scene.[74] Can we find anything like that in Greek? I have not found any convincing examples yet, so I simply suggest the possibility.

Whatever we may think about subtleties of that kind, one type of "ethical" mimesis was widely accepted by the ancient Greek critics,[75] namely, the kind that is effected by rhythms—spondees, for example, with their dignity and *hauteur*, anapaests with their magnificence and emotive power. Even if we find such a doctrine unprovable and implausible, we must acknowledge that it was almost universally held in antiquity.

In concluding this chapter I must apologize if some of it has seemed excessively credulous about the power of words to imitate and embody ideas and emotions. While everyone must admit that there are certainly some clear examples of deliberate mimesis in Greek literature, many may reject the more subtle types which I have tried to establish. If so, I offer an exculpatory analogy. Students of the Homeric poems—and also of any documents embodying legendary material, such as the Arthurian cycle or the Song of Roland—may be divided into two groups, historicists and mythicists. By "historicists" I mean those who try to extract as much firm history as possible from poems and myths: in contrast the mythicists insist that the documents are essentially imaginative. We see the historicists eager to connect references to people, places, and objects with historical and archaeological evidence: so, for example, they identify a cup described by Homer with one remotely like it found by Schliemann at Mycenae; and they rather optimistically identify the palace excavated at Ano Englianos with Nestor's home as described in the *Odyssey*. The mythicists are inclined to regard these equations as unproved and unnecessary.

Seekers of verbal mimesis are like the historicists. Their ear craves a sensory embodiment of the poet's ideas. Sometimes through wishful thinking they persuade themselves that they hear echoes and melodies that few, if any, others can hear, just as the historicists sometimes make identifications that others cannot accept. In every case what sober scholars must do is to assess each claim fairly on a scale of probability ranging from almost certainty to gross improbability. The one thing that is pernicious—and yet not uncommon—is that scholars through lack of sympathy with the other scholar's approach should use his less probable suggestions as a means of rejecting the whole hypothesis—to argue, for example, as many pre-Schliemannian scholars did, that because some places in the Homeric poems were obviously in fairyland, his Troy must have been there, too.

So what I am pleading for is a greater degree of tolerance on the part of eye-readers for ear-readers. I grant, as I have already emphatically granted, that the supreme value of the classics lies in the conceptual content—the myths, the histories, the philosophy, the science—and that this can to a large degree be understood and enjoyed through direct eye-to-brain reading without heed to any word-melody or mimesis. But on the basis of what has been outlined in the previous chapters I assert three things. First: if we ignore the acoustic aspects of Greek literature we ignore an important part of Greek literary theory and practice. Secondly: if we confine our interest in the sound of Greek to metre and rhythm, we neglect the precepts of the ancient teachers and overlook many felicities in the classical styles. Thirdly: since some proportion of every year's new crop of beginners in Greek will be ear-students, not eye-students, we may discourage them and eventually lose them unless we show them that Greek is richly endowed with living sounds for their enjoyment—a disciplined, genius-directed enjoyment which will refine their sensibilities, deepen their understanding, and perhaps even bring harmony to their emotions. In my own teaching I have long been conscious of a kind of hunger among learners for more of the living voice of Greek literature, a sense of some kind of deprivation, as if they had been fed too much on the strong meat of ideas and craved green vegetables or fruits to savour and enjoy. I think we should try to do more to satisfy that hunger.

NOTES TO CHAPTER V

[1] The word ὀνοματοποιΐα first occurs in Strabo 14,2,28,26f. where he cites as examples κελαρύζειν, κλαγγή, ψόφος (more effective when the φ is properly pronounced). The use of the term to mean "onomatopoeia" results from the belief cited on p. 11. For a bibliography of studies on onomatopoeia see Laurand.

Cf. also M. Grammont, "Onomatopées et mots expressifs," *Revue des langues romanes* XLIV (1901) 97–158; Adrien Timmermans *Traité de l'onomatopée* (Paris, 1907); Tylor 200 ff.; and Wilkinson 46 ff. Jespersen 398 ff. has a valuable analysis of sound symbolism in general.

[2] See H. Koller, *Die Mimesis in der Antike* (Bern, 1956) and E. Auerbach, *Mimesis* (Princeton, N.J., 1953).

[3] Aristotle, *Metaphysics* 1,987B 11.

[4] Aristotle, *Poetics* 6,1450B 2.

[5] Socrates in *Memorabilia* 3,10,1 ff. Cf. *Cratylos* 432B–C on the fact that an εἰκών is not identical with the object represented.

6 Richards 135f. and 229. Cf. Quintilian 1,5,72: cf. 8,6,31. See also *Rhetorica ad Herennium* 4,30,42 with Caplan's note.

7 See e.g., Todd and, against him, Wilkinson in *CQ* XXXVI (1942) 121–133. When Todd shows that certain letters like *v*, *t*, and *s* are prominently used at times in passages of widely varying idea and atmosphere, he does not prove that they are never used mimetically. No sane literary critic would argue that prominent use of such letters *always* has a deliberate mimetic motive, just as no sensible person would argue that a music minor key *always* indicates sadness. Cf. Wilkinson 50 ff.: as he notes, verbal mimesis, which he calls "expressiveness" from the French *expressivité*, was regarded by ancient rhetoricians as an aspect of "fittingness, decorum," τὸ πρέπον.

8 Richards 14f.

9 For the fallacious belief that one can "strip off" the poetic qualities of a piece of poetry see, e.g., Plato, *Republic* 601 B.

10 I Cor. 12:14–26.

11 For the voice as the most mimetic of human faculties see Aristotle, *Rhetoric* 3,1,1404A 22 and commentators.

12 On βαῦ, etc., see LSJ. Cf. P. Kretschmer, *Gnomon* 13 (1923) 133, and Wackernagel as cited in n. 14 *infra*.

13 Aristophanes, *Frogs* 209 ff.

14 Aristophanes, *Birds* 227, 243, 260 ff. I have followed the scholia on 227 and 237 in using the oxytone accent "so as to show the sound of the bird by mimesis." For embodiments of such animal cries in normal speech cf. *Birds* 310, 315. McKay, in his notable illustrations of sound-effects in *The Poet* . . . 82–90, detects the screech of the hawk and the song of the nightingale in Hesiod, *Works and Days* 208, τῇ δ' εἰς ᾗ σ' ἂν ἐγώ περ ἄγω καὶ ἀοιδὸν ἐοῦσαν (cf. p. 82). Simpler is Aratos, *Phain.* 1002: ὥρη ἐν ἑσπερίῃ κρώξῃ πολύφωνα κορώνη. On Greek, Latin, and German word-mimesis of animal cries in general and bird cries in particular see Wilhelm Wackernagel's masterly dissertation *Voces Variae Animantium* (Basel, 1867). See note 72 *infra*.

15 Eustathios, *Comment. on Iliad* 768,12 ff.

16 On words of this type (*Schallwörter*) see Schwyzer 716. See also Tylor 219 f., Schwyzer 647, for such *verba intensiva* as μαρμαίρειν, βαμβαίνειν, παμφαίνειν, πορφύρειν, and ποιφύσσω in which the reduplication (with modifications) of the root syllable represents various types of sound (e.g., in βάρβαρος, καχάζειν, παφλάζειν) or movement or change of condition. For literary uses of such words see, e.g., on ποιπνύω in LSJ.

17 *Frogs* 1029.

18 *Odyssey* 6,122.

19 *Od.* 12,369. Similarly Aristophanes (*Pl.* 895) uses ὓ ὓ repeated six times to express delight at an aroma.

20 See G. Herzog-Hauser, *WS* LXIV (1949) 133, who attributes the sound-effect to the alternation of *i* and *u* and the dental consonants: cf. O. Skutsch, *RhM* XXIX (1956) 200; van Groningen 52 n. 1, who finds a similar effect in Moschos, *Europa* 98; and McKay, *Poet* . . . 57 on Callimachos, *Hymn* 5,139. For Virgil's imitative *Tityre tu*, etc., see p. 135.

[21] I Cor. 13:1. For the twice-repeated -αλ- sounds cf. Hesiod *Theogony* 686 (in a richly sonorous passage), μεγάλῳ ἀλαλητῷ. See n. 72 *infra*.

[22] Cf. Philodemos (Hausrath 257), Ὀρφεοτελεστοῦ τυμπάνῳ.

[23] *Agamemnon* 156f. On the verb κλάζω see Schwyzer 1,692 (who compares other *Schallwörter* like ῥέγκω, λύζω): the verb is used elsewhere of the sounds made by birds, dogs, winds, arrows, wheels, bells, trumpets, cicadas, and the sea (see LSJ *s.v.* and at κλαγγή).

[24] *Richard the Second* II,i,73.

[25] G. Rauscher, *De Scholiis Homericis* (diss. Strassburg, 1886) 47–50 lists the scholia which refer to mimesis by metrical means in Homer. Cf. Rossi 43 n. 103. The only true spondaic line in Homer (*Il.* 23,226) might, as Wilkinson 62 notes, be intended to express slow solemnity: but see D. W. Pye, "Wholly Spondaic Lines in Homer," *GR*, ser. 2, XI (1964) 2–6. See n. 40 *infra*. On roughness and smoothness in dactylic hexameters see L. Voltz, *Ph.* LII (1894) 385–394. The phonetic and mimetic intentions of one metrical abnormality cited by Demetrios 255 as an example of how cacophony can produce a forceful effect (δεινότητα) are obscure. The circumstances are these: an eagle has just dropped a snake ominously into the middle of Hector's army as it surges against the Greek rampart; then Homer says (*Il.* 12,208) Τρῶες δ' ἐρρίγησαν ὅπως ἴδον αἰόλον ὄφιν. The unique use of a normally short syllable instead of a long (see Schulze, *Quaestiones Epicae* 2,598) in the word ὄφις (used only here in Homer) is evidently the hub of the effect (for the rest of the line is unremarkable). Suggestions are that the shortening expresses the serpent's slender tail (μύουρος) or that it indicates how the Trojans "shrank" with fear (see Eustathios and the scholiasts *ad loc.*). Perhaps the poet intended to shock his audience with a sudden lapse in the metre. Or was a reciter intended to say ὄ-ο-φιν, as in "It's very co-o-old"? If so, this lengthening would aim at the reverse effect to that in *Il.* 4,125 where (according to the B scholia) the word ἆλτο is syncopated to show the speed of the shot.

[26] *Iliad* 23,116. See n. 40 *infra*.

[27] *How They Brought the Good News from Ghent to Aix* 1 f.

[28] On mimesis through the size of words see Jespersen Cf., and 403 where he cites words like "multitudinous" and lengthened forms like "splendiferous." Cf. the reduplicated forms cited in n. 16 *supra*. Aristophanes' use of long words for grotesque effect is exemplified in *Eccl.* 1169 and *Wasps* 505,1357: cf. n. 41 on p. xxxiv of my edition of *Frogs*. See also *Il.* 15,678.

[29] Tennyson, *Morte D'Arthur* 199. Cf. Homer's λίγξε βιός, *Il.* 4,125.

[30] Cowper, *On the Loss of the Royal George* 1 f.

[31] Milton, *Lycidas* 1.

[32] See pp. 12–14.

[33] *Odyssey* 12,430.

[34] *Iliad* 4,20. Aristotle (*Hist. Animal.* 535ᴮ 32) uses μύζειν to describe the sound made by dolphins. See further in n. 37 *infra* and cf. Lucilius fr. 454 (Warmington).

[35] See LSJ at κνυζεῖσθαι and cf. κνύζα, "wrinkled."

[36] Aeschylus, *P.V.* 357.

[37] Other examples of this very rich class of gesture-words in Greek are the various words beginning in μῦ (μύω, μυστήριον, etc.) where the initial movements of the

lips obviously follow those of someone who knows something important but cannot or will not speak out (as when we say "Mm"): cf. Tylor 185. In contrast, words in μῦ (μύζω, μυκάομαι, μυκηθμός, etc.) with their greater emphasis on the vowel sound give a direct sound-mimesis (as in our "moo") as exemplified in LSJ. Cf. especially *Od.* 12,265f., μυκηθμοῦ τ' ἤκουσα βοῶν αὐλιζομενάων / οἰῶν τε βληχήν. As Eustathios 1721,26 notes, goats *me-eeh* (μηκῶνται), sheep bleat (βληχή). Similarly Tylor 197 f. notes the "primitive" use of *pu-* in words for evil smells, etc. (the lips re*pu*diating the re*pu*lsive or *pu*trid sensation): cf. φεῦ as used, e.g., in *Agamemnon* 1307–12, where it certainly does not mean "alas!" as so many translators take it.

[38] Dionysios 20,202,3 ff. on *Odyssey* 11,593–598.

[39] On the longer kinds of long syllables see chap. ii, n. 74.

[40] This has been taken as supporting the view that caesura was not recognized by the classical Greek metrists: see Samuel E. Bassett, *AJP*, XL (1919) 343–372, and E. H. Sturtevant, *AJP* XLII (1921) 289–308. (The question involves the general problem of word-separation in ancient Greek: see further in chap. vii, n. 46). But the coincidence of the caesuras in *Odyssey* 1,598 and *Iliad* 23,116 (see p. 105) does seem to suggest that some trochaic pattern was audible: cf. A. M. Dale, *JHS* LXXXV (1965) 189. Possibly, too, there is a deliberate suggestion of lyrical anapaestic rhythms in the first line of the Sirens' song in *Od.* 12,184: δεῦρ' ἄγ' ἰών, πολύαιν' Ὀδυσεῦ, μέγα κῦδος Ἀχαιῶν, where the punctuation implies "caesuras" at least in the second and fourth feet.

[41] Keats, *The Eve of St. Agnes* 267: Keats originally wrote "smooth with crannamon." Leigh Hunt remembered Keats reading the line with great relish: see Graves 12.

[42] Dionysios 15,154,12 ff.

[43] Lucretius 4,13. He effectively uses the nasal *n* and liquid *l*'s in a similar description of taste in 2,398 f., . . . *mellis lactisque liquores / iucundo sensu linguae tractentur in ore.* See further in Paul Friedländer, "Pattern of Sound and Atomistic Theory," *AJP* LXII (1941) 22, and Phillip H. de Lacy, "The Epicurean Analysis of Sound," *AJP* LX (1939) 88.

[44] Cf. Macdermott 55: "When sense and mouth-gesture harmonize, mind and body unite to express the speaker's meaning just as they unite when a furious little boy takes to fisticuffs. There is even some truth in the suggestion that the union between mood and facial movement is so intimate that it works in both directions, that, for example, a feeling of happiness can be induced by the deliberate assumption of a happy expression. Surely, then, it is not merely fanciful to think that such a broad distinction as that between high and low sounds must be the survival of something fundamental, and, being so, must still awaken within us something of the sense of fitness and inevitability which such distinctions between sounds evoked in our primitive ancestors hundreds of thousands of years ago?"

[45] Cf. Paget 125: ". . . in recognizing speech sounds, the human ear is not listening to music but to indications, due to resonance, of the position and gestures of the organs of articulation."

[46] *Iliad* 1,248 f.

[47] *Il.* 18,109.

⁴⁸ Swinburne, *August*. Cf. n. 19 *supra*.

⁴⁹ Helen: *Odyssey* 4,279. The Delian women: *Hymn to Apollo* 162 f. (reading κρεμβαλιαστύν). Cleopatra: Plutarch, *Mark Antony* 27 (τὴν γλῶσσαν ὥσπερ ὄργανόν τι τρέπουσα καθ᾽ ἣν βούλοιτο διάλεκτον).

⁵⁰ *Iliad* 2,455 ff. For γλάγος see 471.

⁵¹ *Il.* 2,471. For similar γλ- sounds in connexion with milk cf. *Il.* 4,434 and 5,902; *Od.* 4,88.

⁵² *Il.* 3,363.

⁵³ *Od.* 9,71.

⁵⁴ On cacophony in general see Jespersen 278, Herescu 225 ff., Kourmoules, J. S. Th. Hanssen in *SO* XXII (1942) 80–106 (he is sceptical about many examples), and Wilhelm Schulze, *Kleine Schriften* (Göttingen, 1933) 304; also Dionysios 16,162,14 ff., 22,218,9 ff. and *On Demosthenes* 43, and Aristotle, *Rhetoric* 3,2,11,1405A.

⁵⁵ *Od.* 6,137.

⁵⁶ Catullus 36,1. Cf. Servius on *Aeneid* 2,27 who notes the κακέμφατον in *Dorica castra* (*-ca ca-*: see Herescu 226 ff.).

⁵⁷ *Iliad* 6,344.

⁵⁸ Sophocles, *O.T.* 1397.

⁵⁹ For other examples of the use of *kappa*'s and *chi*'s (= *k–h*) in pejorative or abusive phrases cf. κάκ᾽ ἐλέγχε᾽, Ἀχαιΐδες, οὐκέτ᾽ Ἀχαιοί (*Il.* 2,235), κυλλὸν ἀνὰ κύκλον κυκλεῖς (Aristophanes, *Birds* 1379), and Κᾶρες, Καππόδοκες, Κίλικες, τρία κάππα κάκιστα (cf. the *Souda* at κάππα).

⁶⁰ *Odyssey* 6,162 f., cited by Dionysios 16,162,10 f.

⁶¹ *Od.* 12,430.

⁶² See p. 82.

⁶³ See p. 79 and n. 73 *infra*.

⁶⁴ *Agamemnon* 1343.

⁶⁵ *Agamemnon* 1345.

⁶⁶ *Philoctetes* 745 f.

⁶⁷ *Agamemnon* 1076. On Greek exclamations in general see Eustathios 855,17 (on *Il.* 11,438). For emotional cries (like αἰβοῖ, ἀπαπαῖ) in Aristophanes see E. Moutsopoulos, "La philosophie de la musique et le theâtre d'Aristophane," in ΧΑΡΙΣ *to Constantine I. Vouveris* (Athens, 1964) 208 f. A special type cited by Eustathios, namely, those addressed to animals like ψό, βή, χύρρε, σίττα, φίττα, ψίττα, deserves further study.

⁶⁸ Matthew Arnold, *Rugby Chapel* 1 f.

⁶⁹ R. C. Givler in *Psychological Monographs* XIX 2 (1915) offers support for the view that the sounds of poetry can in themselves create moods. But he goes rather too far, and Richards in his *Practical Criticism* shows how much subjectivism may be involved. Cf. pp. 99 f.

⁷⁰ Dryden, *Alexander's Feast* 77 f.

⁷¹ Sophocles, *Ajax* 677. Cf. Tylor 175 ff.

⁷² For possible examples of deliberate suggestion of threnodic and other exclamations in Greek poetry see McKay *The Poet* . . . 86, and *AUMLA* 22 (1964) 193–195. He cites as examples of ω Theokritos, *Idylls* 10,40, ὤμοι τῶ πώγωνος, and 1,115, ὦ λύκοι, ὦ θῶες, ὦ ἀν᾽ ὤρεα φωλάδες ἄρκτοι. Dr. McKay has also sug-

gested to me that in *Anth. Pal.* 9,129,5, Κηφισὸν κώκυον ὀλωλότα πολλάκι Νύμφαι, the recurrent ολ- syllables may be intended to suggest ὀλολυγή, while in Callimachos, *Hymn* 2,101 f. ἄλλον ἐπ' ἄλλῳ βάλλων, the repeated αλλ- may hint at ἀλαλή. Cf. D. A. Kidd in *AUMLA* 15 (1961) 14 on similar use of ω sounds by Aratos.

[73] On *ethos* and *pathos* (which are not always clearly separated by Greek rhetoricians) see W. Kroll, *Ph.* LXXV (1918) 68–78 (citing W. Suess's *Ethos* [Leipzig, 1910], which I have not seen); L. P. Wilkinson, "Philodemus on *Ethos* in Music," *CQ* XXXII (1938) 174–181; J. F. Lockwood, *CQ* XXIII (1929) 180–185; and Grube 291 f.

[74] Wilson 195.

[75] See, e.g., Dionysios chaps. 17, 18; Aristides Quintilianus, *De Mus.* 2,15; Aristotle. *Rhetoric* 3,8,1408B 21 ff.

VI

Matters of Pronunciation

IN THE FIRST chapter I cited the three main arguments offered by classical scholars for neglecting the sound of ancient Greek literature. The first—namely, that matters of sound are unimportant for the understanding and enjoyment of the texts—has now, I hope, been refuted. But the two other arguments remain unanswered still. Let me put them as questions. Do we know enough about the pronunciation of ancient Greek to justify studying it?[1] And if we do, would the effort and energy spent on learning to speak and hear it correctly be worth while?

The first question arises whenever we try to recover the phonetics of any language from literary documents alone, without any help from native speakers or from recordings of the living speech. Such an attempt is always difficult and often full of uncertainties, except when an agreed phonetic script is used. But in the case of Greek we have an unusually rich and varied body of evidence for the accepted pronunciations in ancient times[2]— far richer than for most of the so-called dead languages. This evidence has been examined in detail elsewhere so here I shall offer only a brief outline.

To begin with, we have some good descriptions of the positions and movements of the lips, tongue, and mouth in pronouncing specific phonemes. For example, Dionysios describes the pronunciation of *rho* like this: "It is sounded with the tip of the tongue fanning out the breath and rising toward the palate near the teeth," [3] which indicates that it was a "trilled" or "rolled" *r* as heard in Italy or Scotland, and not the Irish "retracted" *r*, or the North-of-England uvular *r* or the South-of-England fricative *r*. Some of these ancient phonetic descriptions have serious deficiencies and gaps,[4] but on the whole they give clear information on many important questions.

Secondly, we have definite statements about phonetic changes. I have given examples of these in earlier chapters.[5]

Thirdly, we have comparisons between Greek and Latin phonemes by

Roman rhetoricians. Thus Quintilian states that the Greek *phi* was not pronounced like the ugly Latin *f*. Yet in spite of this definite statement—supported by other evidence—most of us willfully mispronounce *phi* as *f*, instead of approximately as in "shepherd."

Fourthly, we have the evidence of transliterations of Greek words into other languages and the reverse.[6] For example, against the view that *upsilon* was pronounced like *iota* is the fact that the Latin writers did not transliterate it as *i*, but took over the Greek letter in the form of *y*—*i-grec* as the French still call it—to indicate the non-Latin sound. So, too, against the modern Greek pronunciation of *beta* as *v* there are spellings like Οὐαλέριος (not Βαλ-) for *Valerius* (though *B-* for *V-* does occasionally occur) and Φόλουιος for *Fulvius*. (Incidentally, the second example cannot be taken as evidence that the Greeks considered that the Latin *f* was the same as their *phi*, in view of clear statements to the contrary elsewhere.[7] What it does show is the prejudice of the Greeks, unlike the Romans, against innovations in their speech and alphabet, and a recognition that the nearest sound in their language to the Latin *f* was their *phi*, a similarity which became an identity later.) Transliterations into ancient Persian, Hebrew, Coptic, and Gothic also provide useful evidence.

Fifthly, we have references by Greek authors to specific similarities or dissimilarities of sound in their language, in connexion with ambiguities, puns, etymologies, and various types of sound-patterning (mainly assonance, rhyme, and metre). For example, the celebrated confusion between the words λοιμός, "plague," and λῑμός, "hunger," in the prediction quoted by Thucydides[8] shows that the sounds of οι and ι were similar, but not identical. The dispute was not basically about the meaning but about which of two similar sounds (approximately *loymos* and *leemos*) had been uttered by the oracle, just as some years ago a member of Parliament indignantly repudiated the charge that he was a Bulgarian and was mollified on being told that what had been said was "vulgarian" with a *v*. Strictly speaking, these are not verbal ambiguities but the result of audial uncertainties, as when the Cyclopes misheard the name Οὖτις as οὔτις. In contrast, if I were to point to the Agora in Athens and say "That's a fine sight (site)," using a full homophone, the uncertainty would not lie in the sound but in the meaning. An English translator of the phrase in Thucydides gives the phonetic effect aptly by translating λοιμός and λιμός as "death" and "dearth" [9] (more effective when pronounced by a southern Englishman than by an Irishman).

One can also gain some evidence from deliberate puns: for example, when Aristophanes says βλέπειν βαλλήναδε,[10] with a pun in the second word on

Παλλήναδε, he shows that νβ and νπ sounded somewhat alike (as in modern Greek) but were not homophones.

Sixthly, there is the evidence of onomatopoeia, or sound-mimesis as I prefer to call it. This is never conclusive since we never know just how exact the mimesis is. We can hardly assert that Aristophanes' frog-chorus with their *Bre-ke-ke-kex* prove that the classical *beta* was not pronounced as *v*, because the voices of the Attic frogs were scarcely, even in the highly cultivated atmosphere of the fifth-century, quite distinct in articulating the first phoneme of their croak. Certainly, so far as my own ears could determine, contemporary Attic frogs might be saying *brek* or *vrek*. But when the bleating of sheep is written with an *eta* in βῆ βῆ, and when Homer's goats are described as μηκάδας, it will seem to me to be evidence that *eta* was more like the French *ê* than our *ee* until someone leads me to a flock of sheep that says "bee-bee." (In parenthesis we may note that until the eighteenth century "bleat" was pronounced more mimetically as *blayte*.)

Seventhly, we have the fact that the spelling of words in the old Greek alphabet apparently was more reliably phonetical than it is in most of the modern European languages. Though the spelling of ancient Greek in the manuscripts is always suspect, since they have been processed by the Alexandrian editors and their successors down to the present day, yet fortunately in many matters of orthography scribes have been faithful even to what they could not understand. More reliably, inscriptions and early papyri, as well as glossographers like Hesychios, reveal much both by their agreements and disagreements. For example when fourth-century Boeotian inscriptions in the Ionic alphabet use ου for υ, writing words like Πυρρῖνος as Πουρρῖνος, they show that by this time *upsilon* in East Ionic and Attic no longer represented the sound *u* (approximately as in "moon").[11] Similarly, glosses in Hesychios like τούνη for τύνη, and οὐδραίνει for ὑδραίνει, show the same divergency between the narrowing Attic-Ionic *upsilon* and the more open sound still in use elsewhere. A good deal also can be learned from accidental misspellings.[12]

Eightly, among the main sources of evidence for the sound of classical Greek we have the phonetic classifications made by the ancient grammarians and rhetoricians like Dionysios of Halicarnassos and Dionysios the Thracian.[13] For example, when they classify *theta*, *phi*, and *chi* as "mutes" (ἄφωνα), not as "half-voiced" (ἡμίφωνα) letters like *sigma* and *rho*, they rule out our mispronunciations of them as *f*, *th*, and *ch* (as in *loch*). Similarly, when Sigma in Lucian's *Judgement of the Vowels*[14] complains that he has been deprived of his place in words like Σμύρνα, stolen from him by

Zeta, we know that such words were pronounced by Atticizers in the second century A.D. as if they began with *zee* (or *zed*).

To these internal sources of evidence must be added the probabilities to be derived from comparative philology and general linguistics. To take a simple example: the English pronunciation of the letter *i* as in "sight" and "smile"—or, to put it another way, the English use of the letter *i* to represent such a sound—is unparalleled in other European languages and was not developed in England until the fifteenth century, so the likelihood that the ancient Greeks pronounced *iota* in that way is small. On the other hand, the fact that Sanskrit had aspirated *kh*, *ph*, and *th* strengthens the evidence for pronouncing *chi*, *phi*, and *theta* as aspirates. Some of the phonetic developments in modern Greek also help to determine pronunciations in ancient Greek.

Taken together, the evidence from these nine main sources gives a fairly good approximate notion of the ancient Greek sound system. There are a few notable uncertainties especially in the pronunciation of the diphthongs. And the qualification "approximate" must always be emphasized. Without accurate phonographic records or a scientifically precise phonetic notation no exact reproduction is feasible. Even with those scientific aids one could never give a full and intelligible picture of the pronunciations of a single city like Athens or San Francisco during a single day, much less for a year or an epoch or a century. Each citizen sounds his words differently, and even in the case of individuals pronunciation varies from hour to hour· Sophocles would have pronounced his words one way when he was training a chorus in the Theatre of Dionysos in the morning and another way at the end of a symposium that evening. I know one present-day author who sometimes says "ak*ow*stics" and sometimes "ak*oo*stics," sometimes "prīvacy" and sometimes "prĭvacy," sometimes "pātronage" and sometimes "pătronage," without causing confusion or offence, because such variations are normal and accepted. But if he said "ak*you*stics" or "prīv*ay*cy" or "patrōnage" he might well be misunderstood. The spoken word is never stable, except when fixed in a mechanical recording.

Certainly our knowledge of classical Greek pronunciation is far from perfect. But it goes a good way toward giving us the basic phonemes and pitch-variations. As an eminent German scholar once said:

I am perfectly convinced, that, if an ancient Athenian were to rise from his grave and hear one of us speak Greek, on the basis of the best scientific enquiry and with the most delicate and practised organs, he would think the pronunciation horribly barbarous. But if he heard a modern Greek, he would not indeed be so loud in his censure, simply because he would fail to observe that this is supposed to be his own language. . . . Finally if a German came with his Reuchlinian pronunciation, observing quantities with pedantic care [and this applies also to the older pronunciation among English speakers], the ancient Athenian would probably stop his ears at such disfigurement of his language (if indeed he recognized it as such) and at such discordant sounds.[15]

That, then, is our choice—between, on the one hand, an approximate approach to hearing and reading Greek as it was heard and read in classical times, and, on the other, hearing it and reading it in a palpably incorrect way—between a determined effort to get as close as we possibly can to the ancient word-melodies and a decision to use something easier but quite unauthentic.

Here we have to face the third argument against trying to restore the sounds of ancient Greek as far as possible. The effort needed, we are told, would be too great, especially with regard to the pronunciation of the pitch-accent: beginners would be discouraged, advanced students confused. Before I try to answer the assertion about beginners, let me glance for a while at the actual state of Greek pronunciation in schools and universities today.

Confusion reigns, in Ireland and Britain at any rate. The young classical student as he passes from preparatory school to secondary school and on to the university may meet a radically different pronunciation of Greek at each stage. Some countries are, indeed, less chaotic. The United States is better off than many, thanks mainly to efforts by the American Philological Association early in its history.[16] But in the European countries scholars and pupils can be heard using any one of four methods (and there are infinite sub-variations),[17] taking as their models either modern Greek, or the pronunciation as determined from the evidence of the classical Greek as described above, or classical Latin, or their own national language. (I avoid using the traditional terms Reuchlinian, Erasmian, and Henningian for the first three, because they are used too loosely.) In Ireland and Great Britain one can hear all four of these from place to place. For instance, the name of the Greek god of wine and the theater, Διόνυσος, is pronounced in four distinctly different ways (with several lesser variations): those whose model is modern Greek pronounce it something like *Thee-ó-nee-sos* (the hyphens indicating syllable-divisions); the Latinizers say *Dée-o-nóo-sus;* the Anglicizers,[18] *Dye-on-eye-zus;* and those who try to restore the ancient pronunciation, *Dǐ-ó* (with a rising tone of approximately a fifth) *-now-* (or *noo*) *-sos*. Similarly, the Greek for a king may be heard as *va-see-léfs* (stressed on the last syllable), *bá-see-loos* (stressed on the first syllable), *báy-sill-yuze,* or *ba-say-leús* (last syllable as in Spanish *Ceuta* and with a rising tone of approximately a fifth). These differ in stress, quantity, quality (contrast the initial consonants *Thee*, *Dee*, *Die*, and *Dĭ* in the first), pitch-accent, and syllable division.

An actual incident may illustrate the kind of distress that can result. Some years ago a candidate for entrance to a university was being examined *viva voce* by an elderly don celebrated for his skill in composing Greek and Latin verses but who belonged to the old "hoh-hee-toh" school of pronunciation. While reading some Greek the lad pronounced the name of the place where the Greeks defeated the Persians in 479 B.C., Μυκάλη, as *Mickálee* with the stress on the next to last syllable. At such a "false quantity" the don exploded: "Where in the name of Heaven did you learn to say it like that? It's 'Míckaly, Míckaly, Míckaly.' " [19] In fact the student's pronunciation would at least have been intelligible to a modern Greek, while no Greek—ancient, Byzantine, or modern—would recognize the don's Latinizing Anglicism. Such are the anomalies, and sometimes injustices, of the present chaos.

If an enquirer from another planet were to ask us how such a babel came to exist among rational scholars and why pronunciations clearly contrary to the evidence are freely used in reading a highly revered language, we would have a sorry tale to tell him. It has been often told elsewhere,[20] so I must resist the temptation to display its sardonic humours again. As in many controversies about language, decisions about ancient Greek pronunciation have often depended more on chauvinism, sectarianism, political alliances, scholastic migrations, and personal proclivities than on objective evidence or educational ideals. We may smile now—but it was not so funny when it was actually happening—to remember how Bishop Gardiner as Chancellor of the University of Cambridge promulgated an edict that anyone who used the pronunciation recommended by Erasmus should be expelled from the Senate if he were a member of it, be debarred from graduation if a candidate for a degree, be removed from the list of Scholars, if a Scholar, and, if a schoolboy, should be flogged.[21] We may think it regrettable that Lutherans should retain the Reuchlinian pronunciation because their leader Melanchthon had been in controversy with Erasmus. We may deplore the political bias that made the Latinizing absurdities of the Dutchman Henning specially acceptable to the English at the end of the seventeenth century—which is why so many in Ireland and Britain still say *árrety* for ἀρετή and *Míckaly* for Μυκάλη. The resulting babel remains to confound and dishearten many a learner who moves from teacher to teacher.

You **may** be wondering what evidence there is to justify such comments on the present state of Greek pronunciation. I rely mainly on a questionnaire that I sent out in the autumn of 1965 to fifty universities and schools in Ireland and Great Britain and on personal observation. The replies give, I believe, a fair notion of the conflicting traditions.[22] Seventeen out of twenty-five university teachers of Greek, and seventeen out of twenty-four schoolmasters, claim to use the reformed pronunciation of Greek, more or less. (I say "claim" and "more or less" because details in the replies show that few "reformers" have adopted all the established principles of the reformed pronunciation. For example, only four out of thirty-three pronounce *phi* as *p-h*; and only six pronounce the accent by variation in pitch, while twenty-seven do not try it at all.) Six schoolmasters and four university teachers use the Anglicizing pronunciation (e.g., *eta* as in *thee, upsilon* as in *new*): one of these while using it himself recommends the reformed method to his pupils.

Some of the incidental remarks are noteworthy. Two university teachers prefer the Anglicizing method and think it the best one, but use the reformed method because most of their students are accustomed to it. Another says that among twelve colleagues at a university college in North America recently he found twelve different theories on how to pronounce Greek. One schoolmaster confesses to speaking his Greek in "an ignorant and inconsistent hotch-potch." Three out of the total of forty-seven think that pronunciation does not matter. Four deplore the existing chaos and hope for some means of reaching consistency. One is well satisfied with what he was brought up with (the Anglicizing method) and sees no reason to change. Two are firmly in favour of adopting the modern Greek pronunciation: three think that it would be disastrous to do so.

A special question was asked about motives for using any particular kind of pronunciation. Those who favoured the reformed method mostly referred to the weight of the ancient evidence as the reason for their choice: only one mentioned matters of euphony. Supporters of the modern Greek usage admired its consistency and claimed that the evidence for the reformed method is unsatisfactory. Those who retained the Anglicizing method (mixed with a good deal of Latinization apparently) argued that it is easier to understand, is more uniform, and "helps students to spell correctly."

These were frank and helpful answers, and those who took the trouble to provide them deserve our thanks. A much wider and more detailed survey would be needed before one could precisely assess the full extent of the variations and motivations in our present ways of speaking ancient Greek. But, clearly, confusion and contradiction still exist, and those who value the welfare of Greek studies cannot justifiably ignore this chaos, whatever remedy they suggest. It is one of the worst causes of frustration and disheartenment among young learners when teachers tell them to do things in contradictory ways, or tell them "Don't do what I do, but do what I say you should do."

The chief practical argument against speaking and hearing ancient Greek as much as possible in the way the ancient Greeks themselves did, remains to be met. This is simply, "It's too hard, especially if we are expected to pronounce the pitch-accent." I deny this. Of course, it is easier to pronounce every language like one's own; and, of course, it will take more effort, and harder effort, to learn a language that has tonic accents unknown in one's own vernacular. But people are learning other such languages successfully every day of the year—Chinese or Yoruba, for example. Besides, it has already been proved experimentally by at least one gifted and devoted teacher of Greek in England—W. H. D. Rouse at the Perse School in Cambridge[23]—that normal schoolboys can be taught to speak Greek with due regard to quality, quantity, and pitch-variations. From my own experience with first-year classes I can bear witness that ability and willingness to learn the full reformed pronunciation are certainly available for any teacher—and this despite the fact that many entrants to the universities have already been hearing and speaking a defective pronunciation for several years.

This last fact brings us to the greatest handicap in trying to learn the reformed pronunciation—faulty speech-habits already established.[24] The older the learner is, the harder it will be for him to change from, say, *eeta* to *êta* (ἦτα) or from *filos* to *p-hilos* (φίλος). I know this only too well from my own personal experience. To illustrate: I first learned to pronounce the Greek word for Muse, Μοῦσα, as *Mowsa* (with *ow* approximately as in "now"). Then under modern Greek influence I was converted to *Moosa*; now the evidence has compelled me to say *Mowsa* (with *ow* approximately as in "allow" tensely pronounced), and I have not yet tried to distinguish "pure" from "spurious" *ov* by a difference in pronunciation.[25] Changes in speech-habits like this are hard for adults. But if Eliza Doolittle in Shaw's *Pygmalion*, and if other Elizas every year in London, can radically reform their way of speaking from Cockney to standard English, why then must classical students and scholars believe that a similar change is too hard for them?

But what about children? Here the reverse is true: the younger they are, the easier it is to learn new sounds. Psychologists and educationists agree that young pupils have the remarkable gift of being able to reproduce sounds just as they hear them without direction on how to use their vocal organs in the process. As they grow older they gradually lose this ability, partly as the result of having learned to read silently, partly from other psychological and physiological changes. Unfortunately this deterioration in sound-reproduction has usually gone a long way by the time many pupils have begun to learn Greek. This is an argument for teaching the sounds of Greek, or of any non-vernacular language, as early as possible.[26]

There is a second good reason why younger pupils can pick up unusual speech-sounds easily. Infants in their cots and prams spend long hours in experimenting with the capabilities of their voices both out of sheer interest in self-exploration and also—as parents well know—to test the operational effects of their more penetrating and high-pitched vocal sounds. In fact, infants are masters of a far wider range of sounds than adults. Later they learn their native language more by restricting their range of sounds than by extending it. The few unusual sounds of ancient Greek would be literally child's play to them. This inborn versatility has generally been pegged down to the limited gamut of a single language long before the child comes to learn Greek. But something of it remains well on into adolescence, and can be revived, and, what is more, can be revived in a way that will give pleasure to the learner, if properly done.

There is another aspect of the mental attitude of children that deserves consideration by both the opponents and the advocates of the reformed Greek pronunciation. Far from being surprised and repelled by new sounds made by their teachers, children naturally expect a strange-looking language like Greek to have strange-sounding sounds. In the world around them different animals have different cries, and peculiarly dressed people often speak peculiarly. If a cat were to bark like a dog, or a Red Indian in full war paint were to speak like the local clergyman, the phenomenon would be likely to disturb them psychologically. Children find such contradictions suspicious, even menacing. Similarly, when presented with a set of new letters in Greek they are more likely to be perturbed than comforted when they hear that the sounds represented by these new letters are the same old sounds that they know already in their own language. Their instinct is right, of course. Different letters would have different sounds, if the makers and users of alphabets were rational beings like Bernard Shaw, and similar letters would have similar sounds. The fact that the English alphabet is so unsatisfactory in this respect will give children all the more reason for joy when they are told that the Greek alphabet is phonetically far more trustworthy.

For those reasons, mainly, I assert that children will welcome the strangeness of the sound of ancient Greek, when a good teacher opens up this new world of speech-sounds to their adventurous and impressionable young minds.

From these generalities I now turn to face what is widely believed to be the gravest single difficulty in teaching the reformed Greek pronunciation. Even the most earnest reformers often baulk at pronouncing the pitch accent.[27] Forty-one out of the forty-nine who answered my questionnaire either neglect it or pronounce it wrongly by stress, and I have been told that it is rarely pronounced as a tonic accent in North America. Before I try now to show that the difficulty is exaggerated, let me concede that mispronunciation or non-pronunciation of the pitch-accent is probably the least damaging of our present faults in pronouncing Greek. Right quality and quantity matter more, and the evidence for them is on the whole more conclusive. But, as I have already exemplified, the ancient Greeks themselves valued the euphony of the accent, and also it was in fact the only way of distinguishing between many words whose spellings were otherwise identical. (Probably, too, it was one of the means by which the Greeks recognized separate words in phrases.) In general, if we fail to sound the Greek speech-melody as indicated by the accent-marks we lose a constituent element in the total artistic effect of stylized Greek. It is almost as if we were to study an oil painting by Titian in a water-colour reproduction, or a Mycenaean bronze in a platinum facsimile. If we want to understand and enjoy the full effect of ancient Greek we should try to master this basic element in its sound-system.

Can it be done? Most scholars and teachers seem to think not. Here is a typical remark, all the more characteristic in its casual assumption of hopelessness: "it is of course virtually impossible for us to reproduce the pitch accent of Greek." [28] So, too, the editor of the most helpful Greek grammar in English remarks in his preface:

And whatever may be said of the difference between stress and pitch accent, the fact remains that the observance of stress accent is the only device by which we can even remotely approach the ancient enunciation. I regret, therefore, the recent decision of my friends in the Classical Association of England and Wales to adhere to the quantitative or Latin method of pronunciation. [Note, here, too, the assumption that it is impossible to render the pitch-accent in terms of pitch-variation.][29]

Even more formidable is the following proposal for future Greek studies by the President of the Classical Association in 1964:

Some ancient niceties will have to be sacrificed. To take a minor example, we shall have to give up pretending to teach the complex Byzantine rules of Greek accentuation, save in the exceptional cases where the accent governs the meaning. This will be a pity, since it will make it harder for our pupils to learn to speak modern Greek —which for all true lovers of Hellas is a desirable accomplishment. But neither their enjoyment of ancient literature nor their understanding of ancient society will be affected in the slightest degree by ceasing to perpetuate in writing what they habitually disregard in reading.[30]

But is it true, in view of what has already been said in these pages, that the enjoyment of Greek literature will not be affected? And is the best means of coping with a fault in reading to adopt a similar fault in writing? And need the complex Byzantine laws of accentuation (which emerged long after the classical period) come into the teaching of the natural sounds of a language orally, which is the natural and right way of teaching beginners? In fact, the written accentuation is basically a matter of orthography, not of learning how to speak a language correctly. If one began to teach learners of English by expounding the complications of English spelling one would find it hard to succeed.

These are some of the misconceptions and counsels of despair that have stood in the way of attempts to revive the voice-melody of the Greeks.[31] Their total effect has been paralyzing on all but the most independent-minded teachers in the English-speaking areas of classical instruction. Nearly all are based on one fundamental mistake. They treat Greek accentuation as if it were primarily a visual matter. They speak of the accents as if their main function was to distinguish certain similar-looking words in silent reading. When teachers of Greek talk, as they often do, of "writing-in" the accents, or "putting on" the accents, they perpetuate this error. I have even heard the process being described, with reference to students' compositions, as "sprinkling on the accents like pepper from a pepper pot." In fact, as we have seen, these acute, grave, and circumflex marks are a kind of musical notation, indicating what was an indispensable feature of ancient Greek pronunciation—an addition to writing, but not in any sense an addition to correct speaking or hearing. They are no more additional to the Greek language than the tones of Chinese are additional to Chinese. It is true that the conceptual meaning of Greek words, unlike the Chinese in this, does not usually depend entirely on the pitch-accent, but their aesthetic effect always does.

The rudiments of the ancient Greek pitch-variation can, I am convinced, be taught successfully if the right methods are adopted and the right example given. I must not go into details here, but I can show what I mean broadly in a few words. Every man, woman, and child who speaks English already uses approximations to the pitch-accents of ancient Greece. We say "yés?" with a rising inflection (or voice-glide) extending over about a musical fourth or a fifth, when we are questioning a statement or inviting a further statement. That is in essence the ancient acute accentuation. We say "yé-ès" with an upward inflection followed by a downward one when we wish to express doubt or hesitation in affirming something. That is virtually the ancient circumflex. We say "yès!" with a downward inflection when we mean "Of course" or "I told you so." That perhaps (but here the evidence is less clear) is the grave accent. And when, dully or listlessly or apathetically or melancholically, we say "yes" with a low and level tone, it probably corresponds to the intonation of the unaccented syllables.[32] If we can do this effortlessly in English, why not in Greek? There is no question here of its being impossible without "a good musical ear," as is so often said about the Greek accents. (The only people who necessarily find it impossible to acquire these inflexions by instinctive imitation are those who are totally deaf—Helen Keller, for example.)[33] These upward and downward voice-glides are natural and instinctive in all European languages and, indeed, are basic in all normal speech, though not generally used phonemically as in Greek.

Now I do not want to disguise the fact that there are many nuances of voice-intonation left out in this broad sketch—for example, the modification of tones within the phrase, or under emotional stress, or in questions or exclamations, or according to vowel-variation. (What little evidence there is for this in ancient Greek will be given in the last chapter.) There are also many uncertainties of detail in our knowledge of other aspects of ancient Greek pronunciation. But should we not go as far as we can in restoring the ancient sounds, as we do in so many other fields of classical study? Sir Arthur Evans' restorations at Knossos are limited and not always based on certain evidence. Yet they have done much to encourage interest in Minoan civilization.

I come now to my final *credo* on the sound of Greek. I believe that not only will young learners of Greek find it easy enough to learn the full pronunciation, but also that they will enjoy Greek literature all the more on account of the novelty and strangeness of its phonetics. Children are initially more at home in the world of sound than in the world of sight. Even before they are born into the visual world they feel sound-vibrations in the womb through the amniotic fluid. When a pregnant mother sings or sighs or screams or sobs or laughs, her unborn child feels the movements of the vocal organs and lungs, not exactly by hearing but by sensing them tactually—and, indeed, his later hearing is only, in a sense, a concentration of this prenatal, tactile sense. After their birth infants can identify and localize things heard before things seen; and they soon find that they can deliberately make sounds for themselves long before they can deliberately fabricate visible objects. Soon they become greater virtuosos in emitting extraordinary sounds than any adult. They can out-scream or out-cry or out-whine or out-bubble all their elders. In this sphere of sound they are adroit and at home. So why should they not revel in it, and welcome further explorations of this long-familiar territory, so much more congenial at first than the world of books and pictures?[34]

In fact, they do revel in it, as we know from seeing the pleasure that young children take in nonsense rhymes or in game-formulas like "eena, meena, mina, mo" or the one which delighted Sir Walter Scott ". . . pin, pan, musky, dan, tweedle-um, twoddle-um, twenty-wan!" [35] Dylan Thomas has borne witness to this charm of words (and may I remind you that the word "charm" ultimately comes from the Latin *carmen*, "a song"?):

The first poems I knew were nursery rhymes, and before I could read them for myself I had come to love just the words of them, the words alone. What the words stood for, symbolised, or meant was of very secondary importance; what mattered was the *sound* of them. . . . And these words were, to me, as the notes of bells, the sounds of musical instruments, the noises of the wind, sea and rain, the rattle of milkcarts, the clopping of hooves on cobbles, the fingering of branches on a window pane, might be to someone, deaf from birth, who has miraculously found his hearing.[36]

An educationist has stated this from the teacher's point of view:

Children are by nature poets; they delight in speech for its own sake, in rhyme and rhythm, in assonance, alliteration and cadence. . . . Instruction in speech should be directed first of all to the conservation of that interest in sounds themselves and their utterance which every child possesses as a birthright. While we must not neglect the reference to objects and events, yet the aesthetic qualities of sounds, and their articulation, should ever be foremost in the mind of the teacher of linguistics.[37]

This is true of adolescent students, as well as of young children. Here is what a pupil—celebrated both as a scholar in English literature and as a moralist—has recorded about listening to a schoolmaster reading poetry, not, indeed, in Greek but from Milton, the English poet who most successfully, perhaps, of all captured the euphony of Greek:

Every verse he said turned into music on his lips: something midway between speech and song. [We may note here in parenthesis independent support for the "melodic kind of speech" observed by the ancient critics.] It is not the only good way of reading verse, but it is the way to enchant boys; more dramatic and less rhythmical ways can be learned later. He first taught me the right sensuality of poetry, how it should be savoured and mouthed in solitude.[38]

Nothing could be more Greek in feeling and sense than that. How apt the term "right sensuality" is for that aesthetic experience of the sound of poetry so much praised by ancient critics!

Here is one more testimony from another well-known man of letters. After a description of the boredom he felt as a young child in learning Latin grammar, Sir Edmund Gosse writes:

One evening my Father took down his Virgil . . . and then, in the twilight, . . . he began to murmur and to chant the adorable verses by memory.

> Tityre, tu patulae recubans sub tegmine fagi,

he warbled; and I stopped my play, and listened as if to a nightingale, till he reached

> tu, Tityre, lentus in umbra
> Formosam resonare doces Amaryllida silvas.

"O Papa, what is that?" I could not prevent myself from asking. He translated the verses, he explained their meaning, but his exposition gave me little interest. What to me was the beautiful Amaryllis? She and her love-sick Tityrus awakened no image whatever in my mind. But a miracle had been revealed to me, the incalculable, the amazing beauty which could exist in the sound of verses.[39]

Now I must end. Knowable, feasible, desirable—these I have tried to prove are true terms for the right use of the sounds of ancient Greek literature. I know that I have omitted difficulties and uncertainties. But the broad outlines are, I am convinced, firm enough to build on, as firm as in many another field of classical studies where working hypotheses are readily accepted until better ones are established. Let me emphasize once again that in arguing for the value, the limited but positive value, of observing sound-effects in ancient Greek, I have no intention of depreciating the supreme importance of what Greek civilization offers to our intellect and our visual imagination. But I do affirm that the loss of what Wordsworth called "the living voice" [40] has done harm to Greek studies.

Is it too late to repair that harm? I do not think so. If enough younger university teachers, together with those few older scholars who are prepared to re-learn their way of speaking Greek, would decide to practice and preach the full reformed pronunciation for the sake of its literary value as well as for its linguistic accuracy, then perhaps in two generations the babel in our Greek classes might be changed into harmonious order, and the ear-hunger of our students might be fully fed. To quote a last example of the effect of euphony in proverbs: "where there's a will there's a way."

NOTES TO CHAPTER VI

[1] On classical Greek pronunciation in general see especially Havercamp, Blass, Grammont, Lejeune, Schwyzer, Sturtevant, Thomson, Zacher.

[2] On the evidence for the sounds of ancient Greek see Blass 14 ff., Sturtevant 21 ff., Schwyzer 169 ff.

[3] Dionysios 14, 144, 24. There is a v. l. ἀπορραπιζούσης ("cause to vibrate") for ἀπορριπιζούσης. On rho in general see especially Sturtevant 22 and Allen 32.

[4] On deficiencies in ancient Greek descriptions of the use of the vocal organs in pronunciation see, e.g., Sturtevant 24–26, 49, 57, 58.

[5] See chap. i, nn. 45 and 46, and chap. iii, n. 5; also Blass and Sturtevant.

[6] For transliterations in general see especially Blass, Sturtevant, and Schwyzer 152 ff. For Latin see Eckinger, *Die Orthographie lateinischer Wörter in griechischen Inschriften*. For Hebrew, H. E. Dr. Max Nurock has kindly referred me to: Paul Kahle, *The Cairo Geniza* (Oxford, 1959) 252–258; Samuel Krauss, *Griechische und lateinische Lehnwörter im Talmud* (Berlin, 1898–99), H. B. Rosen "On the Use of the Tenses in the Aramaic of Daniel," *Journal of Semitic Studies* VI (1961) 183–203; Franz Wutz, "Die Transkriptionen von der Septuaginta, etc.," *Texte und Untersuchungen zur vormasoretischen Grammatik des Hebräischen 2*; *Beiträge zur Wissenschaft vom Alten Testament* n.f. 9 (Stuttgart, 1933); and G. Zuntz, "Greek Words in the Talmud," *Journal of Semitic Studies* I (1956) 129–140.

[7] Quintilian on *phi* and *f*: see p. 64.

[8] Thucydides 2, 54, 1–3. See K. Strunk, *Glotta* XXXVIII (1960) 87f.

[9] "Dearth" and "death": Rex Warner in his translation (London, 1954) 127.

[10] Aristophanes, *Acharnians* 233; see Blass 97.

[11] Evidence for pronunciation of *upsilon:* see especially Blass 40.

[12] Evidence from misspellings: see, e.g., Robert T. Meyer, "The Linguistic Value of the Papyri," *CJ* XLIX (1954) 161–164.

[13] For dissident views see Sextus Empiricus, *Adv. Gramm.* 1, 102 and Diogenes Laertius 7, 57 (both perhaps Stoic eccentricities).

[14] On Lucian's *Judgement* see refs. in index. See Additional Note *infra*.

[15] Blass 17.

[16] See *The American Philological Association: An Historical Sketch* by Lucius Rogers Shero (Philadelphia, 1964), 9, 14 (reprinted in *TAPA* XCIV [1965] x-l).

[17] On the evolution of the four main types of pronunciation of Greek in western Europe see especially Bywater, Drerup, Havercamp, Schwyzer 174 ff.; also E. O. Dobson, *English Pronunciation 1500–1700* (Oxford, 1957); D.-C. Hesseling and H. Pernot, "Érasme et les origines de la prononciation érasmienne," *REG* XXXII (1921) 278–301; H. Pernot, *D'Homère à nos jours* (Paris, 1921) chap. iv; E. Wiken, "The Itacistic, Etacistic and Henningian Pronunciations of Greek in Sweden," *Eranos* XLIII (1946) 500–510; A. Collins, F. H. Stubbings, and S. J. Papastavrou, "Greek in Our Schools," *GR* ser. 2, III (1955) 78–82. For faults in the German pronunciation see H. Hirt, *Handbuch der griechischen Laut-*

und Formenlehre (Heidelberg, 1912) 79 as well as Drerup. For a strong but, I think, unconvincing attack on the reformed or Erasmian pronunciation see T. Papademetracopoulos, *La tradition ancienne et les partisans d'Érasme* (Athens, 1903). See also Strunk (as cited in n. 8 *supra*) 74–79. For a valiant defence of "the sound and healthy prejudice both of teachers and pupils against the needless and pedantic attempt to reform them" see *GR* II (1932/33) 139–143.

[18] On the special faults of the Anglicizing method of pronouncing Greek cf. E. A. Sophocles, *History of the Greek Alphabet and Pronunciation* (Cambridge, Mass., 1854) vi–vii (as cited by Drerup 772): "And it is worthy of notice that no system of Greek pronunciation conflicts oftener with the direct testimony of the ancient grammarians, as well as with the established principles of the Greek language, than that which takes the English for its basis; for in no other European language is the same letter or combination of letters oftener employed to denote more than one sound, or no sound at all. . . . It cannot be true that an Englishman learns Greek more easily by attempting to pronounce it as if it were English; for English orthoëpy is confessedly complicated and discouraging, even when it confines itself to its own language."

Milton in his *Letter on Education* (speaking of the right pronunciation of Latin) says: "For we Englishmen being farre Northerly, do not open our mouths in cold air, wide enough to grace a Southern tongue; but are observ'd by all other nations to speak exceeding close and inward. So that to smatter Latin with an English mouth is as ill hearing as law French." Cf. his amusing sonnet (XI) on such rugged names as "Colkitto, or Macdonnel, or Galasp . . . That would have made Quintilian stare and gasp" (I owe this reference to L. J. D. Richardson).

[19] On "the English horror of false quantities" and some notorious "howlers" see H. E. P. Platt, *A Last Ramble in the Classics* (Oxford, 1906) 152–158.

[20] For the provisions of Gardiner's edict see Havercamp 2, 207.

[21] See the works cited in n. 17 *supra*.

[22] Summary of answers to questionnaire (U = university professors, S = schoolmasters): using "conventional English" pronunciation, 4 U, 6 S; using "modern Greek" pronunciation, 2 U, 1 S; using "reformed" pronunciation, 17 U, 17 S. Motives: ease, 6 U, 4 S; intelligibility, 11 U, 9 S; lack of sufficient evidence for "reformed" kind, 1 U; belief that the "reformed" kind is the best attested, 5 U, 3 S; congruity with Latin teaching, 3 S; habit, 4 U, 3 S. Attempts to pronounce the accents: no attempt, 15 U, 13 S; pronounced as a stress accent, 4 U, 4 S; pronounced with pitch-variation, 5 U, 2 S. *Eta* pronounced (approximately, as in all following examples) as in *thee*, 2 U, 3 S; as *they*, 18 U, 16 S; as in *then*, 5 U, 3 S: *upsilon* as in *new*, 3 U, 5 S; as in *soon*, 13 U, 10 S; as in French *rue*, 9 U, 7 S: *phi* as in *fat*, 23 U, 16 S; as in *top-hat*, 4 U, 1 S: αι (diphthong) as in *lie*, 21 U, 15 S. Quantity: "longs" pronounced as approximately twice "shorts," 16 U, 8 S; as stressed syllables, 7 U, 9 S; a mixture of both, 2 U, 4 S. One S thought it best to leave matters of pronunciation until the university stage (see n. 31 *infra*); 4 S, 1 U felt an urgent need for removal of confusion; 8 U, 5 S admitted inconsistencies in their methods.

[23] On Rouse's work in the Perse School in Cambridge see F. R. Dale, "W. H. D.

Rouse and the Association for the Reform of Classical Teaching," *Didaskalos* 2 (1964) 106 ff. He remarks: "I remember Verrall . . . once using the reformed Greek sounds for the end of Helen's lament, with electrifying effect."

24 Cf. W. J. Ellis in his vigorous and still well worth reading diatribe, *The English, Dionysian, and Hellenic Pronunciations of Greek* (London, 1876) 14: "Beginners would feel no difficulty [with the pitch accents] if the master would only take the trouble to acquire the Dionysian pronunciation [by which he means the 'reformed' type], and especially to be both ready and steady in distinguishing both accent and quantity. This is no slight trouble, as I know by experience, to organs accustomed to a totally different system of reading Greek. . . . But when the master has privately overcome his own difficulties, he will be better able to lend a helping hand to his pupils, and put them on the right road, for he will have learned where the difficulties lie. This is certainly making a foreign language of Greek. But it should never be forgotten that Greek really *is* a foreign language, differing from English in character of pronunciation, and especially in accent and quantity, as much as in words. When Greek is taught properly, sound and symbol will be learned together, as in French and German. The difficulty mainly consists in getting rid of vicious habits already ingrained." He adds later (p. 17), "But for merely historical, philosophical or theological purposes, this additional and difficult study of pitch accent and quantity is entirely unnecessary."

25 For uncertainties in the pronunciation of ου see Sturtevant, Blass, and Tucker.

26 On the importance of early oral teaching see, e.g., W. R. Lee in *Didaskalos* 1 (1963) 123 ff.

27 See Appendix and its Additional Note.

28 Tucker 500.

29 C. B. Gulick in Goodwin and Gulick's *Greek Grammar*, p. iv. For the decision of the Classical Association referred to see *Proceedings of the Classical Association* IV (1906) 68 ff., V (1907) 95 ff., VI (1908) 100 ff., XXV (1928) 60 ff., XXVI (1929) 46 ff. Cf. E. V. Arnold and R. S. Conway, *The Restored Pronunciation of Greek and Latin* (3d ed.; Cambridge, 1907).

30 E. R. Dodds, "Classical Teaching in an Altered Climate," *Proceedings of the Classical Association* LXI (1964) 17. Perhaps this and similar views go back to Chandler's sardonic and pessimistic remarks in the preface to his *Practical Introduction*, e.g., his reference to "those who are unable to see the absurdity of perpetuating in writing a something to which they never attend in reading."

31 Cf. Maas, *Greek Metre* 57. He recommends the use of the "stressed longs" method of pronunciation (i.e., more or less the Henningian Latinizing type: cf. chap. ii, n. 76) and welcomes the fact that this method would "have the advantage of giving us a good excuse for not insisting on the learning of accents" which "have been of almost no value for the grammatical understanding of the texts." His translator, H. Lloyd-Jones, demurs on the grounds that knowledge of the accents aids the correct writing and pronunciation of modern Greek.

32 On standard English inflexions on "yes?" "yes!" etc., see Jones, *Outline*, 275 ff. and Kingdon, *Groundwork*.

33 See Helen Keller, *The Story of My Life* (London, 1903) 394 (in a report on her

pronunciation): "the principal thing that is lacking is sentence accent and variety in the inflection of phrases"—a remark that might well be applied to much contemporary speaking of ancient Greek. Yet it is only fair to note that Miss Keller despite her disabilities in the understanding of voice melody could write (pp. 110 f.): "It was the Iliad that made Greece my paradise. . . . My admiration for the Aeneid is not so great but it is none the less real. . . . The word-painting of Virgil is wonderful sometimes. . . . How easy it is to fly on paper wings!"

[34] So in my opinion the advice given in *The Teaching of the Classics* (Cambridge, 1954) 47 f. that "accents should be ignored for the first two years, and gradually learned thereafter," is misguided and misguiding.

[35] See Iona and Peter Opie, *The Oxford Dictionary of Nursery Rhymes* (Oxford, 1951) 2, 156–158, 336f.

[36] FitzGibbon 324. Reprinted with permission of Atlantic–Little, Brown and Company.

[37] Ogden, *Hearing* 302–305. Cf. Jespersen 149 on the fondness of children for rhyme and assonance. See also Snell, *Aufbau* 49.

[38] C. S. Lewis, *Surprised by Joy* (London, 1957) 109. With Lewis's reference to a delivery "something midway between speech and song" cf. the ancient writers cited on p. 28.

[39] Edmund Gosse, *Father and Son*, end of chap. viii.

[40] Wordsworth, *The Prelude* VI, 94 ff.:

> I was a better judge of thoughts than words,
> Misled in estimating words, not only
> By common inexperience of youth,
> But by the trade in classic niceties,
> The dangerous craft of culling term and phrase
> From languages that want the living voice
> To carry meaning to the natural heart,
> To tell us what is passion, what is truth,
> What reason, what simplicity and sense.

ADDITIONAL NOTE TO CHAPTER 6

Greek *sigma* has acquired another grievance in modern times: its frequent mispronunciation as *z*.

VII
The Speaking Voice

THE GREEKS called the right way of speaking Greek *Hellenismos*.[1] One ancient writer described it as depending on correctness in the use of rising and falling inflexions, aspiration, lengthenings, shortenings and other modifications. The opposite they named *barbarismos*.[2] This is probably a mimetic word, the reduplicated *bar-bar* suggesting a lack of differentiation between the sounds of successive syllables. (Perhaps, too, the fact that both of its first two syllables ended in a consonant stigmatized a tendency among foreigners to pronounce Greek open syllables as closed, as when we say *Myk-al-ee* for Μυ-κά-λη.) Strabo, who provides the best discussion of the term,[3] says that it was originally used to describe anyone who spoke with an awkward, stiff, and harsh intonation (ἐπὶ τῶν δυσεκφόρως καὶ σκληρῶς καὶ τραχέως λαλούντων), or with a thick, coarse intonation (ταχυστομούντων), including stammerers, stutterers, and lispers. It was only in later usage, Strabo thinks, that it was applied to foreigners in particular. But since the word goes back to the *Iliad* (in the form βαρβαρό--φωνοι), where it is applied to that strange people the Carians,[4] one may doubt his opinion.

The Greek comic writers give us examples of how foreigners distorted Greek sounds.[5] (But we must remember that these are caricatures and no doubt exaggerated.) Their commonest fault, apparently, was to mispronounce certain types of letters. Thus in *Thesmophoriazousai* Aristophanes represents a Scythian policeman as being unable to pronounce the aspiration in the letters *theta*, *phi*, and *chi*, for which he substitutes *t*, *p*, and *k*. So he says αἰτρίαν for αἰθρίαν, πορμός for φορμός, and ἔκοντο for ἔχοντο, though occasionally, if the manuscripts are trustworthy in this, he manages to utter the correct sound. (Here we have further evidence that these Greek aspirates were not pronounced like our *th*, *f*, and palatal *ch*, as in "loch" or German *nach*, since they would not easily be misheard or mispronounced

as *t*, *p*, *k*.) This Scythian also has difficulty with vowel sounds. He sometimes pronounces ει as ῑ (e.g., by saying λέγι for λέγει); he interchanges *o*
and *ω* (πῶτε for πόθεν, ἀπόλωλο for -ω-); and he also elides *ω* as if it were *o*.
Further, he often fails to pronounce a final *nu*, saying τή for τήν and Γόργο
for Γόργον, thereby anticipating a feature of modern Greek. The brief
remarks by the mock-Persian in *Acharnians* and the Triballian in *Birds*
also show some of these features.

In general, what we find in the speech of these barbarians is failure to
give the right quality and quantity to certain sounds. Probably at the
productions in Athens the actors playing the parts of these foreigners also
garbled the variations in pitch-accent, but since written accent-marks were
not used at that time this kind of barbarism could not have been recorded
in the official texts of the plays.

Besides these comic caricatures we occasionally have short descriptions
of how foreigners spoke Greek. For example, a Cappadocian is described
as speaking with "a thick tongue," confusing similar letters, and altering
the quantities.[6] There is some evidence, too, for Roman mispronunciations
of Greek words.[7]

Foreigners were not the only people to deviate notably from *Hellenismos*.
Some of the Greeks themselves did so, either through affectation or through
faulty education.[8] The most notorious of these deviations was the mispronunciation of the letter *rho* as *lambda* (as in the comic stage-Oriental
who says "velly" for "very"). The Greeks called this *traulótes*. Modern
linguists variously name it lambdacism, or lallation, or pararhotacism.[9]
Among those who had it in classical times were Alcibiades and his son,
and Demosthenes and Aristotle. Demosthenes,[10] as is well known, made
efforts with pebbles in his mouth to overcome his difficulties and used to
repeat that very rhotacistic line in the *Odyssey*

$$\text{ῥόχθει γὰρ μέγα κῦμα ποτὶ ξερὸν ἠπείροιο.}^{11}$$

At least, he had no *rho* in his own name unlike his fellow-sufferer Aristotle[12]
—or, worse still, the Roman Hirrus who could only call himself Hillus.[13]

Most notorious of all, because caricatured by Aristophanes, was the
pararhotacism of Alcibiades. He is portrayed as saying

$$\text{ὁλᾶς; Θέωλος τὴν κεφαλὴν κόλακος ἔχει}^{14}$$

for

$$\text{ὁρᾶς; Θέωρος τὴν κεφαλὴν κόρακος ἔχει.}$$

But Alcibiades had a way of making anything he did impressive, so we are
not surprised when Plutarch tells us that he made the defect seem a virtue
in his conversation.[15] Thus he may have cultivated a natural trait into a

positive distinction. At any rate, his son had the same mannerism,[16] perhaps by heredity or perhaps by imitation.[17] Similarly, within living memory the Irish Hellenist Mahaffy made the most of a tendency to say *w* for *r*, as in "vewy" for "very."

The ancient critics and commentators identified several other kinds of speech faults. The term *psellótes* and its cognates were used for two specific defects:[18] first, "lisping" in the modern technical sense of inability to pronounce *s* properly ("parasigmatism"), as in saying πιττεύω for πιστεύω,[19] and, second, omission of a letter ("lipogrammatism"), as in saying ἄρτον for ἄρκτον (which exactly corresponds to the vulgar modern error of saying "artic" for "arctic"). According to Aristophanes,[20] the demagogue Hyperbolos had the peculiarity of pronouncing *gamma* like consonantal *y*, saying olíyos for ὀλίγος. And it may have been he, too, whom another comic poet[21] mocked as saying ἴννος for γίννος and δητώμην for διητώμην.

Sometimes the pronunciation of the diphthongs was at fault. When Socrates in the *Clouds* exclaims about another character, "Look at the stupid way he pronounced κρέμαιο with his lips wide apart. How could a fellow like that learn to plead a case successfully?" the implication, perhaps, was that to succeed in the Athenian law courts one needed a tense shrill voice like that of Cleon,[22] not a drawling, slack delivery.

The ancient writers named other faults: *la(m)bdakismos* (an exaggerated emphasis on *lambda*), *mutakismos* (overfondness for *mu*), *rhotakizein* (using *rho* excessively), *sigmatismos* (excessive use of *sigma*), *iotakismos* (a doubling of *iota* in words like *Troia, Maia*, making them *Troiia* and *Maiia*), and *plateiasmos* (broadening vowels, especially *alpha*).[23] The last mentioned is the source of the amusing incident in Theocritos' poem *Women at the Adonis Festival*: a stranger complains about the accent of some Syracusan women, "they scratch your nerves away, broadening every word" (ἐκκναιασεῦντι πλατειάσδοισα ἄπαντα),[24] and gets a stinging reply from the women.

Other faults consisted in stammering (i.e., speaking with an impediment or hesitation), which is generally called ἰσχνοφωνία,[25] or stuttering (i.e., nervous repetition of syllables), βαττολογία. In one famous case of stuttering shock-treatment was the cure—according to myth, at least—when Battos met a lion in Libya and yelled so loudly that he lost the impediment in his speech.[26] Sometimes defects of these kinds could be cured by therapeutic exercises, such as speaking with pebbles in one's mouth or the use of "tongue twisters." [27]

Two other causes of incorrect pronunciation have been noticed in earlier chapters and need only be recalled briefly here. The first is deliberate distortion of a word or words for an intentional effect as when Demosthenes said Ἀσκλήπιος for Ἀσκληπιός and μίσθωτος for μισθωτός;[28] or when poets lengthen or shorten syllables by "metrical license," or divide or contract diphthongs and vowel groups by *diaeresis* and *contraction* against the norm. Aristophanes' daft εἰειειειειλίσσετε[29] is an extreme example of this. Similarly reciters and actors probably varied the timbre-quality of syllables for dramatic reasons. For example, a rhapsode declaiming the almost treasonable words of Calchas to Achilles,

ἀλλά τε καὶ μετόπισθεν ἔχει κότον, ὄφρα τελέσσῃ,
ἐν στήθεσσιν ἑοῖσι · σὺ δὲ φράσαι εἴ με σαώσεις,[30]

might give added sibilance to the unusually numerous sigmas so as to suggest a conspiratorial whisper. Or an actor would probably emphasize the contemptuous staccato effect of the repetitive *tau*'s in the often quoted passage from the *King Oedipus*,

τυφλὸς τά τ' ὦτα τόν τε νοῦν τά τ' ὄμματ' εἶ,[31]

just as a good reciter grinds out the *r*'s in Milton's

Grate on their scrannel pipes of wretched straw.[32]

This is sometimes why lines which seem to be mimetic to some seem quite empty of mimesis to others: those who believe that it is mimetic emphasize the mimetic elements; those who have noticed no mimesis for themselves object to any such emphasis.

A second cause of mispronunciation mentioned in previous chapters is an error through ignorance or psychological confusion, as when Hegelochos said γαλῆν ὁρῶ for γαλήν' ὁρῶ,[33] or in many of the cases of barbarism cited earlier. This kind of mistake has been a favourite comic device from the time of Homer with his Οὖτις-οὖτις incident.[34]

These voluntary and involuntary deviations from the normal Greek pronunciation of various eras provide a strong argument against the perfectionists who say that, since we cannot hope exactly to reproduce the pronunciation of classical Greece for any period, we should not try to pronounce Greek in the ancient way at all. As we have seen, even celebrated fifth-century Athenians had their phonetic faults, and were mocked for them. But they were not discouraged from speaking Greek as well as they could. If present-day speakers of Greek in the "restored" pronunciation were heard by Aristophanes, no doubt he would make some scathing gibes about our pronunciation. But at least we could reply that we probably pronounce *rho* better than Alcibiades and *gamma* than Hyperbolos, and do better with our quantities, aspirates, and final *nu*'s than the Scythian policemen. Indeed, in the last case our fault is likely to be the reverse of theirs: they deprived θ, φ, and χ of their following puff of breath; we speakers of a Germanic language usually pronounce τ, π, and κ with the following puff of breath which only θ, φ, and χ should have. But, at any rate, both we and the Scythian policeman do something that can be excused more than pronouncing θ, φ, and χ as English *th*, *f*, and *ch*.

The Greeks in their discussions of "right speaking," orthoëpy,[35] emphasized the importance of clear articulation in pronouncing syllables. Their word for this, *diarthrosis*,[36] was a metaphor taken from anatomy, in which it referred to the clear demarcation between the limbs and the rest of the body. As a concept it embodied a principle which is characteristic of all good Greek art, literature, and thought—the distinct perception of the separate parts in a complex whole.[37] We can see it equally well in the structure of a Greek choral lyric and in the architecture of a Greek temple where the joinings of the blocks of stone in the walls or columns are not concealed and, on the contrary, each architectural member is articulate in the total visual effect, yet the clearly visible joinings do not disrupt the integrity of the whole structure. The equivalent of this in the sphere of literature was a composition giving a total impression of unity, symmetry, and order, but also permitting a clear perception of the main constituents. In Greek terms, such a work of art was both architectonically and tectonically explicit: the master builder's plan did not conceal the skill of the stonemasons, and the skill of the stonemasons did not distract attention from the master builder's grand design.

In phrasal articulation the Greeks expected a similar distinctness in the constituent parts. They demanded that each syllable should be clearly perceptible, but also that the euphonic line of the word or phrase should not be disrupted. As in Nestor's speeches, there should be both clarity, which demands moments of motionlessness, and also flow, which demands constant motion—a paradox in words, like Zeno's problem of the arrow, but not impossible for a skillful artist.

Sometimes, however, the continuous phrasal flow was disrupted for literary effect by an exaggerated break between the syllables.[38] For this the Greek poets used a term meaning "make a separation inside" (ἐνδατεῖσθαι, perhaps even "to carve up"), especially when it was used for the purpose of emphasizing a significant etymology. Thus Aeschylus tells how a hero pronounced the name Πολυνείκης, "Núchstrife," as Πολυ-νείκης, "Much-strífe";[39] and elsewhere in tragedy characters say δυσ-πάρευνον and εὐ-παιδίας to stress the meaning of the first component. Shakespeare parodies pedantic uses of this etymological articulation in *Cymbeline*, where a soothsayer says:

Thou, Leonatus, art the lion's whelp,
The fit and apt construction of thy name,
Being Leo-natus, doth impart so much:
The "piece of tender air," thy virtuous daughter,
Which we call *mollis aer*; and *mollis aer*
We term it *mulier*. . . .[40]

Other nuances of meaning could depend on how one marked divisions between syllables at the end of words.[41] Isocrates, for example, is said to have replied to an intending pupil who asked what he needed to bring to his lectures: "You need πινακιδίου καινοῦ (καὶ νοῦ) καὶ γραφιδίου καὶ νοῦ (καινοῦ)." This according to varying articulation and accentuation could mean, "a little new tablet" or "a little tablet and intelligence," and "a little new pencil" or "a little pencil and intelligence." Just how Isocrates pronounced the part in each case is open to question. The most effective way, in my opinion, would be to pronounce it so as to suggest at the same time both καὶ νοῦ and καινοῦ by pronouncing the καὶ with a pitch accent somewhere between the down-glide of the grave and the low tone of the unaccented syllable, and also by slurring the articulation of the καὶ and -νου syllables so as to make it uncertain whether they made one word or two. In other words, Isocrates could have reduced the phonetic differences between καὶ νοῦ and καινοῦ to a point where the two forms were almost but not quite homophones, making a virtue out of uncertainty. In much the same way we might say, "Where no pun-is-meant, there should be no pun-ish-ment."

Ingenious sophists and rhetoricians devised many other examples of articulatory ambiguity. I quote two examples out of many. Suppose a law reads—we must remember, of course, that the Greeks unlike the Romans did not separate words in writing—

ΑΥΛΗΤΡΙΣΠΕΣΟΥΣΑΔΗΜΟΣΙΑΕΣΤΩ,

are we to take it as "If a hall fall down three times (αὐλὴ τρὶς πεσοῦσα), let it become public property," or "If a pipe-player falls (αὐλητρὶς πεσοῦσα), let her become public property"? Similarly, if a father has two sons, Leon and Pantaleon, which son is to inherit his property if his will says ἐχέτω τὰ ἐμὰ ΠΑΝΤΑΛΕΩΝ?[42] In the spoken word these ambiguities would not arise, since the pitch accent would indicate how the words should be understood.[43] But written without accent marks, the words are ambiguous. As such they have special interest for textual critics as well as for phoneticians, since many textual problems depend on questions of word-division, which ultimately are questions of articulation. And the collector of linguistic *curiosa* can gather some of his choicest ghost-words from mistaken word-divisions—among the choicest being Virgil's place-name *Inarime*[44] formed from a misreading of Homer's εἰν Ἀρίμοις.[45]

Another anecdote illustrates how a small matter of articulation could wreck a man's fortunes when the hearer was sensitive, powerful, and vindictive. One of the lieutenants of King Lysimachos permitted himself at a banquet to refer to Arsinoë, Lysimachos' wife, as τήν δ' ἐμοῦσαν, a deliberate misarticulation of τήνδε Μοῦσαν.[46] The point of the pun was in the fact that Arsinoë was notoriously afflicted with a tendency to vomit, so the phrase was fiendishly apt: an English equivalent might be "this puke" for "this spook." Lysimachos punished the punster with atrocious appropriateness.

A familiar kind of articulation is punctuation, division between phrases (διαστολή).[47] The same words can have entirely contrary meanings according to how they are broken up in pronunciation, as, for example, in

ἐγώ σ' ἔθηκα, δοῦλον ὄντ', ἐλεύθερον

and

ἐγώ σ' ἔθηκα δοῦλον, ὄντ' ἐλεύθερον,

or in that amazing French *tour de force* in which two separate lines have almost exactly the same sound, but radically different spelling and entirely different meanings according to the punctuation:

Gal, amant de la reine, alla, tour magnanime,
Galamment de l'Arène à la Tour Magne à Nîmes.[48]

(But this masterpiece of ingenuity gives a more amusing titillation to the senses and mind when seen first in writing.) In fact, normal correct reading, orthoëpy, in which the phrases are properly articulated, destroys the ambiguity in such phrases, making a clear decision for one version or the other.

One aspect of Greek orthoëpy remains almost entirely unknown. This is sentence intonation. Apart from a cursory remark by a late grammarian,[49] there is no evidence to tell us how the normal Athenian voice in ancient times rose and fell above and below the graph-line of the fixed tonic accent on every important word. Some variation is certain. For one thing, while the *relative* pitch-variations within a sentence were controlled by the tonic accent, the *absolute* pitch-levels could doubtless be freely varied. Presumably, too, the average gamut of a fifth between the low-level tone and the high note of the rising acute accent varied slightly—perhaps even considerably—according to a speaker's temperament or mood. We must also reckon with the fact that the vowels of themselves normally impose their own individual pitch-values on a speaker.[50] The mnemonic sentence

> Who knows aught of art must first learn then take his ease

gives a rough indication of the natural vowel-scale in conversational English: the voice rises gradually from the vowel of "who" to that of "art," then drops a little to "must" and then rises to "ease," which is spoken on a distinctly higher note than "art." This is a very broad simplification of a very complex process. But broadly speaking we may take it that the voice-melodies of the ancient Greeks sometimes, at least, followed this natural vowel-melody—which may partly explain the nature of the chant of the seven vowels described in chapter iii. In other words, in speaking a line like

> ἄνδρα μοι ἔννεπε Μοῦσα πολύτροπον ὃς μάλα πολλὰ

the voice besides observing the basic patterns of the pitch-accents would have each tonic-accent modified something like this: if *alpha* is assumed to be the middle-toned vowel, then the ἔ of ἔννεπε would be slightly higher than the ἀ of ἄνδρα or of μάλα and the ὑ of πολύτροπον would be higher still, while the ὃ of ὃς would be lower than the ἀ of πολλὰ: so, too, with the low-level vowels: the o's would be lowest, next the α's and ε's, and the οι highest. The implications of this fusion of tonic-accent and vowel-melody cannot be precisely defined without scientific phonetic analysis beyond the scope of the present study. For practical purposes if we pronounce the Greek vowels with the dynamics of modern French or Italian vowels we shall probably get as near to the ancient pitch-variations in this respect as is possible for any but the expert phonetician.

A little is known about some personal tones of voice. Isocrates raised his voice too high in orating, we are told,[51] and Aeschines disparaged Demosthenes' voice for its shrillness as well as its loudness.[52] Cleon, according to one of his enemies, had a shrill screaming voice like the squawk of a burnt pig.[53] In contrast Prodikos the sophist is said to have pitched his voice too low.[54] On the whole, the general tendency among Greeks seems to have been more toward shrillness than toward deepness. An Aristotelian writer asserts that Greek singers tended to sing sharp when going out of tune.[55] In damper and more northerly climates singers are more inclined to sing flat. The practical conclusion for us from this is that in pronouncing ancient Greek we should try to keep the voice at higher levels than in normal English.

Another source of intonational variation is mood or emotion.[56] This is a common element in all languages and needs no elaborate exemplification from ancient Greek. At one end of the emotional and tonal scale we hear

Ajax in his mood of black despondency uttering deep sounds like a bull,[57] at the other the angry denunciatory shrillness of Thersites ὀξέα κεκλήγων as he shouts abuse against Agamemnon.[58] Actors must, of course, have been adept in choosing the right pitch-levels and intonations for the roles they were playing.

Monotony of intonation cannot have meant the same thing to the Greeks as to us.[59] We understand it as an intonation which remains constantly around one pitch-level. But the ancient Greeks had to follow the basic tone-variations prescribed by the word-accents:[60] their voices had to change pitch in almost every word to the extent of approximately one fifth—*doh* to *soh*, or, say, C to G. Presumably for them monotony consisted in having little or no emotional pitch-variation. Isocrates speaks of someone who read a speech "as if he were numbering something off" (ὥσπερ ἀπαριθμῶν).[61] Possibly, too, deficiency in vowel-melody was also regarded as monotonous.

Another aspect of the speaking voice which the Greeks often mentioned was its quality in terms of timbre and resonance. Modern writers variously describe unpleasant voices as "throaty" or "nasal" or "guttural" or "hoarse" or "thin" or "harsh" or "chesty" or "breathy," and so on.[62] Pleasant voices are "rich," "vibrant," "warm." Shelley, we are told, had an "intolerably shrill, harsh and discordant voice," Milton, one that was "delicate" and "tuneable." [63] The Greeks deployed a rich vocabulary for qualities of this kind. They especially disliked hollowness, coarseness, thickness, roughness, breathiness, throatiness, brokenness. They admired Pericles for "the imperturbable moulding" (πλάσμα ἀθόρυβον) of his voice,[64] and deplored the screaming intensities of Cleon in full demagogic spate. Their ideal was a steady, clear, raised (but not shrill) voice, as will be described later.

In all these features of speech, art was often called in to improve nature. The teachers of voice-production (φωνασκοί)[65] could do much to mold a voice to a chosen pattern, and the teachers of rhetoric had much to say on the art of delivery (ὑπόκρισις)[66] for orators. Unfortunately very little is known of the methods of the voice-trainers in the schools for actors. For their profession a rich and skillfully used voice was the primary necessity. The dramatic masks precluded nuances of facial expression:[67] all feeling had to be expressed by the voices with some help from gestures and poses—in contrast with what happens in our cinemas, and to some extent in the theatres, where carefully calculated (and, in the cinema, hugely magnified) facial movements are expected to have our close attention, diminishing the effect of the spoken word.

Besides teachers and performers, two other professional groups in ancient

Greece took a special interest in vocal qualities. The physicians, as we have seen, listened to them in making their diagnoses. Also the writers on "physiognomics," the art or science of deducing character from physical qualities, had a good deal to say about the supposed relationship between certain kinds of voices and certain kinds of persons.[68] Some believed, for example, that people with deep and tense voices were brave, those with high and slack voices cowardly. If you are kind, you are expected to have a soft and deep voice; if disgruntled, one that rises from low to high. If spiteful and morally lax, you are likely to speak with a nasal quality. Greedy and vain people have high, clangy voices like birds; stupid ones bleat like sheep or goats. If you hear a dry quality in someone's voice, look out—he is probably a wily fellow. And a man's cracked or broken tone should warn you against his gluttony and violence. If he talks with *para-rhotacism* like Alcibiades, he must be haughty, proud, and hardhearted. So, at least, the physiognomists thought.

Much of this physiognomical discussion of voices is either commonplace or silly (especially the deductions based on analogies with the cries of animals). But it gives us some clues to the kind of delivery that we might have heard from character-actors in the ancient theatres, and it tells us about the kind of voice-qualities that the ancient Greeks disliked and suspected.

Most of this chapter has been concerned with faults of the Greek speaking voice rather than its virtues, because the Greek critics are generally more explicit about deviations from the good voice than about the nature of the good voice itself. As a final consideration let us now try to define the Greek ideal of euphony in speech, remembering that this euphony was partly a virtue of the words that were being spoken and partly a virtue of the voice speaking them. A euphonious voice could mitigate the cacophony of ill-composed words, and euphonious words could lessen the cacophony of an ugly voice. The ideal artistic achievement came from beautiful words beautifully spoken, or noble words nobly spoken, or delicate words delicately spoken, or from some similar harmony of word and voice. In other words, the Greek attitude to literature was more like our attitude to music than our attitude to the printed page.

The favourite terms of the earlier Greek poets for describing a beautiful voice is λιγύs and its longer form λιγυρόs (and compounds). They are applied to the voices of the Sirens, of the Muse, of cicadas, of nightingales and other birds, of singers, mourners, and orators, and also to the sounds of the lyre, the winds, metal when stuck, and of a whiplash whistling through the air. Pindar in a daring metaphor, which some editors have tried to eliminate, describes his sensations when the urge to compose poetry strikes him with special force as "the impression of a λιγυρᾶς ('whetstone')" upon his mouth,[69] presumably meaning a sensation of having his tongue made shrill and sharp like a knife on the grindstone. Obviously the term had wide and various meanings. Fortunately an Aristotelian writer[70] defines it—at least, as it was understood in the fourth century or later:

> Voices are λιγυραί which are delicate [or "fine," λεπταί: cf. Homer's description of the note given out by a taut bowstring, λίνον δ' ὑπὸ καλὸν ἄειδεν λεπταλέη φωνῇ][71] and firm-toned (πυκναί), as in the case of cicadas and locusts and nightingales and, generally speaking, of all voices which have no jarring resonance (ἀλλότριος ἦχος). Generally speaking, this quality (τὸ λιγυρόν) is not a matter of vocal bulkiness (ἐν ὄγκῳ φωνῆς), nor of relaxed and low tones (ἐν τόνοις ἀνιεμένοις καὶ βαρέσιν), nor of close intervals of sounds (ἐν ταῖς τῶν φθόγγων ἀφαῖς), but rather of sharpness and delicacy (λεπτότητι) and precision (ἀκριβείᾳ).

In other words, the ideal Greek voice was clear, delicate, light, high, melodious, and distinctly articulated. We in more northern climates tend to be deficient in lightness, delicacy, and highness. Modern Greeks notice this. As a Russian scholar has remarked, a present-day Greek finds our "fullness" of speech very surprising. "Has everyone in your country got such a thick voice (τέτοια χοντρὴ φωνή)?" he was once asked.[72] This is the quality that in antiquity Crantor stigmatized as "unhewn and full of tree-bark." [73]

The low, husky tones of our modern cinema actors and actresses would probably not please an ancient Athenian audience (though we know that in one instance, at least, a skillful orator, Mark Antony, could use a natural huskiness of voice to win confidence and stir pity). We, for our part, may find typical modern Greek voices rather high and thin, just as we cannot easily admire what Homer calls the "lily voice" (ὄπα λειριόεσσαν) of the cicadas.[74] To us their inexhaustible, shrill stridulations sound like some metallic mechanical contrivance. But for the ancient Greeks who had none of our everyday machines and steel instruments the voice of the cicada was supremely endowed with pureness, consistency, precision, and fineness of tone—a miracle not achievable so efficiently and tirelessly by anything else in the world of nature or art. Similarly in the nightingale's song they admired the sheer precision of the notes as well as the melodic line.

This preference for highness rather than lowness of tone runs contrary to what is often praised in English literature. Annie Laurie in the famous song has a voice that is "low and sweet"; Cordelia in *King Lear* is remembered as having had a voice that was

ever soft,
Gentle, and low, an excellent thing in woman;[75]

and we normally use terms like "shrill" and "sharp" in disparagement, not in eulogy. The Greeks, of course, disliked these qualities when excessive: a not uncommon form of abuse in classical times was to call someone's voice over-sharp or over-shrill.[76] But in general the ancient Greeks preferred the higher tones to the lower. The same inclination can be seen in the fact that Greek singers tended to sing sharp when going out of tune, where we more often sing flat.[77] So, too, in the verbal tonic accent the "master tone" (ὁ κύριος τόνος) was the high-rising acute, not the low grave.[78]

Such in broad outline is the evidence for the virtues and defects of ancient speakers of Greek and for the phonetic likes and dislikes of the Greeks in matters of voice-quality. The main practical lesson for those who wish to regain the ancient ideals in their own reading and speaking of ancient Greek literature is this: besides aiming at the ideals of distinctness, melodiousness, and tonal consistency, which every English-speaking teacher of elocution recommends, we should try to raise the pitch of our voices above our normal level, even though our climate and vocal traditions may hinder us. To do this, as well as observing the rise and fall of the pitch accent, will not be easy. But as Socrates insists in the dialogue that has been so useful in these studies, the *Cratylos*, good and beautiful things are hard—

χαλεπὰ τὰ καλά.

NOTES TO CHAPTER VII

[1] On Ἑλληνισμός see LSJ. Philodemos 4, 100 (Hausrath) says it depends on ἀνέσει, ἐπιτάσει, προσπνεύσει, ψιλότητι, ἐπεκτάσει, συστολῇ, προθέσει, πτώσει.

[2] On βαρβαρισμός see chap. ii, n. 16. The adjective σόλοικος is sometimes applied to foreign or defective speech: see LSJ. But the term σολοικισμός is confined to faults in syntax and phrasing and is not applied to mispronunciations.

[3] Strabo 14,2,28 on *Il.* 2,867 (see next note). See p. 142 for stammering, etc.

[4] *Iliad* 2,867, Καρῶν . . . βαρβαροφώνων. (Note also the woman's name Ἀβαρβαρέη.) Cf. the notion that making a confused noise by shouting or speaking together may be taken as a symptom of inferior character: see *Il.* 3,2 ff. (contrasting l. 8), also *Od.* 1,365; 4,768; 17,366; 18,399; 22,21; and see LSJ at λάβρος.

[5] See the scholiasts and editors on the passages cited below and also especially J. Friedrich, "Das Attische im Munde von Ausländern bei Aristophanes," *Philologus* LXXV (1918) 274–303. The chief passages considered by him are *Thesmophoriazousai* 1001–7, 1083–1135, 1176–1201, 1210–25; *Acharnians* 104;

Birds 1678 f. Friedrich does not include *Acharnians* 100 or *Birds* 1615, 1628 f., because there the foreigners are apparently not trying to speak Greek at all, but are speaking a foreign language. He also (pp. 301 f.) examines the barbarisms attributed to a foreigner by Timotheos in his *Persians* 162–173, in which the non-Attic sounds are mainly Ionicisms: but see also Page's text in his *Poetae Melici Greeci*, p. 410, for other abnormalities. For confusions of π/φ, τ/θ, and $\varkappa/\chi$ in Asia Minor and Egypt see Schwyzer 204.

[6] Philostratos, *Lives of Sophists* 594.

[7] E.g., Quintilian 12,10,57 implies that rustic Romans mispronounced the Greek name Ἀμφίων as Ampïon: cf. his remarks on aspiration in 1,5,19 ff. The Romans said Γραῖκοι for Greek Γραικοί.

[8] On speech defects in general see Berry 8 ff., who distinguishes three types: defects of articulation (distortions, substitutions, omissions), defects of voice production (matters of quality, loudness, pitch-variation, duration), and defects of rhythm (stammering, stuttering). See also Robbins.

[9] See Robbins on *pararhotacismos* and *lambdacismos*.

[10] For Demosthenes' τραυλότης see Philodemos, *Rhet.* 197 (Sudhaus); Plutarch, *Demosthenes* 844E, *Mor.* 26B, 650E; Cicero, *De or.* 1,260, *De fin.* 5,2,5, *De div.* 2,46,96; Philodemos, *Rhet.* 206; A. Westermann, Vitarum *Scriptores Graeci Minores* (Brunswick, 1845) 295,62 ff., 299,60 ff., 305,66 ff.; and Krumbacher 25, 88 f. Diogenes Laertius 2,108, calls him ῥωβικώτερος, Aeschines 2,99, βάταλος.

[11] *Odyssey* 5,402: see Eustathios *ad loc.* and Westermann (see n. 10 *supra*) 299,69 f. Cf. Krumbacher 25, 88 f.

[12] Aristotle as τραυλός: see Diogenes Laertius 5,1, and Westermann (as cited in n. 10) 402,2.

[13] Hirrus: Cicero, *Ep. ad Fam.* 2,10,1.

[14] *Wasps* 44 f.

[15] On Alcibiades' τραυλότης: see Plutarch, *Alcibiades* 1 and 41, and the scholia on *Wasps* 44 f.

[16] Plutarch (*Alcibiades* 1) cites Archippos to suggest that the son deliberately imitated his father's lisp.

[17] Vendryès 41 notes that the *Incroyables* of France under the Directory imitated the influential Beauharnais family in not pronouncing *r* distinctly (a trait probably derived from their previous Creole environment). In Linear B *l* and *r* are not distinguished, and they are interchanged in some Greek dialects: see Schwyzer 1,213.

[18] See LSJ on ψελλότης. For the second meaning, "lipogrammatism," see "Aristotle," *Problems* 11,30, 902B 24, where τραυλότης is defined as inability to pronounce a letter, and ἰσχνοφωνία as inability to join syllables fluently (i.e., stammering). But in the *Souda* ψελλός is equated with τραυλός. According to a scholium on Pindar, *Olympians* 6,148A, Pindar suffered from ἰσχνοφωνία. So, too, did Isocrates (Philostratos, *Isocrates* 505). Sophocles' defect was μικροφωνία (*Life* 4).

[19] πιττεύω: see LSJ.

[20] *Peace* 757, *Clouds* 870, *Thesm.* 1183. The Tarentines also had this phonetic peculiarity: cf. Blass 110.

[21] Plato Comicus (Edmonds 168); cf. Blass 54 and Quintilian 11,3,81. *Clouds* 870–874; cf. p. 10.

22 For Cleon's tones see p. 147.

23 See LSJ and Lewis and Short's Latin lexicon on these terms and also on words in βαμβ- (on which see Jean Humbert in *Mélanges Desrousseaux* [Paris, 1937] 225–228, and the scholia to *Iliad* 2,804), βαττ-, βραδύγλωσσος, κέκιλος, κοιλοστομία, κολοβότης, κρεμβαλιάζω, μογιλαλία, μυγμός, παχυστομεῖν, πνευματισμός, πνευματώδης, σιγμός, σπαδονισμός, ταὐτολογία.

24 *Idylls* 15,88.

25 See n. 18 *supra*.

26 See Pausanias 10,157. Cf. Herodotos 4,155 f.; Pindar, *Pythians* 5,55–62. Moses in the LXX version of Exodus 4:10 is described as ἰσχνόφωνος καὶ βραδύγλωσσος.

27 On tongue twisters see chap. iii, n. 6.

28 See pp. 31 f.

29 *Frogs* 1313; cf. 1348.

30 *Iliad* 1,82 f.

31 *O.T.* 371.

32 *Lycidas* 124.

33 See p. 30.

34 See pp. 90 f.

35 On "orthoëpy" see chap. i, n. 24.

36 See LSJ at διάρθρωσις, διαρθρόω, ἄρθρωσις, ἄρθρον, ἀρθρόω, ἄναρθρος, διαίρεσις: also on δυσεκφόρητος, δυσεκφώνητος; and cf. n. 47 *infra*.

37 Cf. p. 92.

38 Presumably by a more marked use of the ψῦγμα mentioned by Dionysios Hal.' 20,202,26. But exactly what that was is not clear to me. Roberts translates "inhalation," but I can see no reason for such in the passage Dionysios is describing there. Was it some kind of "glottal stop" necessary in pronouncing hiatus like ἄλγε' ἔχοντα, τοι ὁ, and ἄνω ὤθεσκε? The etymology of ψῦγμα (presumably connected with ψύχω, -χή) would not support this directly, but a modification of the normal emission of breath is involved. See n. 66 *infra* and Basore (as cited there) 84.

39 Aeschylus, *Seven* 578. Cf. my *Aeschylus* 74–75.

40 *Cymbeline* v, v, 443 ff. For curious examples in modern English of disjoining syllables in words for the sake of etymological emphasis see *The Times Literary Supplement*, 29 April 1965, p. 334.

41 On the following punning ambiguities see my *Ambiguity* 5. Cf. Diogenes Laertius, *Lives of Philosophers* 2, 118, and Walz, *Rhetores Graeci* 1,209,1.

42 See Diogenes Laertius, *Lives* 7,62 (cf. 6,52).

43 It might be argued that the paronomasia on καὶ νοῦ and καινοῦ, αὐλὴ τρὶς and αὐλητρὶς, implies that the final-grave accent was indistinguishable from the low-tone grave. But if the two phrases in each pair were identical there would be no pun at all, only a tautology (see further on λοιμός, λιμός on p. ∞). Besides, πάντα Λέων and Πανταλέων have an undeniable difference in accentuation (though perhaps it may give a clue to the existence of a secondary high-tone accent on the fourth-last syllable of a paroxytone word): so, too, ἀπὸ νοῦ and ἀπ' ὄνου in Plato, *Laws* 7,2, 701D, and Aristophanes, *Clouds* 1273.

44 *Aeneid* 9,716.

45 *Iliad* 2,783.

⁴⁶ See my *Ambiguity* 53–55, and cf. the ambiguity Θρᾷττ' εἶ and θράττει in Aristotle, *Rhetoric* 3,11,6 1412A35. Phrases of this kind raise the question whether any perceptible difference could be heard between, say, τήνδ' ἐμοῦσαν and τήνδε Μοῦσαν in the pronunciation of ancient Greek. Sergej Sobolevskij, *Eirene* II (1964) 43 ff. finds evidence in the rules for division of the comic anapaest and in Porson's law for believing that in elision the consonant preceding the elided vowel was closely attached to the vowel in the following word, so that the phrases quoted would be pronounced τήν-δεμοῦσαν and τήν-δε-Μοῦσαν. As S. notes, there is support for this view in the aspiration of the final consonant in phrases like καθ' ἕν and in the way of writing *synaloiphe* as in τοὔνομα. He also cites Aristarchos' opinion that in *Iliad* 8,206 f. one should read Ζῆν'/αὐτοῦ as Ζῆ-ναυτοῦ (see Eustathios *ad loc.*). The articulatory difference would then be as in ἔστιν ἄξιος and ἔστι Νάξιος. Cf. schol. to Dionysios Thrax, Hilgard 156, or as in English "an aim" and "a name." This could have been an element in the mispronunciation of γαλήν' ὁρῶ as γαλῆν ὁρῶ: cf. K. E. A. Schmidt, *Beitrag. z. Gesch. d. Gr. u. d. Lat.* 147 ff. and H. Ehrlich, *KZ* XXXIX (1906) 583 ff. (I am especially indebted to Professor W. S. Allen in this note.)

⁴⁷ See LSJ on διαίρεσις, διαστολή, στιγμή, ὑποδιαστολή, and see Schwyzer 395 f.

⁴⁸ See P. E. Passy, *Petite phonétique comparée* (Leipzig, 1912) 22.

⁴⁹ Stephanus on Aristotle's *Rhetoric*, 309, 20 ff.: he advises those reading the Holy Gospels to learn the high, low, and συρματική (long drawn-out) kinds of intonation: cf. Hanschke 68 ff., Caplan on *Rhetorica ad Herennium* 3,14,25 ff., and Sonkowsky. See chap. ii, n. 27.

⁵⁰ On the inherent relative pitch-values of the vowels see, e.g., Paget 26.

⁵¹ For Isocrates' voice see Philostratos, *Lives* 505 and Philodemos 198 (Sudhaus).

⁵² Aeschines 2,29, and cf. note 10 *supra*. Aeschines himself was fortunate in being λαμπρόφωνος (Westermann [as cited in note 10 *supra*] 263,5).

⁵³ For Cleon's voice see Aristophanes, *Wasps* 36, 596, 1034 and *Knights* 303, 311; Aristotle, *Ath. Pol.* 28,3; Plutarch, *Nicias* 8.

⁵⁴ For Prodikos' voice see Philostratos, *Lives* 1,12,496.

⁵⁵ "Aristotle," *Problems* 19,26 (cf. 46).

⁵⁶ On variation of pitch according to emotional stress see H. Fairbanks and W. L. Pronovost in *Speech Monographs* 6 (1939) 87–104.

⁵⁷ Sophocles, *Ajax* 322.

⁵⁸ *Iliad* 2,222.

⁵⁹ μονοτονία: see chap. iii, n. 66.

⁶⁰ Perhaps the unusual abundance of particles in Greek may be due to the limitation of tonal variation by the pitch-accent.

⁶¹ Isocrates, *Phil.* 26.

⁶² Cf. Berry: "unpleasant voices are variously described as throaty, nasal, denasal, muffled, guttural, whangy, thin or heavy": cf. LSJ at κεκλασμένως, κλαγγώδης, λαρυγγόφωνος (and cognates), ληκυθίζω (and cognates), πνευματώδης, σαθρός, φαρυγγίζειν, and "Aristotle," *De audib.* 804A 33 ff. The *Scriptores Physiognomici* (see n. 68 *infra*) refer to tones and voices as ἀκαμπές, αὐχμηρός, βληχώδης, εὐκαμπές, κλαγγηδόν, σαθρός, ὑπόσαθρος (see index to Foerster).

⁶³ For Shelley's and Milton's voices see Berry 67, 85 ff. (Cf. the actor Charles Kean's voice as described by Wilson 79 f.)

[64] For Pericles' firm πλάσμα see Plutarch, *Pericles* 5 and Krumbacher 7, 14. See LSJ on πλάσμα and πεπλασμένος and cf. p. 10.

[65] See LSJ at φωνασκέω (and cognates) and Krumbacher.

[66] On ὑπόκρισις see Krumbacher; John William Basore, *The Scholia on Hypocrisis in the Commentary of Donatus* (Baltimore, 1908); Bruno Zucchelli, Ὑποκριτης: *Origine e storia del termine* (Genoa, 1962); the passages cited by Caplan on *Rhetorica ad Herennium* 3,14,25 ff.; Hanschke 68 ff.; and Sonkowsky. The Anonymous Commentator on Aristotle, *Rhet.* 3,1 (1403B 18 ff.) recommends orators to use a high voice for a woman's part or for a mourner, a deep voice for a hero, and a rough, loud one for an angry man. See also Stephanos and Simplicius on the same passage. These commentators follow Aristotle in warning against overdoing such ὑπόκρισις. Cf. Dionysios Thrax §2. A noteworthy feature of the later style of ὑπόκρισις was the κρότος τῆς γλώσσης (or τῶν πνευμάτων) mentioned by Philostratos, *Lives of Sophists* 1,25,7; 2,25,6; Eunapios 489; Dionysios 14; Quintilian 11,3,33; Cicero, *De Orat.* 3,11,41. It seems to have been some kind of percussive voice-quality in orating. Philostratos, *Lives* 590 says that Adrian of Tyre preferred the style of the "ancient sophists" (ἀρχαίων σοφιστῶν) who used "resonance" (ἦχος), not κρότος, in their delivery.

[67] But orators had to care for facial expression: see chap. i, nn. 39–41.

[68] See *Scriptores Physiognomici*, ed. R. Foerster (Leipzig, 1893) 1,20,13 ff.; 1,24,3 ff.; 1,32,2; 1,348,5; 1,404 ff. and his index at ἦχος, φθέγγεσθαι, φθέγμα, φθόγγος, φωνή, φωνεῖν. Theophrastos, *Characters* 6,7 says that the man of ἀπόνοια argues with a loud and cracked (παρερρωγυίᾳ) voice. Cf. chap. i, n. 39. See LSJ at λιγύς, λιγυρός and A. J. Van Windekens in *Glotta* XXXV (1956) 208–213.

[69] Pindar, *Olympians* 6,82.

[70] "Aristotle," *De audib.* 804A 21 ff. Cf. 801B 22 ff., for vocal λαμπροτης.

[71] *Odyssey* 18,570–1. Cf. chap. v, n. 29.

[72] Bachtin 29.

[73] Diogenes Laertius, *Lives* 4,27: ἀπελέκητον ἔχειν φωνὴν καὶ φλοιοῦ μεστήν. Cf. chap. ii, n. 42.

[74] *Iliad* 3,152. Cf. the parody in Diogenes Laertius 3,7.

[75] *King Lear* v, iii, 272 f.

[76] See, e.g., the ref. in n. 52 *supra* and Philostratos, *Lives* 1,8,489.

[77] See "Aristotle," *Problems* 19,26 (cf. 19,46).

[78] ὁ κύριος τόνος: see Appendix, n. 6.

Appendix

REMARKS ON THE PRONUNCIATION
OF THE GREEK PITCH ACCENT

THERE ARE three main questions to be asked:

1. How much does the surviving evidence clearly tell about the nature of the accentuation?

2. Can we on the basis of that information learn to pronounce the classical accents adequately?

3. If the answer to question two is affirmative, then would the expense of time and energy needed for learning to pronounce those accents be justified in terms of literary appreciation?

The third question I have tried to answer in earlier pages.[1] Clearly there are at least some passages in Greek literature whose force depends on pronouncing the accents correctly. The first question has been widely discussed elsewhere.[2] I shall not try even to summarize the complex and controversial evidence here. On the whole I believe that there is fairly wide agreement about the nature of the acute and circumflex accents, but not about the grave. The acute accentuation seems to have been an upward glide of the voice within a gamut of approximately a fifth (say, C to G or *doh* to *soh*). Probably—but this is not attested in the evidence—only the higher tones of this upward glide were clearly audible, and the peak note, *soh*, was probably the salient tone, i.e., the point of maximum audibility. The circumflex apparently consisted in an upward glide similar to the acute on the first part of the vowel— which was always long—and a downward glide, also within the gamut of about a fifth, on the second part. Probably—but here again there is no evidence—the falling tone did not audibly descend all the way from *soh* to *doh*. Perhaps it reached its salient tone round about *mi* or E in the range C–G. As suggested in chapter ii, we use approximation to these pitch-variations in our interrogative "Yés?" and dubious "Yé-ès."

The vowels which are left without any accent-mark in a modern Greek text, e.g., the first two in ἀρετή, were apparently pronounced at a pitch-level approximating to the low note of the *doh-soh* gamut. It must be emphasized that except in actual singing the voice does not normally remain stationary on a single note, but constantly changes its pitch; so that when I use musical notation here, the notes only indicate the focal point, or the terminal points, of the pitch-variation. And it must also be emphasized that the pitch of these focal or terminal points may vary. For example, the top note in the interrogative τίς seems to have been higher than the normal acute as in ἀρετή, and the grave in prepositions (as in ἀνὰ λόγον) seems to have been lower than in, say, ὁ καλὸς λόγος. (The absolute level of the voice's pitch was not, of course, fixed, and would vary with changing moods or from person to person.)

So far, I believe, we are on reasonably firm ground. But the nature of what I shall call the oxytone-grave, as in ὁ καλὸς λόγος, is very uncertain.[3] There are three main possibilities:

1. It was the same as the other kind of grave, i.e., the low-pitch accentuation. If so, both syllables of καλὸς would be pronounced approximately at *doh*. The chief argument in favor of this is the fact that in the earlier accented papyri the unaccented syllables are often marked thus: ἀρὲτη or φιλὸσὸφια. But the evidence against this equation seems to me overwhelming.[4]

2. The oxytone-grave was the same as the oxytone. But, if so, why use a different symbol? And some grammarians state that in these oxytone-grave syllables the oxytone accentuation is "leveled" or "put to sleep." Also it is a characteristic of Indo-European languages to modify tone or intonation within a phrase (in sandhi).

3. The third view, which I consider the most probable, is that the oxytone-grave was a modification of the oxytone. The chief objection to this (especially in contrast with the first theory above) is that the grave sign is normally used in our earliest accented texts to indicate the low-pitch tone.[5] This can be explained if the grave-accent mark was used loosely to mean both "keep the pitch of your voice down" and "bring the pitch of your voice down (from the normal high tone)." So in φιλὸσὸφια, where the grave accent marks the low tone, it means "don't let your voice rise" or "keep your voice low," but in ὁ καλὸς λόγος it means "lower your voice from the normal high tone[6] on καλός (learned as an isolated grammatical entity)."

But, granting this, how was the oxytone-grave actually pronounced? Here there is no certain evidence at all. The best hypothesis, in my opinion, equates it with the rather mysterious μέσος τόνος, "the intermediate tone," mentioned by some grammarians.[7] If this is so, we should pronounce it as a falling tone within the gamut *soh–doh*, G–C, with perhaps a salient note round about *mi* or E. This is only a working hypothesis. But, as I have argued previously, we accept such conjectures in other fields of classics. So why not here?

According to these interpretations a line like *Odyssey* 1,1

Ἄνδρα μοι ἔννεπε, Μοῦσα, πολύτροπον ὃς μάλα πολλὰ

would have sounded, if sung, something like

Ἄν – δρα μοι ἐν – νε – πε Μοῦ___ σα πο – λύ – τρο – πον ὃς μά – λα πολ – λὰ

or, if spoken in the "intermediate" intonation, something like this (the arrows indicate rising or falling *portamenti*):

In conversational tones the musical notes would lose their emphasis and the voice would move continually in micro-intervals.

The general effect of the more musical renderings would resemble a kind of three-note chant. In theory this would seem to imply monotony. But in practice, when the three main pitch levels are slightly modified, as they should be, to meet the inherent pitch-variations in the different vowels[8] and to express emotional variations, the effect would not be monotonous.[9]

In this brief and simplified outline of a very complicated subject I have omitted several far from negligible matters, as, for example, the fact that the Greeks were aware of other types of tone-variation in words (e.g., the inverted, down-up circumflex, now to be heard in Swedish), and the formidable problem of sentence-intonation (see p. 146). But what I have said will, I hope, give a reasonably practicable method of reviving the ancient pitch-accent. There is no need whatever for the learner, with our good modern texts at hand, to study the Byzantine rules for placing the accents on a written text, except when he comes to write his own compositions—and even then, if he has learned his accents well by ear, he will be able to write many of them, as Aristophanes in Alexandria did, without benefit of Byzantium.[10]

Finally, from my own experience in North America, Britain, and Ireland, I can affirm that attempts to pronounce and teach the ancient Greek pitch-accent, far from dismaying and discouraging students, stimulate active interest, enquiry, and emulation. Even for Greekless students the unusual melodic patterns seem to catch their ear and arouse their interest more than Greek spoken in the Neo-Hellenic or Anglicizing ways, as if the archaic voice-melodies still retained some of the incantatory power that the ancient Greeks felt in the mere melodies of Greek.

NOTES TO APPENDIX

[1] See Index at *accentuation*.

[2] See especially Chandler, Galton, Hanschke, Laum, Lejeune, Pernot, Schwyzer, Sturtevant, Vendryès, Wackernagel; also the standard works by Bally, Ehrlich, Juret, Kurylowitz, Meillet, Postgate, A. Schmitt; also W. S. Allen in *In Memory of J. R. Firth* (London, 1966) 8–14.

[3] On the grave accent see especially Galton, Laum, Schwyzer, and Sturtevant.

[4] The chief arguments are: (*a*) in modern Greek final graves are stressed; (*b*) final graves are not lost in elision, but become acutes on the previous syllable; (*c*) dissyllabic enclitics give an acute accent to a preceding word in phrases like ἄνθρωποί τινες (against ἄνδρες τινὲς δή); (*d*) it is unlikely that a phrase like εἰ μὴ μητρυιὴ περικαλλὴς Ἠερίβοια would have eleven syllables all with a low-level tone; (*e*)

occasionally the papyri mark a final grave as an acute (e.g., ἐμὸν ξεινοις: see Schwyzer 386); (*f*) the statements in Plato, *Cratylos* 399B and Dionysios 11,127,20 ff. imply that in words like Διί and λευκὸν the final tone resembled the acute; (*g*) the evidence of Greek music on the whole seems to imply that the final grave was nearer the acute than the low-level grave; (*h*) the final grave was specially retained in Byzantine MSS when the other graves were discarded.

[5] See Laum; Schwyzer; and Wilhelm Schubart, *Das Buch bei den Griechen und Römern* (2d ed., 1921) 81–84, 136. Sobolevskij in *Gardthausen Palaeographiam Graecam* II 394 (Artaxerxes, 1924) notes forms like δὲ and ἐπεὶ in some minuscule MSS and deduces a different tone from, say, νομὸν δή. (Wackernagel 1198 cites Jos. Giessler, *Prosodische Zeichen in den antiken Handschriften griech. Lyriker*, which I have not yet seen.) Schwyzer 377 ff. cites the curious form πὸλλ' ἔπαθεν for πόλλ'.

[6] The acute tone (not the low-level grave) was "the master tone" (ὁ κύριος τόνος): see Dionysios Thrax, *Supp.* 674,32; cf. "Aristotle," *Problems* 19,33.

[7] See Sturtevant 98 ff.; Wackernagel 1072 ff., 1192 f.; and Hanschke 112 ff. The remark in Plato, *Philebos* 17c deserves more consideration.

[8] See p. 147.

[9] See pp. 146 ff. Some modern poets have adopted a rather limited tone-pattern for reading their poems. Cf. chap. ii, n. 8.

[10] See pp. 32 ff.

ADDITIONAL NOTE TO APPENDIX

On the views of eighteenth-century British scholars on accentuation, see M. L. Clarke, *Greek Studies in England 1700–1830* (Cambridge, 1945).

Selective Bibliography

(For abbreviations of titles of periodicals see beginning of footnotes to chapter 1.)

Allen, W. Sidney. *Vox Latina*. Cambridge, 1965.

Aristides Quintilianus. *De Musica*, ed. R. P. Winnington-Ingram. Leipzig, 1963.

Bachtin, N. *Introduction to the Greek Language*. Cambridge, 1935.

Balogh, Josef. *Voces Paginarium*. Leipzig, 1927. Reprinted from *Ph.*, LXXXII (1926–27), 84–109, 202–240.

Bassett, S. E. *The Poetry of Homer*. Berkeley, 1938.

Berry, F. *Poetry and the Physical Voice*. London, 1962.

Berry, M. F., and J. Eisenson. *Speech Disorders*. London, 1956.

Blass, Friedrich. *The Pronunciation of Modern Greek*, 3d ed., trans. W. J. Purton. Cambridge, 1890.

———. *Über die Aussprache des Griechischen*, 3d ed. Berlin, 1888.

Bonner, S. F. *The Literary Treatises of Dionysius of Halicarnassos*. Cambridge, 1939.

Brink, C. O. *Horace on Poetry*. Cambridge, 1963.

Brugmann, Karl. *Vergleichende Laut-, Stammbildungs-, und Flexionslehre der Indogermanischen Sprachen*, 2d ed. Berlin, 1930.

Bücher, K. *Arbeit und Rhythmus*, 4th ed. Leipzig, 1909.

Bywater, Ingram. *The Erasmian Pronunciation of Greek and Its Precursors Jerome Aleander, Aldus Manutius, Antonio of Lebrixa*. London, 1908.

Chandler, Henry W. *A Practical Guide to Greek Accentuation*. Oxford, 1862.

Crystal, David, and Randolph Quirk. *Systems of Prosodic and Paralinguistic Features in English*. The Hague, 1964.

De Lacy, Phillip. *Stoic Views of Poetry*. *AJP*, LXIX (1948), 241–271.

Demetrios. *See* Roberts.

Diels, H., and W. Kranz. *Die Fragmente der Vorsokratiker*, 5th ed. Berlin, 1934, 1935.

Dionysios. *See* Roberts.

Dornseiff, Franz. *Das Alphabet in Mystik und Magie*. Leipzig, 1922 (2d ed., 1925).

———. *Buchstabenmystik*. Leipzig, 1916.

Drerup, Engelbert. *Die Schulaussprache des Griechischen von der Renaissance bis zur Gegenwort*. 2 vols. Paderborn, 1930, 1932.

Edmonds, J. W. *The Fragments of Attic Comedy*. 4 vols. Leiden, 1957–61.

FitzGibbon, Constantine. *The Life of Dylan Thomas*. Boston, 1965.

Fowler, H. N. *Plato with an English Translation*. Vol. VI. London, 1926.

Gerber, Gustav. *Die Sprache als Kunst*. 2 vols. Berlin, 1885.

Gildersleeve, Basil. *Studies in Honor of . . . .* Baltimore, 1902.

Givler, R. C. 'The Psycho-Physiological Effect of the Elements of Speech in Rela-
    tion to Poetry,' *Psychological Monographs*, XIX, pt. 2 (1915).
Gleason, H. A., Jr. *An Introduction to Descriptive Linguistics*, rev. ed. New York,
    1961.
Gomperz, T. "Philodem und die aesthetischen Schriften der Herculanischen Biblio-
    thek," *Sitzungsberichte der kaiserlichen Akademie der Wissenschaften*, 123 Band
    (Vienna, 1891), No. VI, 1–88.
Goodwin, W. W., and Gulick, C. B. *Greek Grammar*. Boston, 1930.
Grammont, M. *Le vers francais, ses moyens d'expression, son harmonie*, 3d ed. Paris,
    1923.
———. *Phonétique du grec ancien*. Lyon, 1948.
Graves, Robert. *The Common Asphodel*. London, 1949.
Grove, G. *A Dictionary of Music and Musicians*, 5th ed. London, 1954.
Grube, G. M. A. *The Greek and Roman Critics*. London, 1965.
Guiraud, P. *Langage et versification d'après l'oeuvre de Paul Valéry*. Paris, 1953.
Gurney, P. *The Appreciation of Poetry*. London, 1935.
Hanschke, Paul. *De Accentuum Graecorum Nominibus*. Bonn, 1914.
Hausrath, Augustus. "Philodemi περὶ ποιημάτων libri secundi quae videntur frag-
    menta." *Jahrbücher für classische Philologie, siebzehnter Supplementband*. Leip-
    zig, 1890.
Havelock, Eric A. *Preface to Plato*. Cambridge, Mass., 1963.
Havercamp, Sigebert. *Sylloge scriptorum qui de linguae Graecae vera et recta pro-
    nuntiatione commentarios reliquerunt*. 2 vols. Leyden, 1736, 1740.
Herescu, N. I. 'Poétique ancienne et moderne au sujet de l'euphonie.' *Mélanges* . . .
    offerts à J. Marouzeau. Paris, 1948.
Hilgard, A. *Scholia in Dionysii Thracis Artem Grammaticam*. Leipzig, 1901.
Jensen, Christian. *Philodemus über die Gedichte*. Berlin, 1923.
Jespersen, O. *Language*. London, 1922.
Johnson, Charles W. L. *Musical Pitch and the Measurement of Intervals Among the
    Ancient Greeks*. Baltimore, 1896.
Jones, Daniel. *An Outline of English Phonetics*, 9th ed. Cambridge, 1960.
Joos, Martin. 'Acoustic Phonetics,' suppl. to *Language*, Vol. 24. Baltimore, 1948.
Kemke, Ioannes. *Philodemi de Musica Librorum quae exstant*. Leipzig, 1884.
Kingdon, Roger. *English Intonation Practice*. London, 1958.
———. *The Groundwork of English Intonation*. London, 1958.
Kourmoules, George I. 'ΚΑΚΟΦΩΝΙΑ ΚΑΙ ΠΡΟΦΥΛΑΞΙΣ,' *Epeteris of the School of
    Philosophy of the University of Athens* (1953–54), 201–218.
Krumbacher, Armin. *Die Stimmbildung der Redner im Altertum bis auf die Zeit
    Quintilians.* Paderborn, 1920.
Lanier, Sidney. *The Science of English Verse*. New York, 1903.
Lasserre, François. *Plutarque de la musique*. Olten and Lausanne, 1954.
Laum, B. *Das Alexandrinische Akzentuationssystem* Paderborn, 1928.
Lejeune, Michel. *Traité de phonétique grecque*, 2d ed. Paris, 1955.
Lentz, August. *Herodiani technici reliquiae*. Leipzig, 1867–70.
Maas, Paul. *Greek Metre*, trans. Hugh Lloyd-Jones. Oxford, 1961.
Macdermott, M. M. *Vowel Sounds in Poetry: Their Music and Tone-Colour*. London,
    1940.

Marouzeau, Jules. *Traité de stylistique appliquée au latin*. Paris, 1935.

McKay, K. J. 'The Poet at Play: Kallimachos, The Bath of Pallas.' *Mnemosyne*, suppl. 6 (1962).

Meisterhans, K., and Eduard Schwyzer. *Grammatik der attischen Inschriften*, 3d ed. Berlin, 1900.

Méridier, Louis. *Platon, oeuvres complètes*. Tome V, *Cratyle*. Paris, 1950.

Miller, D. C. *Anecdotal History of the Science of Sound*. New York, 1935.

Muller, G. A. *Language and Communication*. New York, 1951.

Norden, E. *Die Antike Kunstprosa*, 3d ed. 2 vols. Leipzig, 1915, 1918.

Ogden, R. M. *Hearing*. London, 1924.

Paget, Richard. *Human Speech*. London, 1930.

Pernot, H. *Phonétique des parlers de Chio*. Paris, 1907.

Philodemos. *See* Gomperz, Hausrath, Jensen, Kemke, Sudhaus.

Pickard-Cambridge, A. W. *Dithyramb Tragedy and Comedy*, 2d ed. rev. T. B. L. Webster. Oxford, 1962.

Platt, A. *Nine Essays*. Cambridge, 1927.

———. 'On Homeric Technique,' CR, XXXV (1921), 141–143.

Pulgram, Ernst. *Introduction to the Spectrography of Speech*. The Hague, 1959.

Raymond, G. L. *Rhythm and Harmony in Poetry and Music*. New York, 1895.

Richards, I. A. *Practical Criticism*. London, 1929.

Robbins, Samuel D. *A Dictionary of Speech Pathology and Therapy*. London, 1962.

Roberts, W. Rhys. *Demetrius on Style*. Cambridge, 1902.

———. *Dionysius of Halicarnassus on Literary Composition*. London, 1910.

———. *Longinus on the Sublime*, 2d ed. Cambridge, 1899.

Rossi, L. E. *Metrica e critica stilistica: il termine 'ciclico' e l'ἀγωγή ritmica*. Rome, 1963.

Roussel, Louis. 'Grec ancien parlé.' *Mélanges H. Grégoire*, I (Brussels, 1949), 511–515.

———. *Le vers grec ancien*. Montpellier, 1954.

Schmid, W., and O. Stählin. *Geschichte der Griechischen Literatur*. Munich, 1929 and later.

Schneider, R. *Apollonii Dyscoli quae supersunt*. Leipzig, 1910.

Schwyzer, Eduard. *Griechische Grammatik*. 3 vols. Munich, 1939–53.

Shewan, A. 'Alliteration and Assonance in Homer,' CP, XX, (1925), 193–209.

Skutsch, O. 'Sound and Sense in Virgil,' *Virgil Society Lecture Summaries*, Vol. 33. London, 1954.

Snell, B. *Der Aufbau der Sprache*. Hamburg, 1952.

Sonkowsky, Robert F. 'Delivery in Ancient Rhetoric,' TAPA, XC (1959), 256–274.

Stanford, W. B. *Aeschylus in His Style*. Dublin, 1942.

———. *Ambiguity in Greek Literature*. Oxford, 1939.

———. *Greek Metaphor*. Oxford, 1936.

———. 'Greek Views on Euphony,' *Hermathena*, LXI (1943), 3–20.

Strunk, Klaus. "Sprachliches und Prosodisches zur mykenischen Orthographie," *IF*, LVI (1961), 155–170.

Sudhaus, S. *Philodemi Volumina Rhetorica*. Leipzig, 1892.

Szemerényi, O. *Syncope in Greek and Indo-European and the Nature of the Indo-European Accent*. Naples, 1964.

Thomson, George. *The Greek Language*. Cambridge, 1960.

Todd, O. J. 'Sense and Sound in Classical Poetry,' *CQ*, XXXVI (1942), 29–39.

Tucker, R. Whitney. 'On the Dual Pronunciation of *Eta*,' *TAPA*, xciii (1962), 490–501.

Tylor, Edward B. *Primitive Culture*, 5th ed. Vol. 1. London, 1913.

Uhlig, G. *Dionysii Thracis Ars Grammatica*. Leipzig, 1883.

Van Groningen, B. A. 'La poésie verbale en grecque,' *Medelingen der Koninklijke Nederlandse Akademie van Wetenschappen, Afd. Letterkunde*. Nieuwe Reeks Deel, 16, 4. (Amsterdam, 1953).

Vendryès, J. *Language*, trans. P. Redin. London, 1925.

———. *Traité d'accentuation grecque*. Paris, 1904.

Verdenius, W. J. 'Der Ursprung der Philologie,' *Studium Generale*, 19, 2 (1966), 103–114.

Verrall, A. W. *The Bacchants of Euripides and Other Essays*. Cambridge, 1910.

Wace, A. J. B., and Stubbings, F. H. *A Companion to Homer*. London, 1962.

Wackernagel, Jacob. *Kleine Schriften*. Vol. 2. Göttingen, 1953.

Walz, Christian. *Rhetores Graeci*. Stuttgart, 1832–36.

Wellek, R., and Warren, A. *Theory of Literature*, 2d ed. New York, 1956.

Wilson, Katharine M. *Sound and Meaning in English Poetry*. London, 1930.

Wilkinson. L. P. *Golden Latin Artistry*. Cambridge, 1963.

Wood, Alexander. *The Physics of Music*, 6th ed., rev. J. M. Bowsher. London, 1962.

Zacher, K. *Die Aussprache des Griechischen*. Leipzig, 1888.

Zielinski, Thaddeus. *Tragodumenon Libri Tres*. Cracow, 1965.

Indexes

A. GENERAL INDEX

(For Greek and Latin authors and words, see also Indexes B and C.)

accentuation, 23n. 33, 24n. 45, 24n. 46, 30 ff., 40, 60, 63, 65, 66, 85, 96n. 33, 128 f., 131 ff., 141, 145, 146 f., 153n. 43, 157 ff.
acrostics, 85
acute accent, 133, 145, 157 ff.
Aelius Dionysius, 69n. 31
Aeolic dialect, 66
Aeschines, 31, 37, 154n. 52
Aeschylus, 38, 54, 67n. 3, 81, 88, 97n. 57, 104
aesthetic considerations, 8, 13 f., 15, 48 ff., 56, 57 f., 61, 67n. 5, 79, 80, 112 f., 134 f., 148
agma, 77, 94n. 7
Alcibiades, 53, 141 f., 149
alliteration, 17, 76, 84 f.
alpha, 24n. 51, 51 f., 81, 82, 104
alphabet, 22n. 25, 77. *See also* letters
Ambrose, St., 2, 29
America, 63, 159
Amphialos, 75
amphibrach, 16
anagrams, 75, 85, 87
anapaests, 16, 115, 119n. 40
anaphora, 86 f.
anaptyxis, 60
animals, cries of, 102 f., 117n. 14
Antony (Antonius), Mark, 150
aphaeresis, 71n. 74.
Apollonius Dyskolos, 70n. 48
Aratos, 120n. 72. *See also* Index B
Archinos, 10
architectonic euphony, 79, 92, 144
Aristides Quintilianus. *See* Index B
Aristophanes, 85, 88, 102, 112, 123 f. *See also* Index B
Aristophanes of Byzantium, 32, 159

Aristotle, 6, 17, 58, 80, 92 f., 141 f. *See also* Index B
Aristoxenos, 17, 28
Arnold, Matthew, 114
Arrian, 58
articulation, 144 ff.
asigmatic odes, 8, 69n. 31
aspirated letters, 55, 62 f., 152n. 7. *See also chi*, etc.
assimilation, 62
assonance, 66, 75, 76, 84 ff, 104, 139n. 37
Attic dialect, 11, 18, 54, 62, 73n. 99
Augustine, St., 2
Augustus, 2, 29

baccheios, 16
barbarism, 10, 30, 140
Battos, 142
beauty of sound. *See* aesthetic considerations
beta, 55, 65, 123, 124
Bion, 114
birds, cries and song of, 102 f., 117n. 14
Boeotian, 124
Browning, Robert, 105
Burns, Robert, 66
Byzantine Greek, 130 f., 159, 160n. 4

cacophony, 56, 59, 63, 78, 112, 118n. 25. *See also* unpleasant sounds
Caesar, Gaius, 18, 29
Caesar, Julius, 2
caesura, 107, 119n. 40
Calchas, 104, 143
Callias, *Letter Tragedy* of, 9
Callimachos, 117n. 20
Campbell, Thomas, 89
Cappadocian, 141
Carroll, Lewis, 60, 111 f.
Cassandra, 114
catharsis. *See katharsis*

Catullus, 112
chi, 55, 62, 65, 112, 124 f., 140 f., 143 f.
Chamaileon, 44n. 9
Chinese, 3, 4, 21n. 15, 31, 34, 129
Chremes, 103
Churchill, Sir Winston, 45n. 22
cicadas, sound of, 35, 149, 150
Cicero, 18. *See also* Index B
circumflex accent, 87, 90, 114, 133, 157 ff.
Clare, John, 35
Claudius (emperor), 72n. 85
Cleon, 142, 147
Cleopatra, 111
colours compared with sounds, 34
consonantal groups, 59, 61 ff., 83
consonants, 52 ff., 59, 61 ff., 83 ff., 107 f.
contraction, 71n. 75, 143
conundrums, 85
Coptic, 123
Cowper, William, 105
Crantor, 150
crasis, 71n. 75
Crashaw, Richard, 34
Crates of Mallos, 18
Cyclops, 90 f.

dactyls, 41, 48n. 74, 107 f., 118n. 25
Dante, 34
deictic iota, 72n. 81
Delian women, 111
delta, 9, 13, 55
Demetrios (rhetorician), 18. *See also* Index B
Demokritos, 9, 10, 50, 67n. 3
Demosthenes, 31, 37, 58, 59, 79, 141 ff.
diaeresis, 142
dialects: 65 f., 152n. 20. *See also* under names of dialects

diarthrosis, 144 ff. *See also* Index B

dictation, 3

Dionysios of Halicarnassos, 8, 14–17, 51 ff., 76. *See also* Index B

Dionysios of Thrace, 17, 20n. 5, 68n. 8

diphthongs, 50, 68n. 8, 129, 137n. 22, 141

distorted words, 111 f., 118n. 25

division of syllables, 114 ff., 154n. 46

Doric dialect, 25n. 51, 66, 73n. 99, 81, 106

double letters, 55. *See also zeta*, etc.

Dryden, John, 87, 114

e, 77. *See also epsilon*; *eta*

ear, effect of sounds on, 34, 56

ear-philology, 1, 100, 116

ecstasy, 79

Egypt, 3, 58, 82

elision, 58 f., 61

emotions, and emotive language, 78 ff., 87 ff., 92 f., 103, 113 f., 147 f.

English language, 66, 123, 126, 129, 132, 137n. 18, 147

epanaphora, 86

Epicureans, 18, 51

epsilon, 13, 24n. 45, 52, 82

Erasmian pronunciation, 126 ff.

eta, 13, 24n. 45, 24n. 51, 51 f., 82, 128, 129, 137n. 22

"ethical" mimesis (*ethos*), 115, 149, 155n. 66

etymology, 8, 94n. 2, 153n. 40

euphony, *euphonia*, 2, 6 ff., 48–121 *passim*

Euripides, 10, 31, 39, 54, 84, 87, 88

exclamations, 103, 107, 114, 120n. 67

eye-philology, 1, 96n. 31, 116

f, 64, 123

foreigners, pronunciation of Greek by, 71n. 72, 140 ff.

French, 62, 124, 137n. 18, 146, 147

Galen, 36

gamma, 9, 13, 55, 77, 109 ff., 142

Gardiner, Bishop Stephen, 127

Gellius, Aulus, 18. *See also* Index B

gemination, 52

German, 126

gestures, vocal, 12 f., 105 f., 109

Gladstone, William E., 28

glide sounds, 71n. 77

glottal stop, 57, 153n. 38

Gorgias, 9, 95n. 30

Gosse, Sir Edmund, 135

grandeur in sounds, 13, 25n. 21, 25n. 22

grave accent, 133, 145, 153n. 43, 157 ff.

greatness in sounds. *See* grandeur in sounds

Greek, modern, 62, 63, 125 f., 141, 150, 159n. 4

gutturals, 62

Handel, 111

harmonics. *See* partials

Hebrew, 123, 136n. 6

Hegelochos, 31

Helen of Troy, 111, 112

Hellenism, linguistic, 140 ff.

Henningian pronunciation, 126 ff., 138n. 31

Herakleitos, 8 f.

Hercules, 38, 54

Herodotos, 59, 75, 94n. 3

Herophilos, 47n. 55

Hesiod, 7. *See also* Index B

hexameters, 36, 118n. 25. *See also* dactyls

hiatus, 57 ff., 107

Hippias, 9

Hippocratic writers, 34

Hirrus, 141

Hitler, Adolf, 39

Homer, 7, 9, 36, 54, 66, 70n. 40, 85, 86, 88, 94n. 6, 113, 118n. 25, 139n. 33

homoikatarkton, 83 f.

homoioteleuton, 83

honey in imagery and mimesis, 15, 34

Horace, 52. *See also* Index B

hyperbaton, 94n. 3

Hyperbolos, 142

i, 75, 77, 123, 125. *See also iota*

Incroyables, 152n. 17

indeterminate vowel. *See* schwa

intensity of sound, 38 f.

intersensal metaphors. *See* synaesthetic metaphors

intonation, 5, 7, 28 f., 45n. 27, 114, 138n. 33, 146 ff., 150 f., 157 ff.

Ionic dialect, 73nn. 98–99

iota, 12 f., 51 f., 72n. 81, 82, 123, 125. *See also i*

iotacism, 52, 65, 142

Irish language, 109, 123

isocolon, 84

Isocrates, 37, 59, 96n. 37, 145, 148, 152n. 18

Italian, 53, 62

jingles, 85

Joyce, James, 29

k, kappa, 55, 61, 104, 109, 112, 120n. 59

katharsis, 92 f.

Keats, John, 100, 109

Keller, Helen, 138n. 3

kinaesthetic mimesis, 110 f.

Klangfarbe. See timbre-quality

l and *ll*, 52. *See also lambda*

Lalage, 103

lambda (*labda*), 13, 14, 52, 109 ff., 141 f.

lambdakismos, 141 f.

Lasos of Hermione, 7 f.

Latin, 52, 55, 61–64 *passim*, 72n. 94, 122 ff., 136n. 6, 137n. 18, 145

latinizing pronunciation of Greek, 126 ff.

letter-frequencies, 97 additional n.

letters, alphabetical, 1, 22n. 25, 35, 77, 130. *See also alpha*, etc.

Libanios, 58

Licymnios, 9

Linear B. *See* Mycenaean Greek

lipogrammatism, 152n. 18

liquid letters, 52, 55

lisping, 141 f.

Longfellow, Henry W., 41

"Longinus," 18, 78

long syllables. *See* quantity

long words, mimesis by, 105

loudness. *See* intensity of sound

Lucian, 18, 58, 69n. 24, 124. *See also* Index B

Lucilius, 68n. 15

lullaby, 80 f.

Lysimachos, 146

m, 53, 110. *See also mu*

magic, 15, 81 f., 89, 95n. 22

Mahaffy, John Pentland, 142

Martial, 53

melody in speech, 16, 45n. 29, 75, 114

memory, 3

Menelaos, 37

Messala, M. Valerius, 69n. 24

metre, 16, 36 f., 39 ff., 66, 76. *See also* rhythm

Metrodoros, 73n. 98

Milton, John, 37, 38, 53, 96n. 39, 105, 134, 137n. 18, 143, 148
mimesis, 10, 12 f., 14, 99–121 *passim*, 124
mimicry. *See* mimesis
monotony, 59, 62, 148, 159
Moschos, 114, 117n. 20
mousikē, 8, 23n. 3, 27, 79
mu, 9, 53, 106, 109, 118n. 37. *See also* m
Muses, 27, 50, 149
music, 48–73 *passim*, 77 ff., 92, 120n. 67, 157 ff.
mutakismos, 142
mute letters. *See* voiceless letters
Mycenaean Greek, 69n. 24, 72n. 95, 152n. 17

n, nn, 53, 75. *See also* nu
Nash, Thomas, 103
Nestor, 50, 109 f., 115
neutral vowel. *See* schwa
Nireus, 86
nu, 53, 61, 62, 110, 113, 141. *See* n

o, 13. *See also* omicron, omega
Odysseus, 37, 75, 90 f., 112
omega, 13, 33, 51, 82, 114, 120n. 72, 141
omicron, 52, 82, 120n. 72, 141
onomatopoeia. *See* mimesis
orthoëpy, 7, 9, 144, 146 f.
orthography, 124, 132
overtones. *See* partials
Ovid, 52, 64

p, 119n. 37. *See also* pi
palindromes, 85
pararhotacismus, 141 f., 149
parechesis, 83, 96n. 33
parisosis, 84
paromoiosis, 83
paronomasia, 12, 83, 94n. 2
partials, 8, 33
particles, 154n. 60
pathos, 115
patterns of sounds, 75, 84 ff., 108
Paul, St., 101, 104
Pericles, 10, 148
Persian, 123
Persius, 68n., 15
phi, 55, 64, 65, 123, 124 f., 128, 129, 137n. 22, 140 f., 143 f.
Philodemos, 26n. 73, 71n. 66, 72n. 78, 118, 121n. 72, 151n. 1, 154n. 52
Philostratos. *See* Index B

phonetics, 10, 13, 33, 54, 55 f., 71n. 72, 122–139 *passim*
Phrynichos, 4
physiognomists, 37, 149, 154n. 62
pi, 55, 110
Pindar, 3, 16, 66, 67n. 3, 83, 86, 149, 152n. 18
pitch, 30. *See also* accentuation; intonation
plateiasmos, 142
Plato, 6, 10 ff., 14, 59, 67n. 5, 93
pleasant sounds. *See* euphony
Plutarch, 29, 58. *See also* Index B
Poe, Edgar Allan, 53
Polynesian, 63
Polyphemos, 90 f.
Pope, Alexander, 25n. 65, 41
prodelision. *See* aphaeresis
Prodikos, 9, 11, 147
pronunciation of Greek, 5, 6–7, 24n. 45, 40, 60, 122–139, 140–155 *passim*, 159
prophylaxis, euphonic, 61 f., 72n. 78
prosody, 6
Protagoras, 9
prothesis, 62
proverbs, 84
psellótes, 142
psi, 55
punning. *See* paronomasia
Pythagoreans, 8, 9, 23n. 26, 24n. 42, 46n. 33, 99

quantity, 7, 63, 71n. 56, 72n. 83, 137n. 19, 137n. 22, 138n. 31
Quintilian, 2, 3, 18. *See also* Index B

r, 122, 143 *See also* rho
rate of delivery. *See* speed of speech
reading, 1–7, 148
reduplication, 117n. 16
repetition, 86 ff.
Reuchlinian pronunciation, 126 ff.
rho, 12, 14, 53, 55, 62, 69n. 24, 112, 122, 141 f.
rhopalic lines, 82
rhyme, 74 f., 83 f., 139n. 37
rhythm, 39 ff., 107, 115. *See also* metre
Roman. *See* Latin
rough sounds, 33 f., 55, 107, 112, 137n. 18, 148
Rouse, W. H. D., 129
Russia, 81

s, 8, 110, 117n. 7, 142. *See also* sigma
san, 8
Sannyrion, 44n. 20
Sanskrit, 125
Sappho, 56 f., 87
Schallwörter, 103, 118n. 23
Schliemann, Heinrich, 15, 115
schwa, 63, 64
Scott, Sir Walter, 134
semivowels, 51 ff., 57, 107
seven, symbolism of, 95n. 22
seven vowels, chant of, 58, 82
"shaggy" words, 34
Shakespeare, 12, 42, 80–88 *passim*, 104, 115, 144 f., 151 f.
Shaw, George B., 129
Shelley, Percy B., 148
shibboleth, 55
short syllables. *See* quantity
sight and sound, 34
sigma, 8, 18, 53 ff., 61, 62, 104, 110, 139 additional note
sigmatism, 54, 142
silent reading, 1 ff.
singing, 28 f., 54, 147
Sirens, 81, 83, 149
Sisyphos, 106 ff.
size, mimesis of, 118
smell: mimesis of, 110, 117n. 19; compared with sound, 34
smooth sounds, 33 f., 55
Socrates, 99, 142. *See also* Plato
solecism, 151n. 2
Sophists, 9
Sophocles, 10, 54, 67n. 3, 74, 86, 125, 152n. 18
sound-patterns. *See* patterns of sounds
speech-defects, 51, 140–155 *passim*
speed of speech, 20n. 7, 36 ff.
spelling. *See* orthography
spondaic lines, 115
stammering, 140, 142
Stentor, 38
Stoics, 18
Strattis, 44n. 20
stress, 40 ff., 63
stuttering, 140, 142
Swedish, 159
Swift, Jonathan, 21n. 14
Swinburne, Algernon C., 110
syllable-division, 144 ff.
synaesthetic metaphors, 34
synizesis, 71n. 75

t, 117n. 7. *See also* tau
tarantella, 93
Tarentine Greek, 152n. 20
taste: mimesis of, 108 ff.; compared with sound, 34

tau, 13, 18, 55, 72n. 77, 112.
    See also t
tempo. *See* speed of speech
Tennyson, Alfred, Lord, 28, 41,
    87, 88, 105
Theocritos, 38, 39, 66. *See also*
    Index B
Theophrastos, 17, 38, 79, 113
Thersites, 148
theta, 9, 55, 65, 124 f., 140 f.,
    143 f.
Thomas, Dylan, 4, 134
Thompson, Francis, 59
Thucydides, 4, 58, 75
timbre-quality, 7, 33 ff., 65, 66,
    82, 143, 148
tongue-twisters, 51, 142
touch: compared with sounds,
    35; mimesis of, 108
transliterations, 123
Triballian, 141
trochees, 16, 41, 107, 108

Tryphiodoros, 69n. 31
Tyrrhenius Postumius, 44n. 16

u, 64. *See also upsilon*
United States of America, 126
unpleasant sounds, 51, 56, 78,
    148, 150 f., 154n. 62. *See also*
    cacophony
upsilon, 33, 51, 64, 82, 103 f.,
    123, 124, 128, 137n. 22. *See*
    also u

v, 117n. 7, 123
Valery, Paul, 14, 29, 76 f.
variant forms, 66
variation, stylistic, 59 f., 66
verba intensiva, 117n. 16
Virgil, 64, 68n. 10, 77, 86, 135,
    139n. 33, 146
voiceless letters, 55, 57
voice-qualities, 29, 35, 140–155
    passim

vowels, 24n. 45, 51 ff., 57, 62–
    65 *passim*, 82 ff., 88, 114. *See*
    also alpha, etc.

water-clock, 37
weight: compared with sound,
    34; mimesis of, 106 f., 108
word-division, 144 ff., 154n. 46
Wordsworth, William, 19, 135

x, 59. *See also xi*
Xenophon, 39. *See also* Index B
xi, 55, 69n. 24

y, 62, 64
Yeats, W. B., 29, 29 f., 74 f.
Yoruba, 129

zeta, 55, 64, 69n. 24, 72n. 92,
    124 f.

B. SELECTIVE INDEX OF PASSAGES FROM GREEK AND LATIN AUTHORS

(For modern authors and some other classical authors, see Index A. Passages cited but not quoted are omitted here.)

AESCHINES
2,29................. 147
2,99............. 152n. 10
AESCHYLUS
Agam. 121,139,159..... 89
  156–7................ 104
  1076................ 114
  1343................ 113
  1345................ 113
Cho. 386–7............ 34
Eum. 130............. 88
  306 ff............... 81
P.V. 357.......... 54, 106
  364................ 64
Sev. 578.............. 144
  962................ 88
Anthologia Palatina
  5,291............. 95n. 26
  9,129............. 121n. 72
ANTIPHANES
  fr. 196 (Edmonds)... 21n. 9
ARATOS
Phainomena 1002 . 117n. 14
  fr. 334........... 96n. 39
ARISTIDES QUINTILIANUS
De Musica 1,4........ 28
  1,8................ 28
  1,10............. 43n. 6
  1,20............ 70n. 39
  2,11............ 70n. 39
  2,13............ 73n. 99
  2,14............ 70n. 39
ARISTOPHANES
Ach. 104........... 140 f.
  233.............. 123 f.
  281............ 97n. 51
Birds 227,243,260–3.... 102
  1379.......... 120n. 59
  1678–9......... 140 f.
Clouds 870 ff...... 152n. 20
  1273.......... 153n. 43
Eccl. 21–3......... 45n. 20
Frogs 136............ 85
  184............... 85
  209............... 102
  303–4............ 31
  840.............. 32
  1029............ 117

1313.............. 143
1354–5............. 88
Kn. 954........... 44n. 20
Peace 757............ 142
Plout. 278......... 96n. 39
Thesm. 48........... 36
  1001–7.......... 140 f.
  1083–1135........ 140 f.
  1176–1201........ 140 f.
  1183.............. 142
  1210–15.......... 140 f.
Wasps 36........ 154n. 53
  44–5............. 141
  40 f............ 44n. 20
ARISTOTLE (including spurious works)
De audib. 804A 21 ff.... 150
De color. 3,793A.... 70n. 50
Hist. anim. 535B 32
  .... 118n. 34
Metaph. 1,987B 11..... 98
Nic. eth. 4,8,1125A 12.. 37
Poet. 6,1450B 2........ 98
  20,1456B 30–4....... 6
  25,1461A 22 ff.... 23n. 33
Probl. 5,2.......... 47n. 64
  10,39.......... 20n. 5
  11,11.......... 46n. 36
  19,26............. 151
  19,27 and 29........ 79
Rhet. 3,1,1403B 2 ff..... 17
  3,1,1403B 20 ff....... 6
  3,1,1407B 12.... 26n. 68
  3,11,1412A 35... 154n. 46
Soph. el. 166B 1.... 23n. 33
Top. 107A 11...... 46n. 42
  112B 22.......... 67n. 1
ARISTOXENOS
Harm. 1,8 ff.......... 28
  1,10,9........... 43n. 6
AUGUSTINE
Conf. 5,13............ 29
  6,3................ 2
  8,12............... 2
BIBLE
1 Corinthians 12,14 ff.. 117
  13,1.............. 118
  13,13............. 2

Exodus 4,10...... 153n. 26
Judges 12,6.......... 55
Revelation 1,8........ 82
CALLIMACHOS
Hymn 2,101 ff..... 120n. 72
  5,139........... 117n. 20
CATULLUS
  36,1.............. 112
CICERO
Ad Att. 12,2,6........ 18
De Orat. 3,43......... 59
  3,46............ 68n. 10
Orat. 27........... 44n. 9
  161............ 69n. 24
  177.............. 56
DEMETRIOS
On Style 61–2........ 86
  63................ 86
  68............. 58, 59
  72......... 58, 71n. 56
  140 f............ 86, 87
  174............. 52
  175........... 68n. 20
  176........... 70n. 44
  177........... 73n. 99
  209........... 71n. 56
  255........... 118n. 25
DEMOKRITOS
  various frs..... 23nn. 30–32
DEMOSTHENES
On the Crown 52
  .... 32 f. (Cf. 35.)
DIOGENES LAERTIUS
Lives: 2, 108...... 152n. 10
  2,87........... 46n. 36
  4,27.............. 150
  5,38........... 26n. 70
  7,28........... 23n. 39
  8,65.............. 85
DIONYSIOS OF HALICARNASSOS
De Comp. chap. 11..... 15
  chap. 12.. 25n. 61, 33, 56
  chap. 14... 33, 51 ff., 122
  chap. 15... 33, 34, 109 f.
  chap. 16........... 66
  chap. 17.......... 83
  chap. 19... 59 f., 71n. 64

chap. 20..... 59, 70n. 49,
        106 f., 153n. 38
chap. 22.. 16, 59, 95n. 30
chap. 23............ 56
chap. 25........ 17, 76
De Demosth. 22.... 94n. 10
    38.............. 47n. 46
    40............. 72n. 78
    42................ 59
    43............... 83
EUBULUS
    frs. 26–7 (Edmonds) 69n. 30
EURIPIDES
    Alc. 782.............. 84
    Bacch. 1065......... 87
    Hipp. 621............ 82
    I.T. 763........... 21n. 9
    Med. 476............. 54
    Or. 279.............. 31
    Rhes. 674–6.......... 88
    fr. 382............ 23n. 37
EUSTATHIOS
    on *Il.* 1,1
    ... 23n. 41, 70n. 48, 71n. 56
    on *Il.* 1,54........ 96n. 38
    on *Il.* 10,409...... 69n. 31
    488,12 ff.......... 96n. 38
    768,12 ff............. 103
    855,17........... 120n. 67
    1273,41.......... 72n. 78
    1400,20 .... 71n. 66
    1721,26.......... 119n. 37
GELLIUS, AULUS
    Noct. Att. 10,4.... 24n. 48
        13,21.... 68n. 10, 76
HERAKLEITOS
    various frs..... 23nn. 30–31
HERODOTOS
    1,139............. 69n. 23
    4,155–6............. 142
HESIOD
    Theog. 686....... 118n. 21
    Works 208....... 117n. 14
HOMER
    Iliad 1,1.......... 23n. 41
        45............. 53, 86
        82–3............. 143
        248 f....... 50, 110
        436–9........... 86
        783............. 146
    2,222............ 148
        235.......... 120n. 59
        455 ff.......... 111 f.
        471............ 111 f.
        666............. 63
        671–3........... 86
        867............ 140
    3,152....... 35, 150
        213–24........... 37
        363............ 112
    4,20.............. 106
        125.. 118nn. 25 and 29

6,168.......... 22n. 15
    344............ 112
8,206 f........ 154n. 46
9,67........... 71n. 66
10,228–31......... 86 f.
12,208........ 118n. 25
16,357......... 67n. 2
17,265......... 71n. 66
    756........... 34
18,109........... 110
    576........... 34
20,49......... 71n. 66
21,1–16........... 89 f.
22,127–8.......... 88
23,116........... 105
Odyssey 1,1....... 41, 158
3,272.......... 96n. 40
4,136–7........ 96n. 33
    279........... 111
5,61........... 83
    402........... 141
6,122........... 103
    137........... 112
    162 f........... 113
8,128 ff............ 75
9,71........... 112
    366 ff......... 90 f.
    405–6......... 90 f.
    414........... 90 f.
    422........... 90 f.
    455........... 90 f.
    460........... 90 f.
    515........... 91
10,221........... 83
    227........... 83
11,49......... 96n. 33
    593 ff......... 106 ff.
    596........... 107
    598........... 108
12,44........... 83
    183........... 83
    184 ff........ 19n. 40
    265–6........ 119n. 37
    369........... 104
    430........ 106, 113
15,74........... 84
18,570–1........... 150
19,457 f........... 81
20,19–21........ 90 f.
24,340–342........ 75
See also EUSTATHIOS
on
HORACE
    Odes 1,22,23......... 52
    4,6,35–6.......... 40
    Sat. 1,3,64–5...... 20n. 8
        1,6,122 f....... 20n. 8
        2,5,55......... 20n. 7
Hymn to Delian Apollo
    162–3............. 111
ISOCRATES
    Phil. 26............ 148

"LONGINUS'
    De Subl. 39.......... 78
LUCIAN
    Adv. Indoct. 2...... 20n. 7
    De Salt. 27........ 44n. 9
    Iudicium sept. voc. passim
    .... *See* Lucian in Index A
LUCRETIUS
    4,13................ 109
MARTIAL
    1,101............... 53
MENANDER
    fr. 381 (Edmonds)
        44n. 20
OVID
    Fasti 4,439–40....... 64
PERSIUS............. 68n. 17
PETRONIUS
    Sat. 115.......... 21n. 14
PHILOSTRATOS
    Vit. Soph. 505........ 147
    509............ 147
    590......... 155n. 66
    594........... 141
PINDAR
    Isthm. 1,1........ 83
    Nem. 4,1......... 83
    Ol. 1,1......... 83
        4,13.......... 86
        6,4........... 3
        6,82...... 149 f.
        7,9........... 86
    Pyth. 1,1......... 83
        5,55–62...... 142
    fr. 61,1–2 (Bowra)..... 8
PLATO
    Cratylos passim
        .... 10–15, 67n. 5
        404C.... 68n. 15, 96n. 38
        432B–C.......... 116n. 6
        414C.......... 72n. 79
    Laws 701D...... 153n. 43
    Phaidros 274C..... 21n. 15
    Philebos 17C......... 6
        51C........... 57
    Rep. 601B....... 117n. 9
    Theait. 203B...... 69n. 23
    Tim. 22B........... 3
        80A–B...... 45n. 33
PLATO COMICUS
    fr. 168 (Edmonds)..... 142
PLUTARCH (including spuri-
    ous works)
    Alcib. 1 and 41....... 141
    Brutus 5....... 20n. 8
    De aud. poet. 2,38A.... 79
        7,47D........... 29
    De musica 2....... 21n. 15
    Mark Antony 27....... 111
    Moralia 845B....... 43n. 7
    Pericles 5........ 155n. 64
    Quaest. conv. 9, 2... 24n. 51

QUINTILIAN

1,1,34.............. 20n. 7
1,4,17............. 68n. 10
1,7,31................ 3
1,7,33–35............. 8
1,8,2................ 29
1,10,9............... 27
9,4,51............. 48n. 72
9,4,116.............. 56
11,3,45............ 71n. 66
12,10,23........... 69n. 24
12,10,27............. 64
12,10,31............. 53
12,10,33........... 72n. 94
12,10,57........... 152n. 7

SAPPHO

Aphrodite ode........ 56 f.
maidenhood fr........ 87
Hesperos fr.......... 87

SEXTUS EMPIRICUS

Adv. Prof. 1,169.... 45n. 30
6,44............... 34

SOPHOCLES

Aj. 39............... 54
322................ 148

675................ 86
677................ 114
807 f 96n. 37
El. 1036............. 60
O.T. 371.......... 84, 143
932............. 67n. 3
1397.............. 112
Phil. 101............ 60
745 f.............. 114
frs. (Pearson) 117.. 23n. 37
314............. 97n. 51

STRABO

14,2,28.............. 140

SUETONIUS

Augustus 39.......... 2

TACITUS

Annals 11,14...... 72n. 85

THEOCRITOS

Idylls 1,115........ 94n. 3
2,17,22,27.......... 89
4,45.............. 39
10,40......... 120n. 72
13,58 ff 39
15,87–95........... 66
15,88............. 142

22,39............. 52
24,7–9............ 80 f.
28,1.............. 66

THEOPHRASTOS

Characters 4,1........ 39
6,7........... 155n. 68
See also Index A

THUCYDIDES

1,24................ 58
2,54............... 123
6,1................ 58

TIMOTHEOS

Persians 162–73.... 152n. 5

VIRGIL

Aeneid 2,9........ 86
2,27..... 120n. 56
3,106............. 76
9,716.............. 146
Eclogues 1,1.. 117n. 20, 135
Georgics 3,550........ 64
1,25.............. 76

XENOPHON

Memor. 3,3,13...... 67n. 4
3,10,1............ 99
On Hunting 7,5........ 39

C. SELECTIVE INDEX OF GREEK AND LATIN WORDS

(For references to single letters [such as *alpha*], see Index A.)

ἀάατος, 83
ἄγμα, 77
ἀγωγή, 47n. 53
ἀδινός, 34
Ἀθηνᾶ, 11, 66, 67n. 5
αἰαῖ: 103, 114
αἴλινα, -ον, 89, 114
ἀκούω, 20n. 5
ἀκρίβεια: 150
ἀλαλαγή, ἀλαλάζειν, 103 f.
ἀμβλύζ, 46n. 36, 106
Ἀμφίων, 152n. 7
ἀοιδή, -ος, 27, 83
Ἀρσινόη, 85
Ἄρτεμις, 11
Ἀσκληπιός, 32
ἀϋτή, 103
ἄφϋων, 31
ἄφωνα, 21n. 9, 70n. 38, 124

βαλλήναδε, 123
βάρβαρος and compounds, 44n. 16, 140
βαρύς and compounds, 34
βάττος and compounds, 21n. 14, 142
βαῦ, 102
βῆ, 102, 124
βομβαλοβομβάξ, 36
βομβυλιός, 103
βρεκεκέξ, 102, 124

γαλήν', γαλῆν, 31, 143, 154n. 46
γλ-, words beginning in, 13, 109 ff.
γλάγος, 111 f.
γοητεύεται, 15
γοόωσα, 58

δῆμος, δημός, 44n. 20
διάρθρωσις, 144 ff.
διαστολή, 146
δίδομεν/διδόμεν, 23n. 33
δυσ- compounds, 67n. 2, 153n. 36

ἐλελεῦ, 103
ἐνδατεῖσθαι, 144 f.

ἐνθουσιασμός, 15, 79
ἔρημος, 32
ἑταίρων, ἑταιρῶν, 44n. 20
ἕτοιμος, 32
ἐτυμολογία, 9
εἰειειειειειλίσσετε, 112, 143
εὐ- compounds, 50 ff., 68n. 15

ἡδυ- compounds, 67nn. 2–3
ἠέλιος, 58, 83

θάλασσα, θάλαττα, 18
θιγεῖν, 106
θράττει, 154n. 46

ἰαυοῖ and other exclamations in ι- . *See* exclamations
ἰσχνοφωνία, 142, 152n. 36, 153n. 26

καλλ- compounds, 67
κάρχαρος, 108
κηλεῖν, 15
κεκακωμένος, 112
κελαρύζειν, 116n. 1
κιχλίζειν, 103
κίνησις, 28, 46n. 36
κλαγγή, κλάζω, 104 f., 116n. 1, 154n. 62
κναξζβί, 51
κνυζεῖσθαι, 106
κόκκυξ, 103
κρέξ, 103
κρότος, 155n. 66
Κώκυτος, 103

λαμπρός, 34, 41n. 39, 52, 154n. 52, 155n. 70
λεῖος, 46n. 36, 70n. 44, 108
λειριόεσσαν, 35, 150
λεπτός, 150
λευκός, 46n. 42
λιμός, 123
λοιμός, 123
λουλοῦδι, 65

μακρός, 47n. 63
μαλακός, 33, 46n. 36, 108

μέγας and compounds: 24n. 51, 25n. 52, 37, 47n. 63, 58
μέλι and compounds, 46n. 43. *See also* honey in Index A
μέλος, μελῳδία. *See* melody in Index A
μέσος τόνος, 158
μηκάδες, 103, 124
μῆτις/μήτις, 90 f.
μίμησις. *See* mimesis in Index A
μίσθωτος, 31 f.
μονοτονία. *See* monotony in Index A
μουσική. *See* mousiké, music in Index A
μόχθηρος, 31
μύζειν, 106, 118n. 37
Μυκάλη, 127, 140
μυκηθμός, 103, 118n. 37

νεφεληγερέτα, 66

ξουθός, 46n. 42

ὄγκος, 79, 150
ὀλολύζειν, 103
ὁμοιο- compounds. *See* homoiokatarkton, homoioteleuton in Index A
ὀνοματοποιΐα, 99
ὀξύς, 46n. 36, 47n. 64
ὀρέων, 58
ὀρθοέπεια. *See* orthoëpy in Index A
ὀσμή, 110
ὀτοτοτοῖ, 103, 114
ου for υ, 124
οὐ/οὔ, 23n. 33
Οὐαλέριος, 123
Οὖτις/οὔτις, 31, 90 f., 143

πάθος. *See* pathos in Index A
Παλλήναδε, 123
παρακαταλογή, 43n. 7
πεταλοῦδα, 65
πευκήεις, 47n. 45
πικρός, 108
πιππίζειν, 103
πλάσμα, 148

πνεῦμα, 55
ποιότης, 45n. 30
πόνηρος, 31
Πουρρῖνος, 124
πρέπον, τὸ, 25n. 62, 117n. 7
προσῳδιά. *See* prosody in Index A
πτύειν, 106
πυκνός, 150

σάν, 23n. 28
σείεσθαι, 13
σῆμα, 11
σίζειν, 13, 54
σίττα, 39, 120n. 67
σκληρός, 14, 33, 54, 70n. 44, 146
Σκύλλη, 106
Σμύρνα, σμύρνα, 45n. 30, 53, 69n. 24, 110, 124
σπαδονισμός, 72n. 78

σπίτι, 63
στύφειν, 33, 47n. 46, 108
σύγκρουσις, 70n. 48
συμβολή, 70n. 48
σύμπληξις, 70n. 48
σύμπτωσις, 70n. 48
σφήξ, 103
Σώκρατες, 32
σῶμα, 11

tacitus, 20n. 81
tetigi 106, 108
τετραχθά, 112
τιττυβίζειν, 103
τονάριον, 27
τούνη, 124
τραυλότης, 141 f.
τραχύς, 46n. 36, 70n. 44, 72n. 78, 108, 140

ὑγίεια, 62

ὑπόκρισις, 38, 43n. 7, 148 f.
ὕφος, 79

φαιός, 46n. 42
φίλος, 129
φεῦ, 119n. 37
Φούλουιος, 123
φωνασκοί, 148

χα-, words containing: 103 f.
χάριεν, 32
χάσμησις, χασμῷδες, 70n. 48
χρέμπτεσθαι, 103
χρήστων, 31

ψελλότης, 142
ψιθυρισμός, 103, 104
ψῦγμα, 153n. 38

ὤ-, exclamations in. *See omega* in Index A

Synopsis of Record

THE AIM of this record is to illustrate the main features of spoken classical Greek. It begins with the following passage from Sophocles (*Ajax* 669–77):

καὶ γὰρ τὰ δεινὰ καὶ τὰ καρτερώτατα
τιμαῖς ὑπείκει · τοῦτο μὲν νιφοστιβεῖς
χειμῶνες ἐκχωροῦσιν εὐκάρπῳ θέρει·
ἐξίσταται δὲ νυκτὸς αἰανὴς κύκλος
τῇ λευκοπώλῳ φέγγος ἡμέρᾳ φλέγειν·
δεινῶν τ'ἄημα πνευμάτων ἐκοίμισε
στένοντα πόντον · ἐν δ'ὁ παγκρατὴς ὕπνος
λύει πεδήσας, οὐδ'ἀεὶ λαβὼν ἔχει.
ἡμεῖς δὲ πῶς οὐ γνωσόμεσθα σωφρονεῖν;

There are five main elements in the aural effect of these lines: speed of delivery, loudness, voice-melody, phonetic quality, and rhythm. (See chapter 2 of *The Sound of Greek*.) The last three of these are illustrated in what follows.

Variations in voice-melody can be heard in the rising-falling tone of the circumflex accent on the words ἡμεῖς, πῶς, σωφρονεῖν, in the last line of the passage spoken; the falling tone of the grave accent can be heard in δὲ; the rising tone of the acute, in γνωσόμεσθα; and the low-level tone of the unaccented syllables is exemplified in the other three syllables of γνωσόμεσθα.

A distinction must be made here between the three main types of utterance: singing, speaking, and a poetical delivery intermediate between song and speech. This is briefly discussed. (See further in chapter 2 of *The Sound of Greek*.)

According to the ancient evidence (which is not conclusive on several points; see Appendix in *The Sound of Greek*), the normal voice-melody of classical Greek speech moved within a musical interval of a fifth (say C to G, or *doh* to *soh*), the salient notes presumably being the tonic (*do*) for the unaccented syllables, the major fifth (*sol*) for the top of the acute and circumflex, and the major third (*mi*) for the most noticeable note in the grave. (The accents were glides, not static musical tones.)

The second main element in the sound of speech, namely the phonetic quality of the phonemes (see chapter 2), is illustrated in the difference between the roughness of Homer's line

τριχθά τε καὶ τετραχθὰ διέσχισεν ἲς ἀνέμοιο   (*Od.* 9,71)

or in the word κεκακωμένος (*Od.* 6,135) and the smoothness of his πὰρ ποταμὸν κελάδοντα παρὰ ῥοδανὸν δονακῆα   (*Iliad* 18,576)

There is a similar contrast of phonetic quality between the narrow *u*-sounds in Homer's phrase for the shrill cries of girls

ἀμφήλυθε θῆλυς ἀϋτή   (*Od.* 6,122)

and the mournful *omegas* in Theocritos'

ὦ λύκοι, ὦ θῶες, ὦ ἀν'ὤρεα φωλάδες ἄρκτοι   (*Idylls* 1,115)

Similarly Aristophanes' transcriptions of bird-cries in his *Birds* (228, 243, 260–263; cf. 738, 741, 747, 751) make skillful use of phonetic qualities, for example, in

ἰώ ἰώ ἰτώ ἰτώ ἰτώ ἰτώ

and

τριοτό τριοτό τοτοβρίξ

and

τοροτοροτοροτοροτίξ
κικκαβαῦ κικκαβαῦ
τοροτοροτοροτοπολιλιλίξ

In reading these one must try to get as close to the classical pronunciation as possible, carefully distinguishing, for example, η (as in βῆ, βῆ, for the bleating of sheep) from ει and ε (see further in chapter 5 of *The Sound of Greek*). So, too, the iota subscript should be pronounced, and φ, θ, χ, should not sound like *f*, *th*, and *ch*, but like our emphatic *p*, *t*, and *k* (the Greek π, τ, κ being less aspirated). The pronunciation of some ancient Greek sounds remains uncertain; the diphthong ου, for example, seems to have changed from approximately as in *low* to as in *cool* during the classical period. But one must not demand rigid consistency. Contemporary English allows variations in words like "patronage," "privacy," and "acoustics" without stigmatizing the main variants as "wrong."

The third element, rhythm, is illustrated next. Here the essential thing is to pronounce the short syllables as having approximately the duration of half a long syllable (but see chapter 2), and to put as little stress on the long syllables as possible.

The record concludes with three passages from Greek poetry. The first two (*Iliad* 1, 1–5 and *Odyssey* 1, 1–5) are in dactylic metre (one can also note how the differences in the phonetic qualities of the two passages make a contrast of somberness and cheerfulness), and the third (Euripides, *Bacchai* 72–87) is a swifter and more excited lyric passage mainly in ionic *a minore* (‿‿– –) and choriambic –‿‿–) metres.

(1)   Μῆνιν ἄειδε, θεά, πηληϊάδεω Ἀχιλῆος
οὐλομένην, ἣ μυρί' Ἀχαιοῖς ἄλγε' ἔθηκε,
πολλὰς δ'ἰφθίμους ψυχὰς Ἄϊδι προΐαψεν
ἡρώων, αὐτοὺς δὲ ἑλώρια τεῦχε κύνεσσιν
οἰωνοῖσί τε πᾶσι Διός, δ'ἐτελείετο βουλή.

(2) Ἄνδρα μοι ἔννεπε, Μοῦσα, πολύτροπον, ὃς μάλα πολλὰ
πλάγχθη, ἐπεὶ Τροίης ἱερὸν πτολίεθρον ἔπερσε·
πολλῶν δ'ἀνθρώπων ἴδεν ἄστεα καὶ νόον ἔγνω,
πολλὰ δ'ὅγ'ἐν πόντῳ πάθεν ἄλγεα ὃν κατὰ θυμόν,
ἀρνύμενος ἥν τε ψυχὴν καὶ νόστον ἑταίρων.

(3) ὦ μάκαρ ὅστις εὐδαίμων
τελετὰς θεῶν εἰδὼς
βιοτὰν ἀγιστεύει καὶ
θιασεύεται ψυχὰν
ἐν ὄρεσσι βακχεύων
ὁσίοις καθαρμοῖσιν,
τά τε ματρὸς μεγάλας ὄργια
   Κυβέλας θεμιτεύων,
ἀνὰ θύρσον τε τινάσσων
κισσῷ τε στεφανωθεὶς
Διόνυσον θεραπεύει.
ἴτε βάκχαι, ἴτε βάκχαι,
Βρόμιον παῖδα θεὸν θεοῦ
Διόνυσον κατάγουσαι
Φρυγίων ἐξ ὀρέων Ἑλλάδος εἰς
εὐρυχόρους ἀγυιὰς τὸν Βρόμιον.

Ancient Greek literature was mostly composed for the ear and not for the eye—for hearing, not for seeing. (In fact, silent reading seems to have been a rare accomplishment until after the classical period.) The language of poetry was considered to be closely akin to music. Greek rhetoricians and grammarians emphasized the importance of accurate pronunciation (orthoëpy) and of pleasant and appropriate sound-effects (euphony) in composition and performance. Greek authors—especially but not exclusively, the poets and orators—exploited the rich phonetic resources of their language with great ingenuity and subtlety, employing variations in the pitch-accent and in syllable-timbre as well as metrical techniques.

Professor Stanford discusses the Greek theory and practice in matters of this kind. He emphasizes the importance of regaining the classical pronunciation of ancient Greek as far as the evidence permits, and opposes the view that the pitch-accent had little literary significance. The accompanying record provides aural illustrations of the main views expressed in the text.

W. B. STANFORD is Senior Fellow of Trinity College, Dublin, and Regius Professor of Greek in the University of Dublin. He was Sather Professor of Classical Literature, University of California, 1965-66.

1968